Dissent and Cultural Resistance in Asia's Cities

This book documents urban experiences of dissent and emergent resistance against disjunctive global and local flows of capital technology and labour that converge and intersect in some of Asia's fastest growing cities. Rather than constructing occupants of the city as simply passive victims of globalisation or urbanisation, it presents ways in which people are using everyday strategies embedded in cultural practice to challenge dominant socio-economic and political forces impacting urban space.

Taking the city as a site of contestation and a stage where social conflicts are played out, the book highlights the connections between urban power and dissent; the nature and impact of resistance; how the spatiality and built environment of the city generate conflict and, conversely, how protagonists use the cityscape to stage their everyday and public dissent.

The contributors explore the conditions, strategies and outcomes of such dissent and forms of cultural resistance, and explore the following themes:

- the impact of urban development, gentrification and ghetto-isation;
- urban counter narratives and the re-imagining of city spaces;
- the role of grassroots activism and social movements;
- cultural resistance in the creation of neighbourhoods and communities;
- the impact of gender, class and the politics of identity on forms of dissent;
- the formation of transgressive spaces.

Complementing established work on Asian cities, social change and transformation in the Asia Pacific and cultural politics in Asia, this work will be of interest to students, researchers and academics in the field of Asian studies, Asian cultural studies, urban geography, urban studies, anthropology, sociology and cultural studies.

Melissa Butcher is a lecturer in the Department of Geography, the Open University, UK.

Selvaraj Velayutham is a lecturer in the Department of Sociology at Macquarie University, Australia.

Routledge contemporary Asia series

Dissent and Cultural Resistance in Asia's Cities

Edited by Melissa Butcher and
Selvaraj Velayutham

Routledge
Taylor & Francis Group

LONDON AND NEW YORK

First published 2009
by Routledge
2 Park Square, Milton Park, Abingdon, Oxon OX14 4RN

Simultaneously published in the USA and Canada
by Routledge
270 Madison Ave, New York, NY 10016

*Routledge is an imprint of the Taylor & Francis Group, an informa
business*

Typeset in Times New Roman by
Swales & Willis Ltd, Exeter, Devon
Printed and bound in Great Britain by
TJI Digital, Padstow, Cornwall

British Library Cataloguing in Publication Data
A catalogue record for this book is available
from the British Library

Library of Congress Cataloging-in-Publication Data
Dissent and cultural resistance in Asia's cities / edited by
Melissa Butcher and Selvaraj Velayutham.
p. cm.
1. Dissenters—Asia. 2. Protest movements—Asia. 3. City and town
life—Asia. I. Butcher, Melissa, 1966– II. Velayutham, Selvaraj, 1968–
HN655.2.S62D57 2009
303.48′4095091732—dc22
2008041593

ISBN 10: 0–415–49142–8 (hbk)
ISBN 10: 0–203–88015–3 (ebk)

ISBN 13: 978–0–415–49142–6 (hbk)
ISBN 13: 978–0–203–88015–9 (ebk)

Cover image by Cybermohalla Ensemble

Contents

List of figures

List of contributors

Anne-Marie Broudehoux is assistant professor at the School of Design in the University of Quebec at Montreal. She is the author of *The Making and Selling of Post-Mao Beijing* (2004), which was awarded the 2004–2005 International Planning History Society book prize in 2006. She is currently working on a new book on the socio-spatial impacts of the Beijing 2008 Olympic Games.

Melissa Butcher is a lecturer in the Department of Geography, the Open University, UK. The focus of her research is the impact of transnational mobility on urban space, cultural change and conflict, with an emphasis on questions of identity and belonging. Before joining the Open University, she taught at universities in Ireland and Australia. She presents and writes regularly on issues relating to globalisation, migration, popular culture and global human resources management.

Limin Hee is assistant professor at the Department of Architecture, National University of Singapore, and the Asia Research Institute based in Singapore. She leads the Urban Studies Group at the Department of Architecture in the University. Her research interests include sustainable cities, Asian urbanism, public spaces and design pedagogy. Her research on sustainable architecture and urbanism has been a collaborative effort with the Harvard University Graduate School of Design, and has been the subject of a travelling exhibition shown in major cities in Asia and Europe.

Jennifer Hsu is a specialist in development studies at the University of Cambridge. She has published research on the development of civil society organisations in China, including their role in HIV/AIDS and the changing nature of Chinese state–society relationships in an era of socioeconomic reforms. Her current research examines the development of migrant non-governmental organizations in China. She has recently completed an edited collection (with Reza Hasmath) titled *China in an Era of Transition*.

Sameera Khan is a journalist, writer and researcher. A former assistant editor at *The Times of India* in Mumbai, she writes on issues related to public health, environment, women, and local history and culture. She was an integral part of the Gender & Space project at PUKAR and is currently writing a book based on this project along with Shilpa Phadke and Shilpa Ranade. She is also authoring a book on the old Muslim neighbourhoods of Mumbai. She has a BA in History and Anthropology from the University of Bombay and a Masters in Journalism from Columbia University, New York.

Maurizio Marinelli is a senior lecturer in East Asian Studies at the University of Bristol, UK, specialising in the study of contemporary China's intellectual and urban history. His research investigates how China's relations with the rest of the world have influenced historical narratives and shaped visual representations within their respective intellectual discourses. He is currently researching the socio-spatial transformation of Beijing and Tianjin.

Diya Mehra is a PhD candidate in the Department of Anthropology at the University of Texas at Austin. She is currently researching the urbanisation of post-Independence Delhi including transformations following the introduction of neoliberal policies. Her work on slum demolition has appeared in both popular and academic publications (Brosius and Ahuja, 2006; Mahadevia, forthcoming), and she has been actively involved in campaigns against demolition since 2004. Between 2002 and 2004, she worked at Sarai, Centre for the Study of Developing Societies, New Delhi.

B. Lynne Milgram is professor of anthropology at the Ontario College of Art & Design, Toronto, Canada. Her research on gender, development and globalisation in the Philippines analyses the cultural politics of social change with regard to microfinance, material cultural production and trade, and women's work in the second-hand clothing trade between the Philippines and Hong Kong. This research has been published in edited volumes and journals. She has also co-edited (with K. M. Grimes) *Artisans and Cooperatives: Developing Alternative Trade for the Global Economy*, (with Roy Hamilton) *Material Choices: Refashioning Bast and Leaf Fibers in Asia and the Pacific* and (with K. E. Browne) *Economics and Morality: Anthropological Approaches*. Her current research explores issues in urbanisation and street vending in the Philippines.

Shilpa Phadke is a sociologist, researcher, writer and pedagogue. She is assistant professor at the Centre for Media and Cultural Studies at the Tata Institute of Social Sciences, Mumbai. She has been educated at St. Xavier's College, Mumbai, SNDT University and the University of Cambridge, UK. She conceptualised and led the Gender & Space Project at PUKAR from September 2003 to September 2006. Her areas of concern include gender and the politics of space, the middle classes, sexuality and the body, feminist politics among young women and pedagogic practices.

Shilpa Ranade is a practicing architect and researcher. She trained in architecture from CEPT (Centre for Environmental Planning and Technology), Ahmedabad and has done her MA in Comparative Cultural & Literary Studies at the University of Arizona, Tucson. Shilpa has been associate editor of the South Asian volume in the series 'World Architecture 1900–2000: A Critical Mosaic' and has also published articles in various architectural magazines. She is a partner in the design firm DCOOP in Mumbai, in addition to her work on the Gender & Space project at PUKAR.

Selvaraj Velayutham is a lecturer in the Department of Sociology at Macquarie University, Australia. His current research interests include moral economies of migration, transnational affect and emotion, multiculturalism and the sociology of everyday life. He is the author of *Responding to Globalisation: Nation, Culture and Identity in Singapore* and editor of *Tamil Cinema: The Cultural Politics of India's Other Film Industry*. He has published widely on the subject of globalisation, global cities, transnationalism and migration.

Yeoh Seng Guan is a senior lecturer at the School of Arts and Sciences, Monash University, Sunway campus, Malaysia. He holds a PhD from the University of Edinburgh. He has conducted fieldwork in various parts of Malaysia as well as in Baguio City in the Philippines. His research interests include anthropologies of the city, religion and media with particular focus on the Southeast Asia region. He has published widely in academic journals and produced two ethnographic documentaries on street vendors and cockfighting. He is lead editor for *Penang and its Neighbours* (2008) and has a chapter on cosmopolitanism in Little India, Kuala Lumpur in *The Other Global City*, edited by Shail Mayaram (forthcoming).

Acknowledgements

We would like to thank all the authors in this volume for their contributions and assistance throughout the editorial process. Thanks also to the editorial team at Routledge as well as Vijay Devadas, Tim Bunnell, and the anonymous reviewers of the manuscript for their suggestions.

Melissa Butcher would like to thank the many friends and colleagues who provided hours of conversation and food for thought on the ideas presented in the book.

Selvaraj Velayutham's work on this book has been supported by the Macquarie University New Staff Research Grants Scheme. We would also like to acknowledge the support of the Division of Society, Culture, Media and Philosophy's Research Funding Scheme at Macquarie University towards the cost of proofreading and indexing of the book. Finally and most importantly, as always, here is to Amanda for all her support and intellectual companionship and to the arrival of our sweet little Leela.

Introduction

Cultures of resistance in Asia's transforming cities

Melissa Butcher and Selvaraj Velayutham

From Beijing to Hanoi, Kuala Lumpur to Jakarta and Singapore to Mumbai, Asian cities are bustling with movement and change. The convergence of global capital, technology and labour flows together with the efforts of Asian nation-states vying to position their cities as major nodes in the global economy is bringing about new challenges and opportunities in these urban centres. This is generating what Burawoy (2000) calls a 'transformative crisis' in urban space, in that cities which mediate global economic activity and the movement of goods, capital, technology and people, are doing so under conditions of disparity and segmentation (Knox 2002, Sassen 2005), fracturing urban landscapes into new enclaves of spatial and economic inequality, disrupting former frames of reference and spaces of order within the city.

Overt opposition to these transformations has come from various perspectives: from political groups, NGOs and activists. This volume, however, aims to document these contemporary processes of urban transition from the perspective of everyday resistance, giving voice to the experiences of lives embedded and implicated in these processes, and exploring how ordinary inhabitants of Asia's transforming cities are responding to and actively intervening in urban and social change.

The topic of Asian cities is a burgeoning field of study with many writers examining their history, growth, economic and social dimensions from development studies, political economy, human geography, urban studies, anthropological and sociological perspectives (Dwyer 1972, Dutt *et al.* 1994, Lo and Yeung 1996, Borthwick 1998, Drakakis-Smith 2000). The cultural dimensions of this transformation and the everyday lived experiences of Asian cities have also been documented by Forbes 1996, Kim *et al.* 1997, Olds *et al.* 1999, Bunnell *et al.* 2002, Vasudevan *et al.* 2002, Dutt *et al.* 2003, Evers and Korff 2003, Goh and Yeoh 2003, Wu 2007, Velayutham 2007 and Brosius 2008.

Some researchers have challenged the Euro-American centred theoretical approaches that have taken Western cities and notions of progress as points of reference to interpret Asia's urban dynamics. Without taking for granted the historic conditions, cultural specificities and globalising forces shaping Asian cities, Bishop, Phillips and Yeo (2003) argue that a Euro-American approach not only presents a culturally biased reading reducible to a derivative and homogeneous account of global urbanism but also ignores postcolonial settings. They coin the term 'postcolonial urbanism' to describe the specific, divergent, complex and sometimes contradictory features of urbanism found in Southeast Asian cities (see also Evers and Korff's 2003 work on Southeast Asian urbanism). Other researchers have examined in more general terms political opposition and civil society in Asia (Rodan 1996, Schak and Hudson 2003, Alagappa 2004, Lee 2004 and Callahan 2006) but not specifically centred around the city with the exception of Douglass, Ho and Ooi's (2007) exploration of civil society.

Within this context, the ways in which people are responding to the wide range of economic and socio-cultural forces sweeping through the region and the changing urban milieu remains relatively understudied. In particular, what counter narratives can be told about these emerging world cities? What kinds of strategies have people developed to demonstrate their dissent or resist the transformative dynamics of the city? This volume seeks to critically engage with these questions and document practices of dissent and resistance, sometimes overt, sometimes emergent, against disjunctive global and local flows that converge and intersect in some of Asia's fastest growing cities. More importantly, the volume's grounded approach to the study of such practices as they unfold in Asia's cities will offer a culture and context-specific understanding of dissent and resistance.

Portaliou's historical overview points out that the city is not only a container for social and political struggle but is itself a contested object, 'and a carrier of all resulting changes' (2007: 167). Cities have become central nodes in a configuration of power linking transnational corporations, migrants (professionals and low/unskilled) and the state. The city 'is not simply a backdrop to processes of economic, social and political change, but is seen and has often been used as a tool in the process of cultural change and the formation of (national) cultural identity' (Parnwell 1999: 204). In Asia, urban boundaries have shifted as a result of the introduction or imposition of neo-liberal models of economic development with their concomitant need for new everyday practices (work and leisure), new relationships (between employer/employee or within the family) and values (deferred gratification as a normative ideal versus consumerism, for example), creating fracture lines as existing spaces of order are disrupted. Rapid urban transformation is argued to lead to the demise of heritage and cultural traditions, an increase in disproportionate levels of wealth, and the creation of a new urban underclass through gentrification policies that have displaced marginalised communities. In other instances, these new urban spaces are presenting to their inhabitants the possibility of challenging regimented state policies and inequality whether it be by re-appropriating space itself or re-arranging expected activities within it (see Hee, Velayutham and Phadke *et al.*, this volume).

Various social movements have emerged to challenge the dominant discourse of urban development, to intervene in these social and spatial transformations, and/or to preserve extant cultural spaces. Rather than constructing occupants of the city as simply passive victims of globalisation or urbanisation, the articles in this volume present ways in which people are using everyday strategies embedded in cultural frames of reference and practice to challenge dominant socio-economic and political forces impacting on their particular use of urban space. Taking the city as a site of contestation and negotiation, a stage where social interaction and conflict is played out, these articles highlight the connections between urban power and dissent; the nature and impact of resistance; how the spatiality and built environment of the city generates conflict and, conversely, how protagonists use the cityscape to stage their everyday forms of resistance.

Dissent, as an expression of opposition to a dominant tenet, and resistance, as the agency of opposition, are often used interchangeably to describe and theorise different forms and practices of antagonism that challenge sites of power with the objective of bringing about change. For the purposes of this volume, the term 'resistance' is favoured by the authors to express the action-oriented opposition of protagonists in each case study. There are different conceptual frameworks to theorise the practice of resistance. Chin and Mittelman (1997) offer a useful outline of three major theories: Antonio Gramsci's notion of counter-hegemony, Karl Polanyi's concept of counter-movements and James C. Scott's idea of infra-politics, that is, the invisible, disguised, everyday struggles waged by those subordinate to sites of power.

These three theorists agree that resistance arises from and is constitutive of specific and whole ways of life, that is, there is a cultural framework attached to these forms of resistance. However, there continue to be shifts in the usage and understanding of resistance because of this application of a cultural framework. The main objective and modes of resistance differ from one theorist to another, with 'Gramscian wars of movement and position against the state, Polanyian counter-movements against market forces, and Scott's infra-political activities in the face of everyday domination' (Chin and Mittelman 1997: 34). They observe that all three forms of resistance co-exist and are modified in the globalising process but stress the need for a more grounded analysis that takes into account the forms, agents, sites and strategies of resistance in the current context of globalisation.

For this study, we have gathered together articles from various major cities in Asia to explore acts of everyday resistance that very much speak to the work of James C. Scott. Scott defines resistance as:

> Any act(s) by members of the class that is (are) intended either to mitigate or to deny claims (rent, taxes, dependence) made on that class by superordinate classes (landowners, the State, money lenders) or to advance its own claims (work, land, charity, respect) vis-à-vis these superordinate classes.
>
> (1986: 22)

Resistance rises then from within the tension between structures of power and those affected by them, originating within a consensus of what is just and unjust, what needs to be fought against and what accepted. The type of resistance is bound by the parameters of the knowledge and patterns of actions that a group possesses within its cultural expressions, rooted in everyday patterns of work, social action and even pleasure (Adas 1986: 69).

While Scott's work focused on resistance among rural labourers in Asia, the articles in this volume show that cultural frames of reference that demarcate land use, modes of economic production and participation, are as applicable to the urban context where communities also survive in asymmetrical power relationships that are explicit in these processes. In Foucauldian terms, where there are unequal relations of power 'there is resistance, and [...] this resistance is never in a position of exteriority in relation to power' (Scott 1990: 111). Practices of urban authority, ideological and material, and those that resist this confinement to terminology and circumscribed space are the protagonists in this research. However, the research seeks to move away from simple dichotomies of power. Castells (1983) and Hayter and Harvey (1993) argue that resistance takes place on terms defined by existing structures, in particular the state. Yet, the state is not a unified, monolithic structure and opposition to it is not necessarily informed by a single organisation or process. Inter-connected relationships between individuals; economic activity; national, regional, and local sites of power; historical factors; and religious and communal identities, position protagonists differently within 'unequal and multiple power relationships' (Pile 1997: 3) that inflect choices and possibilities.

Internal and external variables of differing importance in each situation will determine 'how social change will be instigated, accepted, rejected, acted upon, acted out or altered' (Harrison 1988: 163). For example, unequal access to the public domain (Milgram, Phadke *et al.* and Yeoh, this volume), presence of an authoritarian government (Broudehoux, Hee, Hsu and Velayutham, this volume) and lack of control over the direction of change (Butcher, Marinelli and Mehra, this volume), lead to different forms of social organisation and opposition. Therefore we take the view that:

> Resistance can take on diverse forms and strategies, ranging from survival or coping strategies to (more or less) organized resistance and transnational organizing, all of which entail cultural as well as economic struggles and the development of new identities and subjectivities.
>
> (Marchand and Runyan 2001: 146–147)

Attention given to large-scale protest movements which directly threaten the state overshadows acts of constant, ordinary, everyday struggle that can take the form, for example, of lethargy, desertion, 'illegal' activities, sabotage, silences and boycotts. These are part of what Scott (1985) described as 'weapons of the weak'. Even action that appears as spontaneous or unorganised can be embedded in structures, beliefs and habits of a culture that may not be sufficiently recognised or understood. There are popular cultures of resistance, for example, the trickster character or references to religious myths and heroes, that as a shared understanding of what is deviant and impolite underwrite what may be perceived by authorities as a challenge. However, cultural practices and expressions used as part of everyday resistance are not made moribund by tradition, as the articles in this volume demonstrate.

For the protagonists, inbuilt in cultures of resistance is a demonstration of flexibility that enables continued survival (see Hee, Marinelli, Mehra, and Milgram in particular for their examples of flexible boundaries between legality and illegality).

That flexibility is often found in interstitial spaces where action is created outside of existing, prescribed power relations. Therefore it is possible to argue, as Skuse and Cousins (2007: 992) do, that a bricolage of counter-hegemonic practices has emerged that are 'not so easily contained within a narrow structural analysis of politics' (Pile 1997: 23). Resistance has formed around issues of gender, class, the environment, identity, kinship, neighbourhood and ad hoc alliances formed through necessity to alleviate a particular conflict (see Gow 2005). These are struggles over material conditions and needs, and over the practices and meanings of everyday life (Routledge 2002: 318), carried out by excavating new terrain in the city (physical and imaginative) that also incorporates non-material aspects such as affective responses to change (for example fear, pleasure) (Wise 2005, 2009). At the heart of this resistance is a sense of place gained from history, geography, culture, imagination and political definition of contested grounds (Pile 1997: 28). In this sense, resistance occurs within, and is shaped by, a specific place as emphasised by the articles in this volume.

According to Scott (1985), the chances of oppositional success increased if formal definitions of hierarchy and power were not challenged, avoiding direct, symbolic confrontation with authority. He also suggests that everyday resistance requires little or no planning because of an implicit understanding of and informal networks found within cultural frames of reference. The articles in this volume however show a diversity of forms of resistance that relied on the broad consensus that cultural frames of reference can give, but that also at times required coordination and resulted in head-on collisions with government authorities (see Broudehoux, Mehra, Milgram and Yeoh, this volume, for example). The outcome of events discussed in these articles would seem to suggest that direct confrontation with the state incurs greater penalties to protesters but in general these are not the invisible and historically silent movements of Scott's Southeast Asian peasantry. States have responded by either relenting, increasing incentives or increasing coercion. In all instances it could be argued that the strategy of resistance has resulted in change, although its viability in the longer term is questionable in light of the failure of any of the protests to modify the seemingly ineluctable effects of neo-liberal economic development–inspired urban regeneration.

Frustrated economic activity, in particular, led to support for cultural practices as a focus, indeed at times the only focus, for resistance. Several articles highlight the defence of old modes of livelihood from economic development imposed as a form of order incorporating the aesthetics of urban regeneration. The goal of these forms of everyday resistance can then seem more about survival rather than revolution. There is tension evident between protagonists' opposition and their desire to participate in consumption, economic organisation and governance. This is resistance driven by '[t]he dull compulsion of economic relations' (Marx 1954: 737) that, it could be argued, restricts options for real change.

White (1986) would argue that real resistance alters exploitative structures or policies, and other resistance may just be a 'safety valve and contribute to a false consciousness, giving (...) temporary relief and thus obscuring the extent of their powerlessness and exploitation' (Scott and Kerkvliet 1986: 2). Yet the parameters of resistance, as delimited by powerful institutions, may leave no option but individual, covert, informal means of resistance. Scott observed that:

> [These] persistent attempts to 'nibble away' may backfire, they may marginally alleviate exploitation, they may amount to a renegotiation of the limits of appropriation; they may change the course of subsequent development, and they may more rarely help bring the system down. (...) Their intention, by contrast, is nearly always survival and persistence.
>
> (1986: 30)

Like Scott, we are optimistic that resistance provides a 'spirit and practice that prevents the worst and promises something better' (Scott 1985: 350).

The contributions in this volume explore these conditions, contradictions, strategies and outcomes of various forms of resistance including: opposition to urban redevelopment and gentrification; counter narratives in the re-imagining of city spaces; grassroots activism and social movements; the re-creation of neighbourhoods and communities; and the impact of gender, class and the politics of identity on strategies of resistance. Each chapter provides background descriptions of specific cities, conveying the history, dynamics and complexities that are unfolding; demonstrating the relationship between locality and the distinct form, protagonists and tactics that unfold in these spaces. Together, they outline how people as individuals or a collective work towards changing, adapting or challenging particular aspects of daily life in these cities.

As we argued earlier, resistance need not be an overt display of opposition but, following Scott, can be observed in mundane and everyday practices. As such, we would like to regard everyday practices of resistance as forms of intervention that people undertake in order to negotiate, confront and mediate the flows and forces of change in the city. These can be multiple in their form and just as our protagonists adopt various means of resistance, so the authors have adopted a variety of approaches in their analyses, giving insight into opposition that is generated, in particular, in everyday activity, grassroots activism, gendered identity and creative expression.

For instance, Milgram's chapter on women street vendors in Baguio City in North Philippines, and Phadke, Ranade and Khan's piece on women and loitering in Mumbai explore practices of *gendered resistance*. Baguio City is one of the Philippines' most highly industrialised centres. However, as Milgram argues, urbanisation is creating new opportunities for some and giving rise to instances of exploitation and constraint of others. She examines recent initiatives of a pioneering group of female entrepreneurs. Their new market enterprises evidence not only a rise in economic growth, but also fundamental shifts in class structure and the social and economic reconfiguration of urban streetscapes by engaging in everyday forms of activism that unsettle essentialist categories of work, class and space.

Going against the Baguio City council's street vending regulations, the female street vendors drew on local concepts such as favoured relations (*suki*), kinship and community obligation or 'communitarianism', and repositioned resources at their disposal by using cultural and social capital alongside economic capital and non-government assistance. These became parallel means by which to craft power and work in alternative but contested urban spaces. In doing so they challenged taken-for-granted conceptions of what is 'legal' and 'illegal' in Filipino urban space.

While the majority of India's population continues to live in rural areas, internal migration and economic liberalisation have resulted in a rapid growth in urbanisation with major cities such as Mumbai and Delhi now vying for 'global city' status. Phadke, Ranade and Khan argue that in twenty-first-century Mumbai, despite their increased visibility in the public sphere, women still do not have equal right to the city's public spaces. They point out that even in Mumbai, arguably India's most gender-friendly city, safety does not flow from institutional arrangements but has to be systematically produced by women. Women's access to public space is dependent on their ability to demonstrate purpose, circumscribed not only by the threat of possible violence but also the risk to reputation. Therefore, in order to be seen as worthy of conditional protection, women feel compelled to manufacture respectability. The question the authors ask in this essay is – what would change if women could access urban public space in a purposeless way? Pushing this proposition further, they make a case for 'loitering' as 'a politics of publicly visible dissent that might offer possibilities to envision a radically altered city', not just for women but all marginal citizens. They argue that the act of loitering disrupts neat boundaries that otherwise define the city, and that it is precisely this ambiguity that makes the act of loitering potentially liberating, questioning established norms of class and gender.

The chapters by Marinelli and Butcher examine the use of art and multimedia as forms of *expressive resistance* within the changing urban landscapes of Asia's cities. Marinelli observes that since the early 1980s, Beijing has been undergoing a period of phenomenal structural transformation and immense growth as a consequence of the Chinese Government's 'Open Door' policy. The dramatic changes in the Chinese capital have progressively forced its citizens to face the challenge of managing the changing fabric and culture of the city, while burgeoning nationalism and the development of local and international tourism have constructed Beijing as a showcase for national identity. In the last few years, increasing attention has been focused on the vanishing of Beijing's walls and it is these remnants of former histories that are the focal point of Marinelli's article, in particular the protest graffiti and performance artworks of the Beijing-based artist Zhang Dali. Zhang Dali has chosen walls as his canvas to question the relationship between representation and spatial transformation, raising the critical question of artistic agency in public space as a form of resistance in China.

Likewise, Butcher's article examines the use of expressive media as a means of intervention in Delhi's drive to be a global city. Marginalised residential areas are marked by 'unauthorised' housing, transience and deprivation, and many people are facing evictions and demolition of their homes. In two such resettlement colonies, young people gather at multimedia labs established by local NGOs to share their thoughts about their neighbourhood, home and the changing city. They have translated these ideas into a collection of media forms including photographs, animations, sound-scapes, blogs, texts and street murals. Utilising traditional and contemporary popular culture, this work has become a narrative reflecting the contested environment of urban Delhi, challenging preconceived visions of these communities and emphasising that marginalised neighbourhoods also have an intellectual life.

Broudehoux, Hee, Hsu and Velayutham's chapters explore practices of *subtle everyday resistance* in cities marked by authoritarian government. Singapore, for example, has been ranked as the world's most 'globalised' city because of its high trade levels, communication traffic and the number of international travellers (see Velayutham 2007), but its government has closely directed this development and indelibly marks public and private space in the city. Hee points out that public housing and urban design in Singapore are dominated by planned and regulated spaces in keeping with the government's model for Singapore as a whole. However, while design politics is dominated by planned spaces this is not always translated by residents' spatial practice into the prescribed use or desired social outcomes of that space. Hee's chapter outlines one of the clearest indications of how resistance can be generated by the built environment itself. She documents the interpretive nature of spatial practice by residents within the designed environment, and new practices created through the interaction of people and the built environment, at times using poetry as Zhang Dali uses graffiti in Marinelli's chapter. Hee argues that the spaces of public housing shaped from both above, through planning and design, and below, through residents' spatial practices, capture alternative constructions of a Singapore in transition. In many ways this exemplifies migration from a form of 'traditional' society into a society where hyper-real forms of tradition are used to resist the state's and globalisation's demands for a particular use of Singapore's urban space.

Velayutham's chapter examines a relatively understudied and subtle form of dissent found in this highly regulated city-state: the practice of complaint and humour among Singaporeans in their everyday lives. Following Scott's work, these fairly ubiquitous practices when examined closely offer an interesting insight into how Singaporeans deal with the economic and social pressures of living in a global city as well as under an autocratic state. Drawing on anecdotes and web sources, Velayutham suggests that these widely shared practices not only act as a coping mechanism, an outlet for Singaporeans to vent their disaffection, frustration and resignation, but also to express their dissent. He argues that both a culture of complaint and humour represent modes of creative everyday dissent in a city which otherwise provides little space for expressions of opposition.

The consequences of dissent and resistance in China are perhaps more evident but even here the existence of a totalitarian government has not prevented acts of opposition. According to Broudehoux, hosting the 2008 Summer Olympic Games allowed Beijing to carry on and accelerate an urban and socio-cultural image reconstruction programme with impacts ranging from socio-spatial polarisation, massive displacements and evictions, heritage destruction, labour exploitation and loss of civil liberties, to the growing control of urban space by private interests and the channelling of public resources to private beneficiaries under public-private partnerships. Yet even in Beijing, diverse modes of resistance were developed by different categories of actors. Broudehoux's article reveals scattered and timely actions led by isolated groups and individuals to voice dissent, raise awareness or try to limit the negative impacts of the Olympic Games, including: performance artists denouncing the spectacle; intellectuals petitioning to limit public spending; and individuals voicing their frustrations towards uneven development using subtle channels similar to the technologically enabled linguistic slips of the tongue that Velayutham notes.

A hindrance to the establishment of more overt forms of opposition in China is its lack of civil society. Hsu's article argues that developing this aspect of everyday life can also constitute a form of resistance. She suggests that in the relationship between Beijing's migrant civil society organisations (CSO) and the government lie the seeds of shifting power dynamics within Beijing that could contribute to the growth of civil society in the country as a whole. China's economic liberalisation has led to unparalleled rural–urban labour migration, resulting in a substantial segment of China's urban population not under state protection. Consequently, migrant CSOs have emerged to provide services such as health and training to migrant workers in urban areas. Although the space where CSOs are working is restricted by the state it is possible to see that they represent a form of contestation within these boundaries. Resistance in this case is neither public nor vocal. Instead, Beijing's migrant CSOs are operating within the system, adopting the rules of the 'game' and using it to overcome the prevailing order of the city; an order that relegates migrant workers to situations where they have no choice but to accept unsafe working conditions, poor wages, unsanitary living conditions and limited opportunities for their children.

Hsu's work is evidence of growing forms of 'middle class' opposition in China, particularly attempts to intervene in urban development. This resistance is very much in the realm of non-confrontational tactics such as the movement of groups 'going for a walk' in the general direction of local urban authority offices. As with Velayutham's work, a 'softly softly' approach in the face of authoritarianism appears to be the only space of resistance open in which to voice or enact opposition.

The chapters by Mehra and Yeoh discuss more overt, activist-centred, *grassroots resistance* in Asia's cities. In recent years, the streets of Kuala Lumpur have borne witness to a number of high-profile street protests not usually associated with a country that has seen years of buoyant economic growth and strong if not authoritarian rule. The dramatic change in the capital city's skyline and major infrastructural development indexing national prosperity are usually identified with the visionary contributions of the former premier, Mahathir Mohammad. However, Yeoh argues that Mahathir's support of globalised neo-liberal policies and national policies of economic re-distribution also produced an extensive system of graduated sovereignty and ethnic-based governmentality that is now being openly challenged by non-beneficiaries and detractors. Yeoh's chapter maps the different tactics and cultural logics used by contending actors (police, the state and protesters) in demarcating the streets of Kuala Lumpur as a public stage for ostensibly democratic and nationalist expressions. He reminds us that each of these case studies has historical and cultural parameters that frame confrontations as well as situate resistance within a more diffuse but wider network such as cyberspace. In particular, Yeoh's work offers suggestions for what these dissenting actions portend for the pluralised spaces of Malaysian civil society.

Mehra's piece is instructive in the ability of the state to manipulate, control and ultimately contain resistance. As Pile has argued 'one of authority's most insidious effects may well be to confine definitions of resistance to only those that appear to oppose it directly, in the open, where it can be made and seen to fail' (1997: 3). Mehra examines the response of traders whose livelihoods were threatened by the remodelling of Delhi, a process undertaken by government authorities. In 2006, the Supreme Court of India ruled that between 50,000 to 500,000 small, medium and large retail businesses in Delhi would have to close shop because they were illegally operating from their premises. They were in violation of 'permitted land-use'; a technical term indicating that Delhi is legally zoned into separate and distinct commercial, industrial and residential zones. This ruling was despite a lived geography of distinctly mixed land-use. Since economic liberalisation, local retail businesses have flourished, expanding onto main streets, basements, upper and lower floors of neighbourhoods, and into spaces made available by energised local real estate markets seeking to gain from the ever-increasing demand for more shopping and services in boomtown Delhi.

Mehra's chapter follows the massive campaign against the order involving tens of thousands of people organised under the banner of Delhi's 'trading' community. In building the campaign, traders attempted to mobilise 'trader' as an identity and community, one with a long history in Delhi as a centre of distribution and retail; to reopen a dialogue on what it means to be a citizen, distilled through the experience of anti-colonial nationalist struggle and its language of protest; and tried repeatedly to evoke a 'space of disruption', utilising, they suggest, the only language that the government is responsive to. But they also engaged in flexible, discrete challenges such as removing incriminating signage while continuing to trade behind a façade.

In the end, however, the protesters were only able to achieve minimal concessions, and in fact some gains made were lost in the long run. This raises the question of measuring the effectiveness of different forms of resistance, that this book does not attempt to do, and indeed, it is possible to argue that it is meaningless to do so. The strategies adopted by groups in these various localities are very much context dependent. It can be seen from the different Beijing and Delhi case studies that within cities there are multiple attempts to modify change for the needs of specific stakeholders, and that the needs of these groups could be antithetical to each other so that the relationship between subalterns and sites of power is in no way always clear.

However, what the chapters do indicate is that various tactics designed to overcome the impasse between the state and subaltern groups in their contestation over the use of urban spaces can reinvest them with new meaning, and in so doing potentially alter power relations. This is achieved largely through transgression, not only of physical boundaries, but the invisible prescribed and habituated uses of space, in line with Scott's 'infra-politics'. For example: the ignoring of 'rules' by Filipino street traders; the invocation of flexibility by Delhi traders who simply covered up illegal shop fronts with a façade; the using of public space in Singapore in ways it was never designed for; or the simple act of a woman 'being' in public space in Mumbai.

Culture is implicated in these processes through claims of customary rights and traditional use; the valorisation of informal networks based on kinship, cultural familiarity and gendered identity; and the use of forms of cultural production as a means of symbolic resistance. As the protagonists operate within punitive frameworks, often resistance is found in the shadowlands between legality and illegality, and in subtle, non-antagonistic modes. This adaptability, particularly of the subversive kind, along with an implicit understanding of where those boundaries of legality/illegality lie, is a major theme within all the chapters, suggesting that this is one 'weapon', however limited its ability to create long-term structural change in the face of the realities of power, that is available in any contestation of public space.

Increasingly, congested, fragmented and culturally diverse cities are becoming the intersection between global, national and local, between economic change and change in everyday life. They require daily negotiation of their shared spaces, at times inverting relationships between the powerful and the subaltern and at other times reinforcing this relationship evident in the grind of marginalisation. It is hoped that these articles provide an opportunity to 'walk' these cities, as de Certeau (1984) would argue, in order to understand these new power dynamics, transformations and oppositions on the ground.

References

Adas, M. (1986) 'From Footdragging to Flight: The Evasive History of Peasant Avoidance Protest in South and Southeast Asia', *Journal of Peasant Studies*, 13(2): 64–86.

Alagappa, M. (ed.) (2004) *Civil Society and Political Change in Asia: Expanding and Contracting Democratic Space*, Stanford: Stanford University Press.

Bishop, R., Phillips, J. and Yeo, W.W. (eds) (2003) *Postcolonial Urbanism: Southeast Asian Cities and Global Process*, London: Routledge.

Borthwick, M. (1998) *Pacific Century: The Emergence of Modern Pacific Asia*, Boulder: Westview Press.

Brosius, C. (2008) 'The Enclaved Gaze: Exploring the Visual Culture of "World Class-Living" in Urban India', in J. Jain (ed.) *India's Popular Culture: Iconic Spaces and Fluid Images*, New Delhi: MARG Publications.

Bunnell, T., Drummond, L. and Ho, K.C. (eds) (2002) *Critical Reflections on Cities in Southeast Asia*, Singapore: Times Academic Press.

Burawoy, M. (2000) 'Introduction: Reaching for the Global', in M. Burawoy *et al.*, *Global Ethnography*, Berkeley: University of California Press, pp 1–35.

Callahan, W. (2006) *Cultural Governance and Resistance in Pacific Asia*, Abingdon, Oxon: Routledge.

Castells, M. (1983) *The City and the Grassroots: A Cross-Cultural Theory of Urban Social Movements*, Berkeley: University of California Press.

Chin, C. and Mittelman, J. (1997) 'Conceptualising Resistance to Globalisation', *New Political Economy* 2(1): 25–37.

de Certeau, M. (1984) *The Practice of Everyday Life*, Berkeley: University of California Press.

Douglass, M., Ho, K.C. and Ooi, G.L. (eds) (2007) *Globalization, the City and Civil Society in Pacific Asia*, London: Routledge.

Drakakis-Smith, D. (2000) *Third World Cities*, London: Routledge.

Dutt, A.K., Costa, F.J., Aggarwal, S. and Noble, A.G. (eds) (1994) *The Asian City: Processes of Development, Characteristics, and Planning*, Boston: Kluwer Academic Publishers.

Dutt, A.K., Noble, A.G., Venugopal, S. and Subbiah, S. (eds) (2003) *Challenges to Asian Urbanization in the 21st Century*, Boston: Kluwer Academic Publishers.

Dwyer, D. (ed.) (1972) *The City as a Centre of Change in Asia*, Hong Kong: Hong Kong University Press.

Evers, H. and Korff, R. (2003) *Southeast Asian Urbanism: The Meaning and Power of Social Space*, Berlin: Lit Verlag.

Forbes, D. (1996) *Asian Metropolis: Urbanisation and the Southeast Asian City*, Melbourne: Oxford University Press.

Goh, R. and Yeoh, B. (eds) (2003) *Theorizing the Southeast Asian City as Text*, Singapore: World Scientific.

Gow, G. (2005) 'Rubbing Shoulders in the Global City: Refugees, Citizenship and Multicultural Alliance in Fairfield, Sydney', *Ethnicities*, 5(3): 386–405.

Harrison, D. (1988) *The Sociology of Modernisation and Development*, London: Unwyn Hyman.

Hayter, T. and Harvey, D. (eds) (1993) *The Factory and the City: Story of the Cowley Automobile Workers in Oxford*, London: Mansell Publishing.

Kim, W.B., Douglass, M., Choe, S.C. and Ho, K.H. (eds) (1997) *Culture and the City in East Asia*, Oxford: Oxford University Press.

Knox, P. (2002), 'World Cities and the Organisation of Global Space', in R.J. Johnston, P.J. Taylor and M.J. Watts (eds), *Geographies of Global Change: Remapping the World*, 2nd edn, Oxford: Blackwell Publishing.

Lee, H.G. (ed.) (2004) *Civil Society in Southeast Asia*, Singapore: Institute of Southeast Asian Studies.

Lo, F.C. and Yeung, Y.M. (eds) (1996) *Emerging World Cities in Pacific Asia*, New York: United Nations University Press.

Marchand, M. and Runyan, A. (2001) 'Feminist Sightings of Global Restructuring: Conceptualizations and Reconceptualizations', in F.J. Schuurman (ed.) *Globalization and Development Studies: Challenges for the 21st Century*, London: Sage.

Marx, K. (1954), *Capital*, Vol. I, London: Lawrence & Wishart.

Olds, K., Dicken, P., Kelly P.E., Kong, L. and Yeung, H.W-C. (eds.) (1999) *Globalisation and the Asia Pacific: Contested Territories*, London: Routledge.

Parnwell, M. (1999) 'Culture and the City in East Asia', *The Journal of Development Studies*, 35 (4): 204–205.

Pile, S. (1997) 'Introduction', in S. Pile and M. Keith (eds), *Geographies of Resistance*, London: Routledge.

Portaliou, E. (2007) 'Anti-Global Movements Reclaim the City', *City*, 11(2): 165–175.

Rodan, G. (ed.) (1996) *Political oppositions in Industrialising Asia*, London: Routledge.

Routledge, P. (2002) 'Resisting and Reshaping Destructive Development: Social Movements and Globalising Networks', in R.J. Johnston, P.J. Taylor and M.J. Watts (eds), *Geographies of Global Change: Remapping the World* 2nd edn, Oxford: Blackwell Publishing.

Sassen, S. (2005) 'The Repositioning of Citizenship and Alienage: Emergent Subjects and Spaces for Politics', *Globalisations*, 2(1): 79–94.

Schak, D. and Hudson, W. (ed.) (2003) *Civil Society in Asia*, Aldershot: Ashgate Publishing.

Scott, J.C. (1990) *Domination and the Arts of Resistance*, Yale: Yale University Press.

—— (1986) 'Everyday Forms of Peasant Resistance', *Journal of Peasant Studies*, 13(2): 5–35.

—— (1985) *Weapons of the Weak: Everyday Forms of Peasant Resistance*, Yale: Yale University Press.

Scott, J.C. and Kerkvliet, B. (1986) 'Introduction', *Journal of Peasant Studies*, 13(2): 1–3.

Skuse, A. and Cousins, T. (2007) 'Spaces of Resistance: Informal Settlement, Communication and Community Organisation in a Cape Town Township', *Urban Studies*, 44 (5/6): 979–995.

Vasudevan, R., Sundaram, R., Bagchi, J., Narula, M., Lovink, G. and Sengupta, S. (eds) (2002) *The Cities of Everyday Life,* Delhi: Sarai.

Velayutham, S. (2007) *Responding to Globalisation: Nation, Culture and Identity in Singapore,* Singapore: Institute of Southeast Asian Studies.

White, C. (1986) 'Everyday Resistance, Socialist Revolution and Rural Development: The Vietnamese Case', *Journal of Peasant Studies*, 13(2): 49–63.

Wise, A. (Forthcoming, 2009). 'Sensuous Multiculturalism: Emotional Landscapes of Interethnic Living in Australian Suburbia', *Journal of Ethnic and Migration Studies*.

—— (2005) 'Hope and Belonging in a Multicultural Suburb', *Journal of Intercultural Studies*, 26(1/2): 171–186.

Wu, F. (ed.) (2007) *China's Emerging Cities: The Making of New Urbanism*, Abingdon, Oxon: Routledge.

1 Seeds of dissent

The politics of resistance to Beijing's Olympic redevelopment

Anne-Marie Broudehoux

For decades, the Chinese leadership has used large-scale events, including national celebrations and international meetings, as an occasion to initiate urban change and accelerate the modernisation of its national capital. With investments surpassing any other event in Olympic history, Beijing's hosting of the 2008 Olympic Games served as a catalyst for a thorough transformation of the city's physical and social landscape.[1] While this rapid transformation carries important benefits – increasing Beijing's global visibility, boosting civic pride, modernising urban infrastructures, and stimulating the local economy in the tourism and real estate sectors – it also bears important social, cultural and economic costs.

But despite a staggering record in terms of forced evictions, labour exploitation and rights violations, Beijing's Olympic redevelopment has generated surprisingly little organised opposition, especially when compared with previous host cities. Based on an early assessment of the impact of Beijing's Olympic transformations, this article suggests that the Olympics have exacerbated the conditions that limit the possibilities of collective resistance in contemporary China. This article also demonstrates how under such restrictive conditions, people have developed a broad range of alternative ways to oppose urban redevelopment and challenge hegemony, using covert tactics of dissent and symbolic modes of resistance to seek redress and turn oppressive situations to their advantage. This article further suggests that these covert strategies may play a part in helping develop a sense of entitlement among urban citizens and bring them a step closer to organised resistance.

The great transformation

Over the seven-year period after winning its Olympic bid, Beijing embarked on an unparalleled urban redevelopment programme, which included the construction of 31 competition venues, 50 training venues and related facilities, a 42-building athlete village and a 16-building media village, as well as new transportation infrastructure with the construction of 62 new roads, four bridges and the expansion of the subway and light rail network (Beijing 2008). This impressive transformation was supplemented by the construction of the world's largest airport terminal, several spectacular cultural projects, important neighbourhood renewal initiatives, as well as countless environmental beautification and landscaping projects (Broudehoux 2007).

The cost of these achievements was partly borne by some of China's most vulnerable population groups. The Geneva-based Centre on Housing Rights and Evictions (COHRE) estimates that between 2001 and 2008, 1.5 million citizens have been uprooted and had their homes demolished to make way for Olympic facilities and infrastructure projects, often without adequate compensation.[2] Not only did Olympic preparations accelerate the rate of urban redevelopment and cause a surge in evictions, but the sense of urgency generated by the tight Olympic deadline also justified the ruthless ways in which some of these evictions were carried out.[3]

If the state's land ownership and power of eviction allowed for the rapid transformation of the city, Beijing's capacity to finance these spectacular projects, built at a tenth of their equivalent cost in Europe, also depended upon the exploitation of a vast, pliant, and disposable migrant labour force, whose rights are routinely violated (see Hsu, this volume). Working long hours in dangerous conditions without adequate safeguards, they receive few legally mandated benefits.[4] Eviction figures cited earlier did not include illegal migrants who lived in the 171 informal settlements that were demolished to make way for Olympic projects (COHRE 2007). Beijing's pre-Olympic clean-up also forced the closure of dozens of schools for children of migrant labourers as part of a government strategy to expel migrants from the city before the Games (HRW 2006a).

The cost of Olympic fame

The long-term costs of Olympic redevelopment are many, creating lasting impacts on Beijing's urban structure and deeply affecting its socio-spatial configuration. The concentration of investments in certain sectors of the city exacerbated pre-existing inequalities, sharpening the social, economic and spatial divides between the city's new rich and its emerging new poor. Furthermore, the destruction of forms of sociability that used to unite different components of society may carry unforeseen political consequences, such as undermining the social cohesion necessary for the long-term stability of the city and nation. At a more personal level, if some families have improved their living conditions as a result of their relocation, others have suffered economic, social and psychological hardships. Olympic image construction had a direct impact on the livelihood of economically and socially marginalised groups in Beijing, accelerating a process of downward mobility. In fact COHRE (2007) estimates that one out of five people displaced by Olympic projects, or an average of 33,000 a year since 2001, were impoverished as a result of their relocation and suffered a significant deterioration in their living conditions and life opportunities. Olympic redevelopment greatly reduced the affordable housing stock and caused property prices around Olympic projects to rise dramatically, making it less affordable for people to live near the city centre. Displaced Beijingers faced increased costs of living due to relocation to the city's outlying suburbs, away from schools, jobs and basic services. In the absence of public transportation, many had to cope with increased transportation costs and commuting time to be able to earn a decent living. Relocation apartments also carried important hidden charges, such as management fees and unsubsidised utility charges that often exceeded people's capacity to pay.

Olympic redevelopment not only worsened some people's living conditions but it also made them more vulnerable to abuse and exploitation. The massive displacement of the underprivileged from the city centre weakened community ties and made it difficult to rebuild social networks for mutual assistance, and diminished their capacity to organise and fight for their rights.

Olympic pacification

In recent years, civic actions to fight redevelopment, including diverse forms of civil disobedience such as mass sit-ins, traffic blockades and street demonstrations, have been on the rise throughout China (Zhang 2004). However, while these forms of overt, collective and organised protest were uncommon in pre-Olympic Beijing, mobilisation against Olympic projects were generally isolated incidents, which, in spite of their non-political nature, were swiftly repressed. For example, on August 20, 2004, hundreds of disgruntled suburban farmers whose land was confiscated to build an exclusive residential project lined up bicycles to block traffic in a Beijing suburb, and were soon forcibly dispersed (Cody 2004).

Several factors explain this relative dearth of collective mobilisation, among which are an underdeveloped sense of rights and entitlement; the repressive nature of the regime; the limited role of civil society, political actors and the media in debating and criticising demolition and relocation; and the nationalist appropriation of the Games. These factors all played a part in creating a political climate that limited the possibility of resistance.

One of the main reasons for the lack of resistance to Olympic redevelopment was that people were often unaware of their citizenship rights and lacked a clear sense of entitlement that would allow to them to formulate claims and to seek redress for rights violations. Despite evidence of an emerging 'rights consciousness' among citizens (Hsing forthcoming; Zhang and Ong 2008), most people continued to listen to the voice of authority and comply with state orders without questioning their legitimacy. A long-standing cultural aversion to conflict and a general tendency to avoid open confrontation were compounded by relentless appeals for the construction of a peaceful, harmonious society in official state propaganda, especially in the years leading to the Games. As a result, only those who felt that a fundamental right has been violated beyond the tolerable dared contest official eviction orders.

The repressive political climate in the years leading to the games, and restrictions on the rights of freedom of expression, assembly and association also played a part in the lack of resistance to Olympic redevelopment. The state's desire to control every aspect of the event and to live up to its claims of hosting a flawless Olympics brought unpredictable shifts in government responses to popular contention. Widespread repression of outspoken journalists, cyber-dissidents, and rights advocates also intimidated potential protesters and encouraged self-policing.

The ideological instrumentalisation of the Olympics contributed a considerable amount of economic, political and psychological leverage to Chinese authorities and helped limit all forms of challenge to redevelopment. Olympic propaganda was greatly infused with nationalist rhetoric, to the point that the nation and the Olympics merged in the collective imagination so that serving one was like serving the other. In Beijing, embracing the Olympics was not only a civic duty, but also a patriotic gesture and a contribution to the advancement of the motherland. By extension, non-compliance to social reforms and opposition to Olympic projects were condemned as anti-patriotic.

I contend that by converting pent-up frustrations into patriotic fervour and refocusing popular attention away from rising social inequalities, state-induced Olympic euphoria acted as an instrument of pacification, neutralising discontent and dispelling possibilities of contestation. Appeals to nationalist sentiment helped silence and undermine the legitimacy of diverse forms of protest. The discursive construction of the Games as a grand patriotic endeavour exerted public and peer pressure on recalcitrant residents, often discrediting their actions as self-interested. It also displaced attention from the rights violation suffered by victims of redevelopment by blaming them for standing in the way of national progress and causing China to lose face on the international scene. This nationalist appropriation of the Olympics put tremendous pressure on residents to accept relocation and sacrifice their own well-being for the common good. In such a context, self-censorship played a key role in discouraging contention. The importance placed upon the Olympics and their success for the nation helped create a social climate where forced evictions were not only considered acceptable, but necessary as well (COHRE 2007).

Open resistance to the Beijing Olympics was also impeded by the absence of an autonomous Chinese public sphere offering the right to criticise policies, fight state oppression or hold officials accountable. The Chinese Communist Party continues to exert considerable control over society, effectively monopolising the resources available for social mobilisation, resulting in the relative dearth of independent political organisations (Zhang and Ong 2008; CECC 2005b). The last few decades have witnessed the growth of third sector organisations in China, as non-profit organisations such as charities, clubs and associations of all kinds gained latitude to pursue activities. However, far from embodying an independent civil society, third sector organisations are closely monitored and subject to a restrictive regulatory environment, while their activities must remain within the strict political limits set by the state (Béja 2006).

Far from being in structural opposition to the regime, this civil society often helps sustain socialist rule by reducing the government's burden and compensating for the state's disengagement from welfare provision and education. Some even argue that civil society organisations have contributed to the maintenance of national stability by helping pacify the disgruntled, and providing charity rather than helping people organise to defend their rights (Liu 2007; Béja 2006; however see Hsu, this volume, for an alternative view).

Many public intellectuals, including writers, historians, economists and scientists have similarly been co-opted into the service of the state. Throughout the history of modern China, scholars and intellectuals have served as voices of introspection, reform and dissent against the excesses of China's leaders (CECC 2005a). However, over the last 15 years the traditional role of the Chinese intellectual to speak truth to power has significantly declined, in part because outspoken critics of the party have been subjected to intimidation and repression. This decline is also due to the state's ability to buy out scholars and intellectuals with higher salaries, better housing, access to travel abroad, and more publishing freedom, on the condition that they no longer seek to reform the political system. Some intellectuals have exchanged their role of moral authority to serve the state as consultants and expert advisors (CECC 2005a; Marquand 2004). But not all have given up their political role and a few independent scholars provide a critical voice on the Internet and in the international media, though with a limited local impact.

The current political context has also restricted people's ability to appeal to the media to have their voices heard. China's official press and broadcast media remain tightly controlled and are subject to internal censorship that minimises controversial and socially provocative content. Because it represents a sensitive issue perceived to pose a threat to national stability, resistance to urban redevelopment is still considered a banned topic for journalists. The official media generally avoids reporting eviction disputes and relocation controversies, which cannot be openly and critically discussed. Although there have been news reports of unusual candour on the issue, especially in the new electronic media, those who oppose redevelopment, especially Olympic-related, are usually denounced in the official press for their selfish efforts to safeguard vested interests and protect personal rights. By failing to report violations and, instead, carrying out denigration campaigns against those who oppose Beijing's regeneration, China's official media has become complicit in redevelopment and plays a part in containing opposition.

Resisting redevelopment

Because the state has monopolised the capacity for collective mobilisation, popular resistance to the Beijing Olympics has been mostly individual and family based, unorganised and unconcerted. The following section surveys the most common forms of resistance used by Beijing residents to oppose redevelopment, and illustrates some of the creative strategies developed to circumvent the system, subvert the conditions of their oppression and turn them to their advantage.

Despite the implicit and explicit controls on resistance noted earlier, Beijingers have refused to remain passive victims of redevelopment and have mobilised available resources to advance various causes. Over the last decade, urban renewal has become a growing object of contention as residents became more aware of their civic rights, especially with regards to property (Zhang and Ong 2008). However, the systematic repression of collective action and conventional forms of civil disobedience has pushed people to develop and deploy subtle and covert forms of resistance and camouflaged strategies of dissent. These represent the 'weapons of the weak' as defined by James C. Scott (1985), or everyday acts of subversion and ordinary forms of resistance devised by the powerless to challenge hegemony, destabilise their oppressor or simply vent their anger.

Usually, people first turn to the few legally sanctioned means available to them to seek redress, taking local cadres, developers and demolition companies to court, and petitioning high-level officials. However, in the absence of an independent judiciary, there exist few legal remedies for the victims of redevelopment. Legal actions against illegal evictions and unfair compensation are rarely successful, as plaintiffs often lack legal titles and evidence of entitlement to ownership or tenancy rights. The legal process can also be lengthy and by the time people do get a court order, their house – which often constitutes the only material evidence to prove their case – is generally gone. Private developers and demolition and relocation bureaus excel in carrying out speedy demolitions so as to limit possible litigation. Protesters, lawyers and housing rights defenders are also routinely intimidated into dropping charges, by being detained, harassed or put under police surveillance. Some have been arrested and charged with bogus allegations (Markus 2003). As a result of such a repressive climate, many lawyers are dissuaded from taking on eviction cases and few victims have access to legal aid. Furthermore, since 2005, lower courts can no longer hear cases brought by evictees and new government regulations restrict lawyers from representing such plaintiffs (HRW 2006b).

Some people have developed clever legalistic manoeuvring to circumvent developers' and local governments' manipulative tactics. You-tien Hsing has documented the inventive ways in which relocatees have turned a legal dead-end into their own advantage, finding cracks in the legal system and using their wit to transform an exploitative situation into a small victory (Hsing forthcoming; 2008). The first strategy takes advantage of an opportunity offered by the central government's 2005 order for the compulsory renewal of the national identity card. Part of the information to be updated on the new card was the card owner's official place of residence, for which displaced residents were instructed to put down the address of their relocation home. But to contest the legitimacy of the relocation process, some insisted on putting their old address on the card even if their house had been demolished. They argued that they could not recognise their new home as their legal address since it was acquired as the result of an illegitimate government action. These residents would later use this official identity card in court cases as a legal proof of entitlement to the demolished property (Hsing 2008).

Many relocatees, believing they had full ownership of their newly allocated home, realised they had become tenants of the private developer, owing him rent, management fees and other charges. Many have refused to pay, because it would sanction the legality of what they view as a fraudulent contract. Developers have taken defaulters to court without realising that it would warrant an entry into the judicial system that had been denied to them since 2005, when Beijing's People's Court had stopped hearing disputes initiated by evictees. Having their day in court as defendants, they could now expose the developers' unlawful practices and plead their case in front of a judge. Only through this creative role reversal from 'reactive defendant to proactive challenger' could they enter the legal system and attempt to challenge urban redevelopment (Hsing 2008).

Even though these creative means of détournement of an illegitimate and exploitative situation were generally practiced by individuals, they spread like wild fire, through word of mouth, Internet blogging and media reports, as ever growing numbers sought redress for injustice. Although getting a day in court did not necessarily result in improved conditions, the clear sense of vindication it afforded people is empowering, allowing them to reclaim their sense of pride, dignity and entitlement after having suffered dispossession.

Petitioning is another popular approach commonly used to collectively seek reparation. In China, there is a long tradition of using petitions as a way of making contentious claims for the redress of collective grievances (Esherick and Wasserstrom 1991). This centuries-old approach, which allows anyone to submit a petition at various levels of government, is often used as an avenue of last resort when other legal options are exhausted, or as a complementary measure combined with other forms of mobilisation. It permits petitioners to bypass corrupt and ill-advised local authorities and appeal directly to prominent politicians in the central government, thought to be less corrupt and more concerned with fairness and stability than low-level officials. However, the popularity of the petitioning system weakened its impact, as the ever-growing number of petitions was becoming too large for the state to handle, and many ended up in bureaucratic limbo, as they were transferred from bureau to bureau without reaching the right authority (COHRE 2008). Furthermore, to have any weight, a petition must represent the collective interests of an impressive number of people, or bear the names of well-established public figures either in the cultural, scientific or intellectual spheres.

In spite of these shortcomings, the petitioning system still has advantages: it may promote an embryonic form of mobilisation in its search for the greatest possible number of signatories, and help crystallise the collective engagement of individual plaintiffs. For example, in 2000, a group of evictees decided to unite and form 'the 10,000 plaintiffs coalition' in order to collectively sue Beijing's Land Management Bureau over unlawful urban renewal practices. Although the court never accepted the case, people resubmitted it every February for seven consecutive years. Through mass mobilisation and legal education initiatives, by 2003, the coalition had grown to 30,000 people who signed a petition to the central government demanding that their rights be recognised (Hsing 2008). Although their demands are yet to be fulfilled, this kind of mobilisation carries important social implications. Recognising the injustice they suffered as a violation entitled these plaintiffs to make a moral claim to the right to the city, an important step forward, according to You-tien Hsing (2008), in demanding citizenship rights.

The petitioning system may also help reactivate the historical role of public intellectuals. In recent years, important public figures, including members of the Chinese Academy of Sciences, historians, preservation activists, academics and other public figures, have intervened on urban renewal issues, by sending petitions to the central government to voice specific concerns or to condemn corruption and exploitation.[5] In Olympic Beijing, prominent members of society have kept a vigilant eye on redevelopment, sending in 2004 a series of petitions to the central government demanding a re-examination of many venues, especially with regard to safety and cost. Although it is unclear what weight these petitions carried, later that year construction on all major Olympic venues came to a halt as the government called for a complete reassessment of the projects. This resulted in important spending reappraisals, improved working conditions and design modifications as several venues were scaled down, and their construction deadlines pushed back a year (Broudehoux 2007).

After legal avenues have failed, one of the most common measures of resistance to redevelopment in Beijing is 'stand-off', carried out by recalcitrant residents who resist eviction by refusing to vacate their house, because they are dissatisfied with the proposed compensation package (Zhang 2004). Known as *dingzihu* or nailed-in households, these families spend months, sometimes years, living in precarious conditions, often without basic services such as electricity and running water, and in constant fear that their house will be torn down if left unoccupied. Although the physical and psychological violence endured at the hands of demolition crews, and the wait and insecurity can be insufferable, people hold on to the hope that this passive resistance strategy will afford them some leverage in the negotiation process for fair compensation, and be rewarded by the settlement of their contentious claims.

One interesting example is the story of the Li family.[6] In 2005, residents of the eastern part of the Qianmen district received eviction notices and were offered the choice between a monetary compensation and a relocation apartment in exchange for their homes. Owning two houses in the neighbourhood, the Li family opted to get cash for one and an apartment for the other. But after their first home was demolished, they realised that the compensation they had received was well below the actual market value of the property. Feeling cheated, they decided to be more prudent with their remaining property. Since the relocation units promised by the developer were still under construction, most of the residents who had signed away their old houses had to rent elsewhere in the city while awaiting the delivery of their new home. The Li family decided that they would rather wait for the new apartment to be ready before surrendering their house to demolition, both to save on rental cost and to make sure the new unit suited their needs.

When I first met the Li family in 2007, they had camped out for over two years in a field of rubble, in the one remaining room of the courtyard house they had shared with neighbours. Mrs Li and her daughter were taking turns guarding the broken house for fear of demolition and robbery. They suffered from lack of sleep due to the road construction work being done at night at their doorstep. The sight of this courageous act of resistance had attracted a silent commentary from Zhang Dali, a local artist long engaged in denouncing Beijing's massive redevelopment (Broudehoux 2004). On one of the interior walls that had been left exposed by the demolition of contiguous structures, Zhang had spray painted one of his trademark graffiti figures developed in the 1990s to condemn Beijing's destructive redevelopment (see Marinelli, this volume), stamping the lone surviving house with a powerful mark of outrage.

I returned to the site a year later, during the 2008 Olympics. The Li family still lived in the scarred 10 square metre house but their patience had paid off with an

Figure 1.1 The Li home with Zhang Dali's graffiti figure, July 2007 (photograph by the author).

unexpected twist of fate. The house was now surrounded by a lush green lawn put down by the city as part of Olympic beautification. Spending her days sitting on the lawn under an umbrella, Mrs Li now hoped for relocation to be delayed another year so she could enjoy living in this quiet cottage on a professionally landscaped lot in the city centre, 300 metres from Tiananmen Square. Even the most rich and powerful in Chinese society, she said, do not have such a chance.

Other victims of redevelopment have taken more desperate measures to have their voices heard. The psychological trauma of being uprooted, compounded by the distress of being powerless and disenfranchised, has taken its toll on some Beijingers, especially older residents, some of whom did not survive relocation (Lai and Lee 2006; Du Plessis 2005). The prospect of being forcibly evicted was so terrifying that some risked their lives in an attempt to resist. In certain cases, after fruitless attempts to obtain fair compensation and when eviction could no longer be averted, suicide was used as an ultimate protest strategy to attract attention to a cause, as people took their lives in very public displays of desperation, often through self-immolation.[7] But even these extreme measures failed to move authorities and were often harshly repressed. In April 2007, an elderly woman threatened to commit suicide by jumping from her apartment window on the construction site of China Central Television (CCTV) Network's new headquarters, one of Olympic

Figure 1.2 The Li home with its new lawn, during the 2008 summer Olympics (photograph by the author).

Beijing's spectacular projects, after all her possessions had been forcibly removed. She was arrested by the district government for causing a public disturbance, along with a witness who had expressed sympathy for her cause (COHRE 2007).

Another well-documented example is the story of the Ye brothers. On October 1, 2003, China's National Day, Ye Guoqiang tried to kill himself by jumping off a bridge in the Forbidden City in front of hundreds of onlookers, to protest the forced demolition of his family's home and restaurant and the compensation offered. Ye Guoqiang survived the jump but received a two-year prison sentence for disturbing the social order. Also briefly jailed, his brother, Ye Guozhu, continued working with a lawyer to obtain rightful compensation for their loss while organising local residents to fight unfair evictions. In August 2004, after applying for permission to hold a mass protest against forced relocation in the capital, Ye Guozhu was jailed for four years, having been found guilty of 'picking quarrels and stirring up trouble' (BBC 2004). To this day, Amnesty International is still exerting pressure on the Chinese prime minister for his release, claiming he has been subjected to torture during his detention (Amnesty International 2008).

More often, people deploy a mixed repertoire of strategies of resistance, combining more familiar tactics including taking legal action, petitioning, leafleting, contacting the media and holding out, with more symbolic strategies of protest and dissent. A good example is the story of recalcitrant property owner Zhang Jinli (Ou 2006). In December 2004, demolition began in the historical district of Dazhalan, as part of the Qianmen district redevelopment project, one of Olympic Beijing's most spectacular and controversial slum clearance interventions, involving some of the highest levels of evictions (COHRE 2008; Meyer 2008; Lin 2006). Once the commercial centre of the city, this densely populated neighbourhood south of Tiananmen Square was also an important site for the absorption and acculturation of poor newcomers to Beijing and housed some of the centre's most destitute inhabitants.[8]

Considered substandard when compared to more upscale shopping districts like Xidan and Wangfujing, the neighbourhood had recently fallen into disrepair, and lagged behind other parts of the city in terms of modernisation. Labelling it as a slum, Beijing authorities decided to rid the city centre of this eyesore by redeveloping this prime real estate into a pedestrian shopping district, housing a mix of traditional Chinese stores and international brand name outlets in Qing-dynasty inspired buildings.[9]

Because of the sensitive nature of the project, plans remained undisclosed to the public, and residents received a few weeks' notice of their eviction. After demolition began, scholars, preservationists and concerned residents tried to save what was left of the neighbourhood, generating enough public discussion to turn the situation into a political controversy. In 2006, a group of Beijing scholars filed a petition with the National People's Congress, denouncing this violation of Beijing's preservation policy and warning that demolishing Qianmen would be more devastating to the cultural heritage of Beijing than the destruction of the ancient city wall by Mao (Yardley 2006).

Local residents also tried to fight to save their own property from destruction and to preserve their close-knit community. Zhang Jinli would become one of the most famous defenders of Dazhalan, a maze of small alleyways and lanes in the western section of the district.[10] Zhang owned a house and restaurant, property acquired by his father just after the revolution on Meishi street, a busy north–south street selected for road widening in order to accommodate the vehicular traffic diverted as the result of Qianmen's pedestrianisation. Zhang waged a long battle to save his home and family's livelihood. He contested the compensation offered by the developer, which ignored the existence of his restaurant and was based on outdated market values. Zhang first resorted to legal means to plead against the unfair treatment he had been subjected to, and called on journalists to witness and report his plight. He also tried to organise a resistance movement to oppose the demolition of Meishi street, distributing flyers around the neighbourhood to raise awareness of the injustice being committed. As these efforts failed and demolition proceeded, Zhang decided to hold on and was labelled a *dingzihu*.

Becoming emboldened and defiant, he turned to less orthodox tactics to elicit reactions from the demolition company and local housing bureau, and to gain visibility to rally others for his cause. Using both wit and irony, Zhang began staging theatrical actions in appealing for his citizenship rights while avoiding overt political criticism. Zhang hung banners on his house denouncing the National Bureau of

Land Resources for their handling of the relocation process, and accused the demolition company of falsifying agreements. He placed a discarded mannequin on his rooftop wearing a shirt bearing the words: 'I strongly demand to see Bao Gong', a reference to an ancient Chinese judge renowned for his fairness and integrity. He also greeted the local police who came to take down his banners by singing the revolutionary anthem, *Without the Communist Party, there is No New China* (Ou 2006).

Zhang's efforts, however, remained individualised, as he failed to organise the community to collectively resist eviction. His house was finally demolished in March 2006. Yet his engagement and determination did prompt others to further his cause. Among them were artists Cao Fei and Ou Ning, who had set out in 2005 to record everyday life in Dazhalan on the eve of its transformation, as part of a China-wide urban documentation project.[11] Zhang's courageous struggle prompted them to place a camera in his hands and let him document his daily protest actions. Zhang gladly seized the opportunity to record the last days of old Meishi street and keep a trace of it for posterity. The result was a 90-minute documentary depicting the conflict between local authorities and the inhabitants of Dazhalan on the eve of the 2008 Olympics.[12] Widely accessible on the Dazhalan Project's extensive website, the film was shown around the world at different events discussing Beijing's transformations and played a major role in keeping Beijing's redevelopment in the international spotlight.

In this case, artist and activist united in a beneficial partnership. While Zhang's filming helped Ou and Cao document a passing way of life from an insider's perspective, the attention paid to Zhang in return helped embolden and intensify his actions and afforded him a greater visibility. The result is a rarely recorded testimony of a lone struggle to save a home, a livelihood and a way of life, that bears no political message other than the powerful images and stories it captured (reminiscent of work by the Cybermohalla Project in Delhi, see Butcher, this volume). While Zhang failed to save his house, he has become an emblematic figure in the fight against greed and power. Ultimately, the message sent by his actions, which reached beyond Beijing's frontiers, may have a lasting impact.

This example underlines the growing importance of the Internet as a tactical tool in the battle against redevelopment, as blogs and websites become privileged places for disseminating information, sharing resources and strategies, and providing a vast forum for discussion. Ou Ning is also behind alternativearchives.com, a group of volunteers racing against time to document the disappearing lifestyles and architecture of Beijing's traditional neighbourhoods. Armed with cameras, these volunteers are compiling a web-based photographic record of this disappearing landscape, collecting images of ancient gates, courtyard houses and ornamental details.

Recent years have seen the multiplication of groups, at times organised as NGOs and many with a preservation agenda, using the Internet as a platform to raise awareness, recruit volunteers, coordinate activities and expose their views to the widest possible audience. These websites often seek to record the transformation of the city, building visual archives and virtual museums to document old Beijing's vanishing urban landscape.[13] As individuals have turned to these websites to share their stories, make their cases heard and to gain moral support from a broader public, these platforms helped compensate for the lack of coverage of redevelopment issues in the official media. I argue that this simple means of keeping the debate alive and refusing to be silenced constitutes an act of resistance, that, given the media attention generated by the Olympics had the potential to exert pressure on Chinese authorities and on the International Olympic Committee as well.

Symbolic strategies of resistance

Other, less visible strategies of voicing dissatisfaction, eluding domination and usurping power have also emerged. One example of covert resistance to redevelopment was the graffiti war that was waged on the walls of neighbourhoods awaiting demolition, using one of the oldest Chinese traditions of urban communication.[14] These walls bear the evidence of a battle of words fought between local authorities and residents. The former painted slogans instructing residents that it is in their best interest to comply with eviction orders and urging them to serve the great Olympic cause. Typical examples included: 'Welcome the Olympics, Leave early receive benefits, Wait around and lose out'; 'Welcome the Olympics, Treasure the Opportunity'; or 'Demolish quickly, Welcome the Olympics, Switch to a New Look'. Residents fought back with their own slogans denouncing the unfair compensation process: 'Calculative developers who undervalue houses make families miserable; the only fair price is the market; can truth prevail?' 'Oppose use of threats, fear, swindles, and other means to carry out evictions.' In other cases, residents posted newspaper clippings about urban renewal on the exteriors of their homes, accompanied by a handwritten commentary underlining the differences between official policy and their own collective reality, especially with respect to compensation rates.

If official slogans were encoded with the imperative yet ambiguous tone of state propaganda and shamelessly brandished the Olympic spirit in their appeal for compliance, the residents' reply to this thinly veiled intimidation campaign was more direct and explicit. While safely avoiding political criticism or allusions to the Olympics, they appealed to basic universal values such as honesty and truth, thus cleverly taking the moral high ground to underline injustice. This tactic afforded residents the ability to retain their integrity while undermining the claims of their adversaries. Even if it has limited public visibility, the anonymity of this mode of communication allowed people to powerfully articulate what they would not be able to say in person, and to publicly enunciate what many were silently thinking.

Further tactics, increasingly common in the battle against urban redevelopment, were popular practices of linguistic resistance and verbal expressions of symbolic discontent, reminiscent of those described in another context by Pred (1992). The Chinese language is especially conducive to the development of oral recalcitrance and linguistic forms of reworking. Its numerous homonyms and tonalities facilitate the playful generation of clever ditties, malicious double entendre and irreverent word games that have long been used to unsettle authority and skirt domination. For centuries, Chinese people have used similar narrative strategies to remodel official slogans and transform dominant discourse into absurdist, derogatory or cunning expressions.

Today, extensive criticism can be found in the popular 'rhythmic sayings' *(shunkouliu)* that abound within China's underground grapevine and travel all over China through word of mouth, and, increasingly, text-messaging (Zhou and Link 2001). Because they have no known author, cannot be put into print, broadcast or recited openly in public, these blunt, satirical rhymes remain free of censorship. But they do carry sufficient weight to be collected by a state office, which monitors popular opinion. A similar strategy described by Patricia Thornton (2002a) is the transformation of traditional couplets *(menlian)* that have long adorned private and public doorways with auspicious and poetic greetings at the occasion of the New Year or other celebrations, and are now turned into covert political criticism through a strategic combination of irony, ambiguity and metonymy.

Bakhtin (1984) referred to such irreverent idiomatic reworkings as grotesque realism, which afforded an absurdist parody of elitist good taste and a baroque laughter at the expense of power. While betraying a keen sense of humour, they represent acts of defiance and symbolic discontent that carry important ideological underpinnings. Butler (1997) insists on the subversive potential of parody, which, once disruptive, becomes domesticated and recirculated to destabilise the primacy of hegemonic meanings. Similar practices of using language to give expression to emotions, attitudes, and preoccupations that cannot be expressed openly have been recorded in other totalitarian states (Wierzbicka 1990).

One of the most widely used weapons of contention for signalling dissatisfaction with urban beautification and discrediting Beijing's Olympic projects has thus been the uttered word. Long before the construction of some of the more grandiose projects, colourful nicknames were devised by the population, using ambiguity and double entendre to unmask government pretence and ridicule design pretensions. These renaming practices often amounted to a usurpation of the official interpretation proposed by designers and political leaders, as individuals attempted to reinterpret and manipulate the symbols that encode specific meanings into the landscape.

One of the main targets of these verbal attacks was the highly controversial design for the new headquarters of CCTV, the party's main propaganda machine. Popular reception of this US$700 million gravity-defying loop had been harsh, as suggested by its prosaic, even demeaning likening to a bench, a kneeling man, a pair of pants, or, more often, a doughnut. The building's common reference of *weifang*, the dangerous or crooked building, expresses general suspicion about its structural integrity and criticises the state's demagogy in choosing such an outlandish design. The use of this particular epithet is also a clever commentary on the numerous evictions this project has required, as the term *weifang* is usually used to classify houses earmarked for demolition, marking them as substandard and unfit for habitation.

The National Centre for the Performing Arts (NCPA), another Olympic-related building, also suffered public scorn.[15] The project was heavily criticised for its spectacular price tag and futuristic design, unfit for its location next to Tiananmen Square. The poetic metaphors used to describe this titanium dome, such as the water drop or the pearl, have been reworked into crude, at times vulgar popular nicknames, endowing it with an air of ridicule and absurdity. Ranging from light mockery such as the bubble, the flying saucer or the pillbox, to more insulting variations on the egg concept, to less equivocal evocations of tomb, or a funeral mound, these sarcastic renaming practices conceal a deeper political commentary. More than a simple reference to its shape, descriptions of the National Centre as a 'tomb' reveal a biting critique of president Jiang Zemin, who sponsored this vanity project a stone's throw from Mao's mausoleum, to immortalise his reign and ensure his elevation to China's pantheon of venerable political leaders.

Those resorting to these weapons of the weak are often close neighbours of Olympic projects, who suffered the partial demolition of their home, lost neighbours to relocation, endured displacement, or awaited a fair settlement. The daily insecurities they suffered, as their city was literally being remade under their feet, are palpable in their irreverence towards Olympic mega-projects. The simple presence of these buildings in the landscape is a constant reminder of their limited control over their destiny, and of their exclusion from China's new prosperity. While reflecting their frustration and resentment at the way the rich and powerful are remaking their city, discursive forms of resistance represent an important coping mechanism and afford a certain sense of control to the powerless and disenfranchised. The prosaic quality of these creative resistance strategies and their apparently non-political nature allows the safe delivery of a subversive message under the cover of anonymity and without the fear of repression.

Conclusion

There remains, however, little evidence to suggest that any of these symbolic strategies and minor acts of subversion have directly inspired groups to collectively organise or openly confront state authorities. As such, these weapons of the weak do not constitute well-organised social movements nor represent the sort of collective action generally addressed by social movement theorists due to their un-institutionalised nature and lack of direct impact upon political institutions and the overall power structure.

However, while some of these strategies may appear suboptimal and their impact limited, by allowing people to voice their frustrations and to criticise, by proxy, the regime that condoned such transformation, they potentially bring them one step closer to organised opposition. Partaking in these symbolic acts may create an imagined community of resistance, of a collectivity of interests, that can empower inhabitants to take things one step further and lay the groundwork for more concrete actions, as in the case of the '10,000 plaintiffs coalition'. Therefore, by allowing for the deliberate expression of critical and dissenting views in the public realm, these strategies have helped open up spaces within which new collectivities may be forged and political agendas refined. The broad public circulation of these subversive messages may also encourage collusion between different social actors, mobilise potential followers and garner popular support, thereby contributing to the formation of a social consensus that can inspire political action.

In this sense, these symbolic strategies should still be considered as part of the overall process of social mobilisation, because they have been known to support and advance, in other contexts, more overtly oppositional social movements in modern Chinese history (Thornton 2002b). These apparently innocuous forms of resistance can also register a cumulative effect, especially when used as a complement to more traditional forms of protest, slowly building a greater impact.[16] Whatever the limitations of these diversified modes of resistance, subsequent changes in official regulations and policy regarding urban redevelopment suggested that the state was taking notice. State efforts to rein in forced evictions, to improve compensation, to control corruption in housing allocation and to increase the supply of affordable homes demonstrate that grievances were being heard (Zhang 2004; Hsing 2008).

It is still too early to make a sound assessment of the legacy of the Beijing Olympics. If the event carried important social impacts, by accelerating the rate of redevelopment and justifying harsh repression of dissent, it may also have unanticipated outcomes. By enhancing awareness of the rights and responsibilities of citizenship and helping to develop a clear sense of entitlement, the Games may have contributed to the emergence of new forms of social mobilisation and encouraged the growth of civil society. As Olympic euphoria dissipates, media controls are lifted and new assessments are made in the Games' aftermath, people have begun to reach a full realisation of both the costs and the impacts of recent urban transformations. The coming years will show if the seeds of resistance that were sown will be allowed to bloom and bring about more change.

Notes

1 In early August 2008, Beijing officials evaluated total investment in the 2008 Beijing Olympics, including operational fund, venue construction costs and infrastructure investment, at US$43.13 billion since 2001 (*Shanghai Daily* 2008).
2 Over the period between 2006 and 2008, an average of 60,000 homes were demolished each year, some 13,000 a month. Although not all households were forcibly and unfairly displaced, COHRE estimates that one out of five were (2007: 157).
3 COHRE evaluates that the eviction rate for the 2000–2008 Olympic preparation period is nearly 2.3 times higher than the average for the 1991–1999 period, going from an average of 70,000 people per annum to about 165,000 people a year (2007: 161).
4 Labour rights organisations evaluate unpaid migrant salaries to be more than a billion dollars and estimate that 72 per cent of construction workers suffer from pay arrears (York 2008).
5 One famous case is regarding the National Centre for the Performing Arts in Beijing. In June 2000, two separate petitions, one signed by 49 members of the Chinese Academy of Science and Academy of Engineering, and the other endorsed by 109 leading Chinese architects were submitted to president Jiang Zemin, demanding an unconditional reversal of the decision to build the project (Broudehoux 2004).
6 Li is a pseudonym used to protect the identity of the family.
7 For example, in September 2003, Beijing resident Wang Baoguan committed suicide by self-immolation while being forcibly evicted in Beijing (Pocha 2004).
8 According to official data, at nearly 45,000 people per square kilometre, the population density in the area was twice the average for the city centre.
9 A report published by the Beijing Academy of Social Sciences in July 2005 entitled

'Investigation of Urban Corners in Beijing', identified the area as a typical slum and gave it first priority for redevelopment, although it figured among Beijing's 25 protected inner-city neighbourhoods designated for historic preservation (Dazhalan Project).
10 Zhang Jinli's story is told in detail by Ou Ning on the Dazhalan project website, Dazhalan-project.org
11 See alternativearchives.com
12 Ou Ning's 2006 documentary film is called: *A Line in the Hutong: The Story of Zhang Jinli.*
13 Among such groups are Friends of Old Beijing (www.oldbeijing.net) and Hutong to Highrise (www.hutongtohighrise.com).
14 While the use of 'large character posters' or *dazhibao* is a long established way to express discontent and criticise power, graffiti remains a relatively new phenomenon in China. Some of the first graffiti in Beijing were initiated by artist Zhang Dali in the 1990s as an early criticism of urban redevelopment, and were a response to the ubiquitous *chai* (demolish) character put up by local authorities to mark buildings to be torn down (Broudehoux 2004: 219–225).
15 For more on this controversy, see Broudehoux 2004: 229–234.
16 In a vivid metaphor, James Scott describes how millions of microscopic organisms can form great barrier reefs onto which even the most powerful vessels can run ashore (Scott 1985: xvii).

References

Amnesty International (2008) 'Permission denied – Housing rights activist in prison', April.1. Online. Available http://www.amnesty.org/en/appeals-for-action/permission-denied-housing-rights-activist-prison (accessed 14 August 2008).
Bakhtin, M. (1984) *Rabelais and his World*, trans. by Helene Iswolsky. Bloomington: Indiana University Press.
BBC (2004) 'China eviction protester "jailed"', *BBC News*, 18 December, Online. Available http://news.bbc.co.uk/1/hi/world/asia-pacific/4107609.stm (accessed 14 August 2008).
Beijing 2008 Olympic Games Official Website (2008) 'Olympic venue distribution, Online. Available http://en.beijing2008.cn/venues/ (accessed 14 August 2008).
Béja, J-P. (2006) 'The changing aspects of civil society in China', *Social Research*, 73 (1): 53–74.
Broudehoux, A-M. (2007) 'Delirious Beijing: Euphoria and despair in the Olympic metropolis', in M. Davis and D. Monk (eds), *Evil Paradises: Dreamworlds of Neoliberalism*. New York: New Press.
—— (2004) *The Making and Selling of Post-Mao Beijing*. London: Routledge.
Butler, J. (1997) *Excitable Speech: A Politics of the Performative*. New York: Routledge.
CECC (Congressional-Executive Commission on China) (2005a) 'Public intellectuals in China', roundtable with Merle Goldman, Perry Link and Hu Ping, Online. Available http://www.cecc.gov/pages/roundtables/031005/index.php (accessed 14 August 2008).
—— (2005b) 'On the development of civil society' Annual Report, Section V(a), Online. Available http://www.cecc.gov/pages/annualRpt/annualRpt05/2005_5a_civilsociety.php (accessed 14 August 2008).
Cody, E. (2004) 'China's land grabs raise specter of popular unrest', *The Washington Post*, October. 5: A1.
COHRE (Centre on Housing Rights and Evictions) (2008) *One World, Whose Dream?*

Housing Rights Violations and the Beijing Olympic Games. Geneva: COHRE Special Report.

—— (2007) *Fair Play for Housing Rights: Mega-Events, Olympic Games and Housing Rights*. Geneva: COHRE Special Report: 154–169.

Du Plessis, J. (2005) 'The growing problem of forced evictions and the crucial importance of community-based, locally appropriate alternatives', *Environment and Urbanization,* 17: 125.

Esherick, J.W. and J.N. Wasserstrom (1991) 'Acting out democracy: Political theater in modern China', in J.N. Wasserstrom and E. J. Perry (eds), *Popular Protest and Political Culture in Modern China*. Boulder: Westview Press.

HRW (Human Rights Watch) (2006a) 'Beijing closes schools for migrants children in pre-olympic cleanup', Online. Available http://www.hrw.org/english/docs/2006/09/26/china14263.htm (accessed 14 August 2008).

—— (2006b) *A Great Danger for Lawyers: New Regulatory Curbs on Lawyers Representing Protesters*. New York: HRW.

Hsing, Y. (2008) 'From property rights to residents' rights: Urban construction and grass-roots resistance in Beijing', Paper presented at the Centre for Chinese Studies, University of California, Berkeley, May 2.

—— (forthcoming) 'Urban housing protest in Beijing' in You-tien Hsing and Ching Kwan Lee (eds), *Reclaiming Chinese Society: Politics of Redistribution, Representation, and Recognition*. Abingdon, Oxon; New York: Routledge.

Lai, G. and R.P.L. Lee. (2006) 'Market reforms and psychological distress in urban Beijing', *International Sociology,* 21 (4): 551–579.

Lin, S. (2006) 'Dashilan deadline', *China Daily,* March 24: 3.

Liu, S. (2007) 'Social citizenship in China: Continuity and change', *Citizenship Studies,* 11 (5): 465–179.

Markus, F. (2003) 'Chinese eviction lawyer jailed', *BBC News,* 28 October, Online. Available http://news.bbc.co.uk/1/hi/world/asia-pacific/3220643.stm (accessed 14 August 2008).

Marquand, R. (2004) 'China "gray lists" its intellectuals', *The Christian Science Monitor,* November 30: 1.

Meyer, M. (2008) *The Last Days of Old Beijing: Life in the Vanishing Backstreets of a City Transformed*. New York: Walker.

Ou, N. (2006) *The Story of Zhang Jinli*. Online, Available http://www.alternativearchive.com/ouning/article.asp?id=52 (accessed 14 August 2008).

Pocha, Jehangir (2004) 'Demolitions Straining Families in China', *Boston Globe*, 9 July: p. A6.

Pred, A. (1992) 'Capitalisms, crises, and cultures II: Notes on local transformation and everyday cultural struggles', in A. Pred and M. Watts, *Reworking Modernity: Capitalisms and Symbolic Discontent*. New Brunswick; NJ: Rutgers:106–117.

Scott, J.C. (1985) *Weapons of the Weak: Everyday Forms of Peasant Resistance*. New Haven: Yale University Press.

Shanghai Daily (2008) 'Balance the key to Olympic cost', August 2, Online. Available http://www.shanghaidaily.com/article/?id=369055&type=National (accessed 14 August 2008).

Thornton, P.M. (2002a) 'Framing dissent in contemporary China: Irony, ambiguity and metonymy', *The China Quarterly,* 171: 663.

—— (2002b) 'Insinuation, insult and invective: The threshold of power and protest in modern China', *Comparative Studies in Society and History,* 44 (3): 597–619.

Yardley, J. (2006) 'Olympics imperil historic Beijing neighbourhood', *The New York Times*, July 12: A1.

York, G. (2008) 'China: migrant workers like slaves to Olympic projects', *Communicating Labour Rights*, March 21, Online. Available http://communicatinglabourrights.wordpress. com/2008/03/12/ (accessed 14 August 2008).

Wierzbicka, A. (1990) 'Antitotalitarian language in Poland: Some mechanisms of linguistic self-defense', *Language in Society*, 19.

Zhang, L. (2004) 'Forced from home: Property rights, civic activism, and the politics of relocation in China', *Urban Anthropology & Studies of Cultural Systems & World Economic Development* 33 (2–4): 247–281.

Zhang, L. and A. Ong (eds) (2008) *Privatizing China: Socialism from Afar.* Ithaca: Cornell University Press.

Zhou, K. and P. Link. (2001) 'Shunkouliu: Popular satirical sayings and popular thought', in E.P. Link, R. Madsen and P. Pickowicz (eds), *Popular China: Unofficial Culture in a Globalizing Society.* London: Rowman & Littlefield.

2 Negotiating Beijing's identity at the turn of the twentieth century*

Maurizio Marinelli

Old Beijing was a cultural space characterized and confined by walls (Wang, 2003; Lu, 2005). In the last few years increasing attention has been focused on the socio-spatial transformation of Beijing, and a common denominator identified by many scholars is the vanishing of the city walls. This pivotal element is immediately associated with material loss. However, some scholars have taken this analysis a step further, addressing the city without walls as a "microcosm of what has happened to Chinese culture." (Wang, 1990; quoted by Zha, 1996: 67).

This chapter concentrates on the work of Zhang Dali, an artist who has chosen the Beijing walls as his canvas. The focus is on the significance of his work and the relevant reaction. The analysis of the association between wounded walls, urban culture, and history re-writing, will demonstrate that the physical loss of the walls has deep implications for Beijing's identity at the turn of the twenty-first century. Zhang Dali's work is indicative of a counter-discourse of intellectual resistance, both to the homogenizing transformative dynamics of the city and to the accompanying dominant narrative of progress, forwardness, and globalizing "newness." Traditionally, walls were the pillars of Beijing's construction as a space of order. Their disruption offers Zhang Dali the opportunity to create a "dialogue" on the city and denounce, looking through the walls, the emergence of spaces of exception.

Walled culture or walls of culture

Wang Yi refers to Beijing's architectural engineering as an apparently perfect but dangerously interlocking organism:

> The degree of sophistication classical Chinese city design had attained was so high, it had become a completely self-referential system, a perfect expression of a codified aesthetics that had gone static. [...] It was like an elaborate structure in which every single building block was placed on a precise spot in a precise relation to the other parts and to the whole, so if you removed any single block, *the entire structure would collapse in a heap*.
>
> (Wang, 1990; italics added)

The intricate framework of the city is like a syntactic structure where walls and gates are the punctuation marks of the public space within which the urban community can act and move. Yang Dongping defines the whole Chinese nation as a land of the "walled culture," where "the walls not only block people's vision, they build up psychological barriers for city people … reshape and change personalities" (Yang, 1994: 29–33).

The architectural structure of Imperial Beijing was that of a model compound city surrounded by a city wall. During the Ming dynasty (1368–1644), Beijing assumed its compound structure consisting of four tiers, each cordoned off by a wall:

> Long before the Ming decision to return the primary capital there, the walls of the former Mongolian imperial city had been rebuilt and reinforced. Work had begun on the outer wall in 1370 … The imperial city Beijing as it is known today was essentially complete when the outer city was walled in 1553.
>
> (Steinhardt, 1999: 169)

Beijing was to be protected by four strongly fortified walls, plus the Great Wall, located near the city in the mountains, but the city was not as impregnable as it looked.

Walls marked the division between the outer (*waicheng*) and the inner city (*neicheng*), walls surrounded the Forbidden City (*zijincheng*), the Imperial City (*huangcheng*), and all the subsidiary units down to the rural town, village, and private home. Traditionally, the basic architectural form of residency in China was the walled compound household (*siheyuan*). This was the typical residential style of the northern farmers[1]: a spacious courtyard located at the centre of four rooms that are connected to each other becoming a walled structure. The walls are a sort of "natural surrounding," concentrically materializing the architectural and social mimicry of the notion of the family-state. This structure both reflected social relations, and also played a part in moulding and structuring them. Behind every wall, other spaces opened up as discrete sites of activity. The function of walls was not only for security, to keep strangers out, but also to support the Confucian-based patriarchal order among those living inside. Traditional architecture and the hierarchical system of social control were closely related. In the mimesis of the compound household form (as in the case of the Emperor's palace), walls demarcated the space of expression and set rules for ordering the members of the family. During the Ming and the Qing (1644–1911) dynasties, precise regulations stipulated building forms, house size, and wall length suitable to the different social classes (Zhao, 1990: 2–6; Zhao, 1989: 18–22).

Hwang Ming-Chorng emphasizes the importance of the symbolic and psychological implications of Beijing's walls more than their practical defensive aspect (Hwang, 1986). A wall sets the clear demarcation line between what is significant and powerful and what is not: what is inside the wall is sacred and what is outside is human. From a psychological perspective, the wall can be symbolically considered as a womb, it has a feminine shape; it serves the purpose of embracing, enclosing, securing, and protecting those within its space. At the same time walls must have a gate, which is the way out. Therefore two functions are simultaneously implied: inclusion/exclusion and conjunction at the gate where the two realms meet.

Zhang Dali's inspiration

Zhang Dali's work on walls seems quite simple but it is in fact extremely sophisticated, full of symbolic meaning and implications.

When he was living in Bologna, Italy from 1989 to 1995[2], he saw some walls covered with murals, tags, and incendiary slogans (Leng, 2000: 170). But his real artistic inspiration came from the leading figures of the New York graffiti movement of the seventies (Rammelzee, Haring, etc.).

The art critic Francesca Alinovi has defined graffiti as a "frontier art," the art of "unsettled outposts" (Alinovi, 1984). Keith Haring's work, for example, is a pictorial form of writing, made up of a tangle of marks in ink or white chalk, which run like streams of images in perennial permeation and metamorphosis. Haring used to draw in public spaces what was to become his symbol: the "Radiant Child."

Back in China, after a few years spent abroad, Zhang Dali perceived, in all its violence, the abrupt change of the Beijing cityscape, which is officially celebrated as a result of the "modernization" and "beautification" urban program. Zhang Dali felt that he had a specific aim: to invite the citizens to discuss the transformation of the city. A fundamental distinguishing factor, compared to other graffiti artists, lies in the fact that Zhang Dali chooses wrecked walls that already have a personality of their own, especially in Beijing.

Zhang Dali is an artist for whom the deconstruction of walls is an "incitement to discourse" (Foucault, 1978: 17–35, 106) on the transformation of the city. His action on physical walls suggests an investigation of metaphoric walls as codified symbols of national identity. Zhang Dali calls his art "conceptual art" (*guannian yishu*), meaning an art based on the strict connection between the artist's life and his artwork. He argues: "In the 1990s, art has transcended the limits of aesthetics (*meishu*). It is not a question anymore of whether something is beautiful or not, my art is conceptual, it asks questions about the basic problem of existence" (Stuart, 1999: 2).

Zhang Dali started using silkscreen to print his scribbles and environmental artworks but, in the second half of the nineties, the work that had the greatest impact belongs to what he calls the "Dialogue" (*duihua*) series. Essentially, it is a stylized head profile drawn or chiselled into the walls of Beijing's traditional buildings that have been partially razed or are destined to be torn down. His prototype graffito[3] appeared for the first time on Beijing's walls in 1995 and it was quite shocking, especially because it was a disruption both of the barriers imposed by formalized language and of the official use of walls. Within a few years, the head profile had become the symbol of the artist himself and a recurrent motif for anyone walking the streets of Beijing.

Starting from the axiom that "painting has an extremely limited effect on society" as only "a tiny number of people" go to art galleries in Beijing, Zhang Dali draws the human head profile in the open to offer his message to everyone endowed with eyes. Zhang Dali argues: "In the studio, painting is just a style. On the street, it has meaning: it becomes part of people's lives" (Personal interview, May 1999). As Zhang Dali says: "Human beings leave signs in the cities" and "this is a kind of

Figure 2.1 Dialogue, Forbidden City, Beijing 1998 (photograph by Zhang Dali).

living art" (Zhao, 1998: 2). These declarations suggest an awareness of the potentiality of graffiti as a medium for an active dialogue. Zhang Dali had the opportunity to live in two microcosms of the "East" and the "West," and even though revealing a certain degree of essentialization, he reached the following conclusion: "Asians always want to avoid expressing themselves, letting their thoughts get trapped in their heart, but [they are] your ideas, why do you want to keep them inside?" (Personal interview, June 1999).

But the walls came a-tumbling down

The series named "Dialogue" is a single project but consists of two groups of connected works: both are based on the key element of the head profile, although they use different vehicles of expression. The first group is expressed by means of a visual language based on action symbols, connected and integrated in a symbiosis with environmental structures. In the late nineties one could find these graffiti

Figure 2.2 Demolition, Forbidden City, Beijing 1998 (photograph by Zhang Dali).

works in the streets and in the residential districts of Beijing undergoing radical change due to urban modernization.

The second group consists of collage, oil painting on canvas or silk-screened photographs of the imagery presented in the first group of works. The artist puts this material together in a frame, on a canvas or inside a light box, in which the human head and instant social characters, words or trendy vocabulary (e.g., the computer-based characters-input system called *ma-gen-ma*) become even more closely interrelated and can be perceived as superficial objects.

Zhang Dali finds his material in the streets: he works with images that are accessible to anybody at any time, extracting the essence of urbanity. Through his artwork, Zhang Dali offers the possibility of a dialogue on what is, in the artist's mind, the heart of the matter: the material and spiritual change of the metropolis. The collage logic applied by Zhang Dali combines and animates the images in a new context. The final result is hybridization of languages and cultures. His works create a new reference paradigm of biological and structural chaos, which charac-terizes our epoch and dominates the metamorphosing urbanity of contemporary Beijing as well. The most significant examples are the light boxes. The artist suggests that they should be ideally placed back on the streets, positioning them in the middle of a scene shared between the advertising industry and the state-administered propaganda. The art critic Mathieu Borysevicz argues:

Taking the head from the street (amid deconstruction, turmoil, and change) and placing it back onto the street (of cosmopolitanism, modernity, and

Figure 2.3 Demolition and Dialogue, Chaoyangmenwai Avenue 1998 (photograph by
    Zhang Dali).

chicness) is a strategy that draws attention to the degree of contrast in today's
China. It is a gesture that addresses the strides capitalism has made into a
system that still professes socialism, and it demonstrates the continued enve-
lopment of the individual in both.

(Borysevicz, 1999: 52–58)

The content of the work

The key elements of Zhang Dali's "conceptual art" are three symbols of cultural
resistance:

- A human head profile spray-painted on condemned walls and freeway
  bridges, or engraved, using hammer and chisels, to destroy the inner part of the
  profile knocking it through the wall. This double act of graffiti plus physical
  destruction gives a sense of double aggression, alluding both to the aggression

of the city per se, and to the way the transformation of the city affects the lives of the citizens.

- The tag AK-47 sprayed on the walls is a "word image" used like a *nom de guerre*. The Soviet assault weapon AK-47 represents the violence of a community being ripped apart. Zhang Dali wants to talk about destructive violence and he shoots, using spray paint and hammer instead of a real gun: "If I use this name, I make people think about the Third World, the violence of the cities, and the wild hooligan culture. That's not what people want to think about in Beijing today!" (Personal interview, May 1999). AK-47 is an imagery Zhang Dali uses to talk about a war (and in Beijing, during the last few years, old buildings have been erased at a pace faster than that of wartime Berlin and London), but what Zhang Dali is exposing is also a dialectic war of signifier (the sound-image AK-47) and signified (the violence *of* the city and *in* the city).
- 18k is chosen as the "word image" of commoditization: it stands for 18-carat gold and represents a symbol for the "economic life of the city." It indicates the demystification of the "get-rich mentality" (which is one of the core reasons for the destruction of the old buildings) and a condemnation of the avarice that has gripped the city. The artist uses word images, but he does not use shock as a commercialization strategy.

The title chosen, "Dialogue," indicates Zhang Dali's intention to exchange ideas and personal experiences related to the repercussions of urban change on the life of individuals. This raises the critical question of the meaning of artistic agency in public space as a form of cultural resistance. Zhang Dali's work aims at creating a dialogue on the mechanisms of spatial transformation and their dominant narratives. His work sets the preconditions to analyze, in a dialectic fashion, a set of interrelated opposites like "demolish houses"–"build houses," "development of the city"–"violence of the city." The artist offers his insights on the network of these antinomies: he humanizes the buildings marked for demolition, spraying on the walls the stylized profile of a human head, which could be his own or everybody's. "Dialogue" was also the title chosen for the installation by Xiaolu and Tang Song (the full title was: *Two gunshots fired at the installation "Dialogue"*) at the opening of the China Avant-garde Exhibition at the National Gallery of Beijing. This large group show, including 297 works in various mediums by 186 artists, was held in February 1989, two months before the beginning of the students' demonstration which led to the tragic epilogue of the Tiananmen Square Massacre on June 4, 1989. Not coincidentally, "Dialogue" was repeated over and over again as one of the fundamental keywords during the students' movement in 1989 – expressing one of the main requests of the students, in the sense of a dialogue with the government (Marinelli, 1993: 65–81).

Beijing's transformation

The works by Zhang Dali embody his view of Chinese cities, which he defines as "ruralized cities" or "cities involved in a process of urbanization" (Personal interview, June 1999): these cities are constrained within the vicious circle of urban destruction and construction, without preservation of the historical dwellings. His work resonates as a criticism of the "fever" of building houses without taking into due consideration the aesthetic and historical relation with the pre-existing topography.

His art has also been called "social art" (Zhao, 1998: 2) and "ecological art" (Dao 1998, 14). The artist is a witness who intends to contribute, with his work, to preserve as a document the urban transformation process that has amputated and vandalized the environment. This is the real disfigurement of the cityscape, much more than Zhang Dali's works.

In the run-up to the 2008 Olympic Games held in Beijing the government did its best to convey the idea of "same world, same dream" (*tongyige shijie, tongyige mengxiang*), and to project the image of Beijing as the hyper-realistic plasticized city of "triumphant modernization" (Broudehoux, 2004: 148–207; 2007). From the year 2000, Chinese magazines have been full of articles like "Beijing becoming an international metropolis" (*Beijing Review*, 2000: 12–25).[4] The 2000 agenda of the Chinese economic reform program has set among its priorities the commitment "to quicken the pace of urbanization during the next fifteen years" as "cities are playing the role of the engine of the economic reform" (*Beijing Review*, 2000: 11). In Beijing, the regime of power is trying to project a façade of hypermodernity: "As the cultural and political centre of China, the city is expected to become an international metropolis in the 21st century" (*Beijing Review*, 2000: 12). Along with the demolition of walls in the post-Mao period, we have witnessed a new version of the demolition of "the soy-jar" of traditional culture. This process was perceived in the eighties as a *sine qua non* to achieve political reforms (Zhu, 1987; Bo, 1985; Cui, 1988). In reality, after the "nuclear fission" (*liebian*) of June 4, 1989, the erasure of traditional culture created a vacuum that is quite difficult to fill with anything more consistent than the consumerist culture of disposable goods.

The wording of the official articles reads as a macabre version of the nationalistic inheritance of the ancient sacred city of Beijing. In the meantime, avant-garde artists have shown what Zhang Dali calls "a sense of commitment to the metropolis," which means a willingness to examine urban transformation (*bianqian*) and its semantic counterparts: marginalization (*bianyuanhua*), and estrangement (*gehe*) (Personal interview, May 1999).

Rapid urbanization causes estrangement among urban dwellers, estrangement from the official image of reality, and from the formalized language used to represent it. The avant-garde artists have started to experiment with new creative languages, using the stimuli of urban references to find an individual path of subjective expression amid the chaos and clatter of real life and real people. For these artists art means working in any place with any means: life, creation, and art can happen together. They have thrown themselves into the wreckage of reality and the rubble of society to collect and re-propose the signs of slums, trash, decay, violence, and the spread of AIDS across China. This apparently eccentric, cultural avant-garde group has invented a private jargon, which has attracted the attention of many Asia watchers and art critics around the world.[5] They have succeeded in finding a new language, legitimizing their minority status, and the territorial violation of a consolidated majority language: the formalized language of the Party and the encomiastic official discourse on Beijing, a story of success.

Walls as canvas

Zhang Dali did not choose the walls of condemned buildings around the city as canvases for his "conceptual art" by chance. During the Ming (from Emperor Yongle onwards) and Qing dynasties, Beijing had traditionally been the residence of the Emperor, the occupant of the dragon throne, also identified as the Son of Heaven. Therefore, the act of breaking a wall can be interpreted as desecration, as wounding the body of the dragon/Emperor. Zhang Dali can spray (in other words, shoot) on the walls of Beijing today since the city without walls is no longer a sacred city, or, in Foucauldian terms, the regime of power does not correspond anymore to the regime of truth (Foucault, 1980: 109–133).

Now that the city has been secularized, the broken walls may be chosen by the artist as the screen on which the multifaceted spectacle of city life is projected. The walls of the ruined buildings are humanized: Zhang in an interview used the word *biaoqing*, which means "expression," and often refers to facial expressions or to feelings. Actually, the ancient city walls seem about to express a physical resistance against impending death. Walls are the structures on which "human beings leave their signs" (Zhang, 1999: 24) so that they may be used to narrate the fluctuating consciousness of sight as they are able to register the hopes of the city (through their reinforcement or remodelling), to give voice to the people (through the shadows of their bodies passing by), to express the different feelings and opinions as walls are part of the social discourse. Now that "icy skyscrapers have taken the places of the old houses and the memory of the past is becoming vague and disrupted" (Zhang, 1999: 24), walls seem to cry out for revenge with vital, frozen energy. Zhang Dali gives shape to this inner force acting as a contemporary astonished witness of the disruption of harmony between cosmic and terrestrial forces that characterized traditional Beijing.

Zhang Dali's "conceptual art," especially the silk-screened works, reflects mutation at the level of cognitive and sensory perception. It testifies to the artist's desire to capture forever the very last moment of life of the old houses: "Old houses should be preserved: they are part of the history and the story of a city. The old houses are the city's roots and they are important to our cultural life" (Stuart, 1999: 3). His works can be interpreted as an attempt to defeat, through the subjective reproduction of images, the annihilating force of the modernization drive with "Chinese (or global?) characteristics."

In the late nineties, some of Zhang Dali's works could be found on the main avenues, others in the surviving tiny alleyways (*hutong*) that ran through the old housing area, crossing the traditional old area of the capital. His works had increasingly become a permanent part of the impermanent urban landscape, even though it was clear that their life was temporally limited, due to the demolition of those same buildings, and spatially confined, due to the progressive lack of walls as "canvases." The walls are for Zhang Dali "the projection screen of the modification of this city" that is changing without any rule, without "anybody knowing how the environment and our city will change" (Zhang, 1999: 24).

In front of this "screen" that is changing in the twinkling of an eye, the artist has transformed his traditional self-positioning. Resorting to the insight of the cultural historian and the acumen of the sociologist, he has decided to exercise the right of a citizen who takes responsibility. Zhang's declaration of intent is: "I want to create a dialogue between the image and a real person." Zhang Dali seems to agree with Zhang Nianchao's assertion that "the city is a form of expression of the modern society," as if it was a sort of miniature version of it, and "an artistic work is a form of expression of an artist's thought" (Zhang, 1999: 24).

Harmonious Beijing?

As Zhang Dali suggested in an interview, the transformation of the city is perceived in his works as a metaphor for the transformation of the individual microcosm. His work is the symbolic representation of the personal sense of violence, the feeling of uneasiness, and psychological insecurity. Violence, uneasiness, and insecurity: these words offer a completely antithetic mental picture compared to the official image. The narrative which dominated the Deng Xiaoping–Jiang Zemin era was based on the necessity "to preserve order and stability" (Deng, 1983, 207–214; Jiang, 1999: 313–332). This reached its climax with Jiang's all-inclusive affirmation of the "three represents." In May 2000, on the eve of the 11th anniversary of the Tiananmen crackdown, Jiang Zemin, during an inspection tour to Jiangsu, Zhejiang, and Shanghai, in line with his obsession with "stability above all," stressed the future role of the Chinese Communist Party (CCP) as "a faithful representative of the requirements in the development of advanced productive forces in China, the orientation of the advanced culture in China, and the fundamental interests of the broadest masses of the people in China."

Today, under the Hu Jintao–Wen Jiabao regime, the eulogistic official narrative has been partially mitigated, due to the increasingly emerging demand to address social inequality[6] and the dictat of "building a harmonious socialist society" (Wang, 2005; Xiong, 2005).[7] The master narrative of the country's spectacular growth over the last 27 years is still very much alive,[8] but it cannot obscure the growing income inequality, the widening urban–rural divide, and the increasing rich–poor gap. In 2004 the GDP passed the threshold of 9 percent, but this growth is causing a series of imbalances both at the national and international level: for example, from 2000 onwards China has contributed two-fifths of the growth in the world demand for raw materials, with a consumption in 2004 equal to 30 percent of extracted petroleum, 30 percent of produced steel, and 40 percent of cement. The estimates are that in the next 20 years China's demands for energy per person could quadruple (overtaking the American rate of consumption). All these factors are creating a picture which could be also described using the words violence, uneasiness, and insecurity, at a macroscopic level.

After a performance held in 1997 on a building demolition site along the second Ring Road of eastern Beijing, Zhang Dali declared:

Just as in my life, many things are happening in this city: demolition (*chai*), construction, car accidents, sex, drunkenness, and violence infiltrate every hole. In the vastness of the city, many things that happen are not clear, nor do we know the ultimate result as people are made nervous, scattered, and insecure. Moreover, the corners of the city are in total chaos and disorder. Waste builds up in every corner of the city. People eat, defecate, and sleep among the garbage. Children look for toys. The water running through the city is oily, bleak, and stinking. On the grass or hanging from the branches of trees, plastic bags dangle, moving with the wind as heads without soul or like gashed hands. People wearing starched suits walk into the main entrance of hotels and exit through the back door onto dark, dirty, muddied lanes. I choose these walls that are spray painted with the image of a human head. They are the screens onto which the show of this city is projected. The screen becomes a normal but realistic working place … nothing else. Only one and a half hours. The sound of the hammer and chisels. Bricks fall, stirring up clouds of dust. Behind the wall a modern neoclassical, shiny mansion appears.

(Cao, 1998)

Reactions to Zhang Dali's work

The works of Zhang Dali remind us of the youth of New York, who at the end of the sixties started to draw their signature or tags on the passenger cars of the subway (Castleman, 1984). When at the beginning of the seventies, the black tags became bigger and the drawings progressively developed into the enormous colourful murals that covered the entire passenger car, "people were astonished and in the subway stations reacted as if they felt threatened by an enemy" but "it was now too late to fight" (Nelli, 1978).

Newspapers and magazines wrote about this growing phenomenon. The connection between graffiti and petty crime was taken for granted. The New York City Government and the Metropolitan Transportation Authority began a campaign against graffiti and initiated a cleanup of the subway.

In China, at first Zhang Dali was labelled a "vagrant artist," and the mildest description of his work was "strange thing" or "weird image" (Jiang, 1998; Bo, 1998). Hang Cheng, editor of the *Shenghuo Shibao* (Life times), in his special investigation on the intentionally unnamed artist's work declared:

Since the journalist of the newspaper interviewed "18k," the creator of the head profile, this newspaper has received many phone calls from citizens expressing numerous opinions. At the same time, our journalists have gathered materials from artists from different fields. The focal point at issue is: "Is the human head on the streets art or not?"

(Hang, 1998a: 8)

It took time for Zhang Dali to be recognized as a "graffiti artist" (Yang and Jiang, 1996: 42) or, better yet, as a "conceptual artist" (Hang, 1998b; Xiao, 1998; Lao, 1998) and, finally, an "eco-artist" (Dao, 1998: 2).

The conclusion was that "the fundamental attitude of the public towards this kind of graffiti in the capital is that they do not understand, they are disgusted, and want to boycott it" (Yang and Jiang, 1996: 42). His graffiti work was immediately label-led by the neighborhood committee members as "sabotage" or borderline "vanda-lism." Some local officials demanded his arrest and that he should be forced to clean the dirty walls. His work was condemned as "detrimental to the beauty of the city." Some local officials of the bureaus for comprehensive improvement – in charge of what is called "the maintenance of a clean and tidy city" – described the artist's work as "a problem which mars the appearance of the city, a violation, a disordered writing and painting" (Yu, 1997). An "old resident of Beijing" demanded that Zhang "be put in prison for years" (Yang and Jiang, 1996: 42).

It is important to point out that as far as the usage of walls is concerned, in China, only the government is allowed to use this space. Walls are monopolized by notices about parking, garbage, and venereal diseases, as well as being tools of the public symbology of the state-administered propaganda. Every unofficial usage of walls in the past has brought forth a tragic epilogue, as in the case of the posting of *dazibao* on the wall of Xidan during the pro-democracy movement in 1978–1979.

In order to understand the negative official reaction, it is necessary to take into consideration two factors. First, the same "dirty" walls on which Zhang Dali per-formed his works had been already slated for demolition and were marked by the Chinese character *chai* (Zhao and Bell, 2005: 489–503). There is a paradox here: the destruction of the "old and shabby" (*pojiu*) buildings in Beijing is not conside-red an "act of vandalism" or "sabotage" if this measure is decreed by the municipal government, while the partial knocking down of a wall targeted for demolition is promptly condemned as an act of "vandalism." Second, these broken walls with graffiti have been transformed into props for the artist calling for a *dialogue* (not necessarily an official one) focused on the social implications of the rapid surge of modernization that has destroyed old houses and traditional *hutong.*

Zhang's work has also been labelled a kind of pollution (*wuran*). The artist's res-ponse is as follows: "Aside from the air, the real pollution in this city is the large number of ugly buildings. The buildings on Chang'an Avenue are all built in diffe-rent styles, but the one thing they have in common is their unsightliness" (Stuart, 1999: 3). On the other hand, the official press describes Chang'an Avenue as "spacious and clean" (*Beijing Review*, 2000).

One Beijing resident spoke of a sense of psychological oppression, as he had to look at the "threatening" head profile on his way to the office every day: he decla-red that he felt depressed and he was unable to work the whole day (Personal inter-view, June 1999). The repetitive figurative symbolism employed by Zhang Dali has a persuasive, even violent, strength, but eventually it is the viewer that projects his own imaginary expression, trying to fill the vacuum of the hole or interpret the line of the spray-painted profile. Therefore, according to the viewer's subjective perception, the graffiti work can produce an effect of wonder or oppression (that can be felt as physical aggression too), or it can be perceived as humorous, melan-cholic, even serious.

The artist insists on calling his work "outdoor art" and defending himself from the accusation of committing a crime states: "I don't know what law exists against outdoor art." Zhang's works are performed on Beijing's walls so that the citizens cannot escape them. They are created outdoors as a way to mobilize Beijing citizens' minds and souls, challenging and ultimately inciting them to be aware of their subject positions. He calls his work "Dialogue" as he believes that this visual image can act as an incitement to discourse on a society in transition. The citizens of Beijing cannot just simply pass by; they are undoubtedly called, stimulated, and incited by the subjective visual code of the artist, so that they have to reckon with his iconographical language resulting from the synthesis of repetitive stylized primitive – even childish – images, alphanumeric figures, and material deconstruction.

Zhang Dali has an epidermal relation with Beijing and its walls: these are the surfaces where he draws, sprays, and chisels his graffiti works. Some brash foreign journalists interpreted Zhang Dali's work as a "declared graffiti war on the demolition of the old quarters." They tried, somewhat dubiously, to link this protest against the changing city to some previous more famous and dramatic "protest acts," like the Democracy Wall that was suppressed in the spring of 1979 and which cost many dissidents years of prison *ante litteram* (Fathers, 1999). One critic, interpreting the head as the portrait of the artist himself, emphasized the emotive characteristics of the head profile haunting all corners of the city: the huge forehead perhaps symbolically expresses the effort of thinking and pondering an uncertain reality, the gaping look embodied by the open mouth, indicated by the absence of eyes, the height of the head (sometimes nearly two meters tall), might be interpreted as a silent astonished sign of stupefaction looking at the change of the city (Fathers, 1999). Another enthusiastically proclaimed his work as a "quixotic mission to halt the bulldozing of huge tracts of the capital's traditional lanes and courtyards to make way for apartment blocks, flashy department stores and subway stations" (Fathers, 1999).

Attainment of his goal: Public dialogue

Evidence of the proliferation of intentional and unintentional attention to Zhang Dali's work can be found in the local newspapers. While giving voice, by reporting the reactions of the public, both to the complaints and comments of the art critics, the newspapers have become the most suitable means of expression for the artist's desire for a dialogue among Beijing's citizens. At the very beginning, the obvious and inevitable questions were: "What is that head? Why did somebody do that? Who did it? How can you call that art?!" In so doing, the newspapers have created a channel of communication, and offered a space to exchange ideas on the city's transmogrifying identity. Readers and writers alike participated in the public dialogue which Zhang Dali was advocating on the issue of the last powerful, and probably the most successful, campaign launched by the regime: "the campaign to produce cities" (Cao, 1998).

The reactions of the citizens to Zhang Dali's work can be considered as a series of signals of cultural resistance, testifying to the appearance of symbolic markers of subject positioning: a changing sense of self and place relation was emerging. A city is an ensemble of many things: an amalgam of memories, emotions, and signs of language. Cities are places for exchange of goods and also words, desires, recollections, and ideas. As Italo Calvino demonstrated with his masterpiece *Invisible Cities*, there are inner cities that exist in people's minds, beside and beyond the visible cities (Calvino, 1972). Zhang Dali suggests the possible existence of other cities (precisely inner cities) for people who do not accept the "urban reform plan" of demolition without preservation. While material walls have come down and mental walls have gone up in the new China with its "socialist economy of the market," the artist goes beyond mere denunciation, suggesting through his subjective creative process, the possibility of building an alternative new city to live in – in one's own mind – seeing but not looking, hearing but not listening to the sound of the metropolis paradigmatic of globalizing modernization.

Zhang Dali's work can be considered, like Calvino's work, "the last love poem to the cities," at the exact moment when it becomes more and more difficult to live in them. The "invisible city" of Beijing that Zhang Dali seems to suggest is a dream built of desires and fears, a dream that derives from the heart of a progressively uninhabitable and inhuman city. Beijing today reveals a striking contrast between the idea of the ancient city and the new one: it is no more "the place of indivisible existence" (to paraphrase Calvino's definition), but it might have "an additional attractiveness: through what it has become one can rethink with nostalgia what it was like" (Calvino, 1972: 29).

Zhang Dali is a witness to what Beijing was and is like at the turn of the twenty-first century. In Calvino's book, the visionary traveller Marco Polo tells stories of impossible cities to the melancholic emperor who has realized that his immense power is progressively vanishing: "In the life of the emperor there is a moment, a desperate moment when you discover that this empire that seemed to be the summa of all the marvellous things is collapsing into a endless and shapeless decay" – or one could say going to pieces like an ancient wall – that "its corruption is too gangrenous for the imperial sceptre to find a remedy, that the triumph over the opposing sovereigns has made of us the heirs of their long ruins" (Calvino, 1972: 1).

Zhang Dali tells the story of the microscopic city that is increasingly expanding, resulting in a city that in reality consists of many concentric cities in expansion. But today the emperor pretends to be unaware that the empire "is putrefying like a corpse in the quagmire": he seems not to realize that his empire "is ill and, what is worse, tries to become inured to its sores" (Calvino, 1972: 59).

Negotiating Beijing's identity

The wall is the Chinese traditional element par excellence. Zhang Dali's artwork on walls uses perspective to encapsulate the complexity of the historical process of transformation of the city. Zhang Dali's wounded walls reveal what is otherwise concealed behind them: they propose a visual allegory of a multi-plane and invite a spectator-centred projection into Chinese time and space. This operation is a process of historical foreshortening: the artist is aware of the existence of the vanishing point and decides to place himself at a "distance" (by working at night) but he does not disappear. His artistic agency is an incitement to open a discourse on the spatial and temporal multi-planes of the city, which leads to the opening of a discourse through the walls of homogenous history.

Zhang Dali invites the spectator, who in this case is the passer-by citizen, to look behind (temporally) by means of looking (spatially) through the wall. In this sense, Zhang Dali is indeed a traditional Chinese painter who believes that to compel belief in reality where there is only a flat surface is contrary to nature, but his work reveals also a post-modern nuance as he proposes to remain even more faithful to the structure of reality by breaking the surface (the wall) to reveal another historical dimension.

Zhang Dali acts like a historian, according to Walter Benjamin's 1917 definition: "The historian is a prophet who is looking behind" (Benjamin, 1996: 6). Zhang Dali's work invites his audience to look through the walls, offering them the possibility to navigate through the past and reunite in the present the undermining disruption of historical continuity. Here I am also referring to other artworks by Zhang Dali, such as "One hundred Chinese" (*Yibaige zhongguoren*) and "A Second History" (*Dier lishi*). In the first body of work, human beings – and specifically migrants – became the focus of his attention to reconsider the present and the issue of identity (Zhang, 2002). In "A Second History," Zhang Dali presents archival photographs, which were published in magazines, newspapers, and posters during the Mao era, after having being appropriately "doctored." Zhang exposes the "doctored" version of each photograph together with un-doctored images made from the original negatives that he found in the archives (Zhang and Wu, 2006). By unmasking the intentional alterations, Zhang Dali contributes to re-writing both the history of official public discourse and the history of Chinese aesthetics.

With "Dialogue" Zhang Dali's reduplication, or better anticipation, of the breach in walls that are doomed to be torn down, is not simply a sign of melancholic nostalgia for the past or a wishful thinking for a better tomorrow. It's an emergent resistance, which reveals a completely different way of thinking about the city, and suggests a different way to conceive history and culture, conceptualizing their intimate relation in a new continuum, which runs parallel to the continuum created by the interconnection of gates and walls in shaping the block diagram of old Beijing.

At the centre of this relation with history, there is an attempt to connect to the present the interrupted possibilities of the past, revaluating them as instruments for a possible future. In this sense, the symbolic representation of the history of the city through the wounded walls becomes a way to re-appropriate the past, by means of translating it in a political act of resistance to forgetfulness and in this sense redeeming it. One of the interrupted possibilities from the past would have been the alternative urban development plan envisioned for Beijing by Liang Sicheng (1901–1972), an architect trained at the University of Pennsylvania in the twenties, and vice-chairman of the Beijing Urban Planning Committee, who in 1950 proposed a plan for the preservation of the historical city enclosed within its city walls, along with the construction of a new city centre in the western suburbs, next to the cultural centre (Lin, 1996; Liang and Chen, 2005). In 1953, the municipal government voted against Liang's plan, judging it "mistaken" and "impractical" when compared with the plan advocated by the Soviet expert team who arrived in Beijing in September 1949 and proposed a blueprint derived from the 1935 Moscow General Plan to transform Beijing into the symbol of the newly founded socialist state. The Soviet-style modernization of Beijing led in the late fifties to the first large-scale dismantling of the city walls, now considered a symbol of "feudalism" and an obstacle for modern-day traffic.

Looking through the walls today creates a new discourse on the history of the city and a new space for negotiating its identity. This idea of "appropriating the past" harks back to Benjamin's concept of "antihistory" which suggests the possibility of rediscovering a "forgotten" or "hidden" dimension but implies also the necessity to learn from the past what is *oppositional* to this present.[9] The image that Benjamin proposes is that of the past converging with the present in a new constellation, and this is something that exists and pulses in Zhang Dali's walls project.

Benjamin's "theses" argue: "History, in a rigorous sense, is therefore an *image* that derives from the involuntary recollection. An *image* that suddenly imposes itself on the subject of history in the moment of danger" (Benjamin, 1991: 69–78; italics added). In the process of recollection, there is a space for action or counter-action and this is the place where dialogue should intervene.

Zhang Dali is proposing the *image* Benjamin refers to: his "Dialogue" is not simply a way of re-evoking the past; it embodies, rather, an active and creative process. Zhang's work is a declaration of an intellectual subject position: the use of artistic structural foreshortening[10] indicates the possibility of re-emerging from a previous condition of oblivion, and points in the direction of voluntary historical recollection. Zhang Dali reopens the wall and guides the eye to look behind the surface. This raises critical questions about the time, the present, the past, a past which "is not even past" (as William Faulkner pointed out in a quite different context [Faulkner, 1992]) and a present which is not past yet. The new constellation formed by the present and the past together contains all the horrifying images of the past but also its unexplored possibilities. "There is no such thing as was" (Faulkner, 1990) that one might consider far away and finally overcome, put behind us once and forever, pretending not to know that the present/past has always the possibility to arise again.

Zhang Dali is an individual voice of resistance, and the perspective that animates his work does not necessarily lead to ideological consistency or indicate the path to a collective strategy. Nevertheless, his search for dialogue is an attempt to reclaim the urban space. The localization and repetitiveness of his signs indicate the possibility of re-appropriation, although only temporarily, of a space which shows (through the wall) a historical dimension with a highly symbolic capital. The dismembered walls are discriminating lines between past and present: the artist's intervention denounces the end of the walls of semiotic signs of a space of order, and unmasks the emergence of spaces of exception in today's Beijing. The human head profile is Zhang Dali's profile but is also the profile of the multitude caught (in China but not only) in the problematic between catastrophe and progress. Zhang's work points at the connection between the two which appears behind the scenes of "modernization" when *we* look at the "storm" that has hit and is still hitting China and us all: "This storm is what *we* call progress" (Benjamin, 1969: 257).

There is no salvific escape in the meditation on history and the past, but perhaps there is a possibility to reinvent, to experiment, and to find new ways to avoid being once again inexorably defeated. Looking at the past through the breach created by Zhang Dali inside the wall alludes to this possibility: it is a cry for cultural resistance. Echoing Lu Xun's metaphor of the iron house (Lu, 1973: 273),[11] which is also a cry for cultural resistance, I would conclude by saying that only the awakening and awareness of what happened can produce energy to reverse the imperative logic of the present, one which mystifies the catastrophe of Beijing's present/past and sells it as progress.

Notes

*   A former version of this work appeared in *China Information*, Vol. XVIII (3), Fall 2004, 429–461.
1   It was born as the result of the adaptation to the natural environment and to the agricultural economy based on the single family.
2   Before going back to Beijing where he is still living now.
3   The Chinese word for graffiti is *tuya*, literally 'poor handwriting, scrawls, crow tracks' and reverberates with synonymy to *luanxie* and *luanhua* (write or draw in a confused and disordered way).
4   According to statistics, in 1994 the projected floor space to be constructed was 6,537.42 million m^2, out of which 2,868.48 million m^2 was completed. The construction sector employed 1,139.14 million people.
5   The most emblematic case is the international attention drawn by the 798 Art Zone, or Dashanzi Art District in Beijing, which opened in 2002.
6   In China, the GINI coefficient used by economists to measure income inequality has reached the value of 0.496. Above 0.40 is considered alarming.
7   The Sixth Plenary Session of the 16th Central Committee of the Communist Party of China (CPC) concluded on October 11, 2006 with the adoption of the "Resolution on major issues regarding the building of a harmonious socialist society," http://english.peopledaily.com.cn/200610/12/eng20061012_310923.html.
8   Constructed on the emphasis, for example, that in 2005 China's volume of goods exchange has exceeded that of countries like Italy and the UK, while the growth in GDP has spiked 10.7 percent in 2006.
9   Nevertheless, as Wu Hung demonstrates, the design of Beijing after 1949 reveals in some aspects a distinctive adherence to the old architectural symbolism of imperial city planning (Wu, 1991: 84–117).
10   This is emphasized even further by the prospective dimension added upon deciding to photograph his works.
11   Lu Xun (1881–1936), in the Preface to *Nahan* (Call to Arms), his first collection of short stories (1922), wrote:

> Imagine an iron house without windows, absolutely indestructible, with many people fast asleep inside who will soon die of suffocation. But you know since they will die in their sleep, they will not feel the pain of death. Now if you cry aloud to wake a few of the lighter sleepers, making those unfortunate few suffer the agony of irrevocable death, do you think you are doing them a good turn? ... But if a few awake, you can't say there is no hope of destroying the iron house.
>
> (Lu, 1922)

References

Alinovi, F. (1984) *Arte di frontiera*, Milan: Mazzotta.

Beijing Review (2000) 'Beijing becoming an international metropolis', *Beijing Review*, 31 January: 12–25.

Beijing Review (2000) 'China to quicken the pace of urbanization', *Beijing Review*, 20 March: 11.

Benjamin, W. (1969) 'Theses on the philosophy of history', in H. Arendt (ed.) *Illuminations*, New York: Schocken Books, 253–264.

Benjamin, W. (1991) 'Über den begriff der geschichte', in R. Tiedemann and H. Schweppenhauser (eds) with T.W. Adorno and G. Scholem, *Gesammelte Schriften* vol. I, 69–78, Frankfurt am Main: Suhrkamp.

Benjamin, W. (1996) 'The metaphysics of youth', in M. Bullock (ed.) *Selected Writings, 1913–1926*, Cambridge: Belknap Press.

Bo, M. (1998) 'Qiangshang de biaoji' (Marks on walls), *Yinyue shenghuobao* (Musical life), 16 April, B1.

Bo, Y. [Guo, Yidong] (1985) *Chouloude zhongguoren* (The ugly Chinese), Taipei: Linbai chubanshe.

Borysevicz, M. (1999) 'Zhang Dali's Conversation with Beijing' *ART AsiaPacific*, 22: 52–58, reprinted in Anon. *Zhang Dali: duihua he chai* (Zhang Dali: demolition and dialogue) (Beijing: The Courtyard Gallery), 12.

Borysevicz, M. and Cao, W. (1997) *Second Wave* (pamphlet, CIFA Gallery exhibition).

Broudehoux, A. (2004) *The Making and Selling of Post-Mao Beijing*, New York: Routledge.

Broudehoux, A. (2007) 'Pékin, ville spectacle: la construction controversée d'une métropole Olympique', *Transtext(e)s-Transcultures*, no. 3 (12/ 2007): 5–25.

Buck-Morss, S. (1989) *Dialectics of Seeing: Walter Benjamin and the Arcades Project*, Cambridge, MA: MIT.

Calvino, I. (1972) *Le Città Invisibili*, Turin: Einaudi.

Cao, W. (1998) 'Chengshi jianshe yu dushihua' (City construction and urbanization) (pamphlet), Beijing sheji bowuguan (Beijing Art Museum), 23 May; reprinted in the catalogue *Zhang Dali: duihua he chai*.

Castleman, C. (1984) *Getting up, Subway Graffiti in New York*, Cambridge, MA: MIT Press.

Central Committee of the Chinese Communist Party (2006) 'Resolution on major issues regarding the building of a harmonious socialist society', http://english.peopledaily.com.cn/200610/12/eng20061012_310923.html, accessed on 20 July 2007.

Cui, W. (ed.) (1988) *Heshanlun* (River's elegy), Beijing: Wenhua sanjie chubanshe.

Dao, Z. (1998) 'Shengtai yishu de wenhua luoji: lu yishujia Zhang Dali yu huanjing de "duihua"' (The cultural logic behind eco-art: traveling the 'dialogue' of the artist Zhang Dali and the environment), *Zhonghua dushubao* (China readers) 14, 6 May: 2.

Deng, X. (1983) *Deng Xiaoping Wenxuan Dierjuan* (Selected Works of Deng Xiaoping, Vol. II), Beijing: Renmin chubanshe, 207–214.

Fathers, F. (1999) 'Democracy Walls', *Asiaweek*, 23 April, www.cgi.cnn.com/ASIANOW/asiaweek/99/0423/feat3.html, accessed on 30 June 2004.

Faulkner, W. (1990) *The Sound and the Fury*, New York: Vintage Books.

Faulkner, W. (1992) *Intruder in the Dust*, New York: Vintage Books.

Foucault, M. (1978) *The History of Sexuality, Vol. I: An Introduction*, Translated by Robert Hurley, New York: Pantheon Books.

Foucault, M. (1980) *Power/Knowledge: Selected Interviews and Other Writings, 1972–77*, Edited and translated by Colin Gordon, New York: Pantheon Books, 109–133. 'Truth and power' is an excerpted version of an interview conducted by Alessandro Fontana and Pasquale Pasquino in June 1976, which initially appeared as 'Intervista a Michel Foucault' (Interview with Michel Foucault) in Foucault, M. (1977) *Microfisica del Potere* (Microphysics), (Turin: Einaudi), 3–28.

Hang, C. (1998a) 'Benbao dujia fangdao jietou tuyaren' (Exclusive interview with the street graffiti artist), *Shenghuo Shibao* (Life times), 18 March 1998.

Hang, C. (1998b) 'Jietou renxiang shibushi yishu?' (Street human portraits: are they art?), *Shenghuo Shibao* (Life times), 21 March 1998: 8.

Hwang, M. (1986) 'Study of urban form in 18th century Beijing' MA thesis, MIT.

Jiang, T. (1998) 'Jujiao Beijing rentouxiang' (Focus on Beijing street human portraits), *Lantian zhoumo* (Blue sky weekend) 1471 (27 March 1998): 1.

Jiang, Z. (1999) *Jiang Zemin lun shehuizhuyi jingsheng wenming jianshe* (Jiang Zemin on the construction of spiritual civilization), Beijing: Zhongyang wenxian chubanshe, 313–332.

Lao, M. (1998) 'Ta yingxiangle women de shenghuo' (He has influenced our lives), *Shenghuo shibao* (Life times), 21 March: 8.

Leng, L. (2000) 'He chengshi "duihua" – Zhang Dali fangtan' ('Dialogue' with the city – conversation with Zhang Dali), in Leng L. (ed.) *Shi wo!* (It's me), Beijing: Zhonglian chubanshe, 167–180.

Liang, S. and Chen, Z. [Wang Ruizhi (ed.)] (2005) *Liang Chen Fang'an yu Beijing* (The Liang-Chen plan and Beijing), Shenyang: Liaoning jiaoyu chubanshe.

Lin, Z. (1996) *Jianzhushi Liang Sicheng* (The architect Liang Sicheng), Tianjin: Kexuejishu chubanshe.

Lu, D. (2005) *Remaking Chinese Urban Form: Modernity, Scarcity and Space, 1949–2005*, New York: Routledge.

Lu, X. [Zhou Shuren] (1973) 'Nahan' (Call to arms), in Lu X., *Lu Xun yanjiu xueshu lunzhu ziliao huibian, 1913–1981* (A corpus of scholarship and essays on Lu Xun), 6 vols. Beijing: Zhongguo wenlian, Vol. I, 273.

Marinelli, M. (1993) 'Analisi del Movimento Studentesco del 1989: l'Opinione di un Intellettuale Cinese', in L. Tomba (ed.) *Se io Fossi il Governo*, Milan: Franco Angeli, 65–81.

Nelli, A. (1978) *Graffiti a New York*, Cosenza: Lerici.

Steinhardt, N.S. (1999) *Chinese Imperial City Planning*, Honolulu: University of Hawai'i Press.

Stuart, L. (1999) 'Dialogue: The Graffiti Art of 18k', *Beijing Scene* 5 (4): 2–3.

Wang, G. (ed.) (2005) *Zouxiang heqie shehui* (Towards a Harmonious Society), Beijing: Shehuikexue wenxian chubanshe.

Wang, J. (2003) *Cheng Ji* (The Tale of a City), Beijing: Sanlian shudian.

Wang, Y. (1990) *Yuanlin yu Zhongguo wenhua* (Gardens and Chinese culture), Shanghai: Wenyi chubanshe.

Wu, H. (1991) 'Tiananmen Square: A Political History of Monuments', *Representations*, 35: 84–117.

Xiao, M. (1998) 'Jietou renxiang de chuzhong shi yishu' (The original intention of the human head on the streets is art), *Shenghuo Shibao* (Life times), 21 March 1998.

Xiong, Y. (2005) *Heqie shehuilun* (Theses on Harmonious Society), Shanghai: Shanghai shehuikexueyuan.

Yang, D. (1994) *Chengshi jifeng: Beijing he Shanghai wenhua jingsheng* (City monsoon: the spiritual culture of Beijing and Shanghai), Beijing: Dongfang chubanshe, 29–33.

Yang, F. and Jiang, Z. (1996) 'Kan! Beijing jiedao de tuya' (Look! Graffiti of Beijing's streets), *Jiedao* (Street), 6: 42.

Yu, Z. (1997) 'Tuliao penhui "zuopin" nanca – Ping'an dadao you ren tuya' (The 'artworks' spray-painted are difficult to clean – there is a graffiti head on Ping'an Avenue), *Beijing wanbao*, April 1997.

Zha, J. (1996) *China Pop: How Soap Operas, Tabloids, and Bestsellers are Transforming a Culture*, New York: New Press.

Zhang, D. (2002) *Yibaige zhongguoren* (One hundred Chinese), Beijing: Beijing guaxinda yishu.

Zhang, D. and Wu, H. (2006) *Zhang Dali. A Second History*, Chicago: Walsh Gallery.

Zhang, N. (1999) 'Zuopin xuanyan' (Art declaration), in *Zhongguo xinruiyishu* (China new art), Beijing: Zhongguo shijieyu chubanshe, 24.

Zhao, D. (1989) 'Beijing zhanlüe fazhan yanjiu' (Studies on Beijing's development strategies), *Zhongguo jianshi* (Building in China) March: 18–22.

Zhao, D. (1990) 'Xiandai fazhan he jiucheng baohu' (Modern development and old city preservation), *Jianzhu xuebao* (Architectural journal), 4: 2–6.

Zhao, G. (1998) 'Weihe qiangshang hua renxiang?' (Why paint a human profile on the wall?), *Beijing qingnianbao* (Beijing youth daily), 18 March 1998: 2.

Zhao, X. and Bell, D. (2005) 'Destroying the Remembered and Recovering the Forgotten in *Chai*: Between Traditionalism and Modernity in Beijing', *China Information*, 19: 489–503.

Zhu, W. (1987) *Zouchu Zhongshiji* (Coming out of the Middle Ages), Shanghai: Shanghai renmin chubanshe.

3 Quietly, quietly, quietly

Beijing's migrant civil society organisations

Jennifer Hsu

Economic growth since the late 1970s is largely responsible for Beijing's physical expansion and transformation. The adoption of market reforms, shifting from a command economy to market-driven one, has created an unparallel movement of people from China's rural to urban areas in search of employment. Prior to economic reforms, the household registration system or *hukou*[1] governed and restricted the movement of people across the country. Despite the relative relaxation[2] of the *hukou*, large cities such as Beijing[3] continue to use the system to prevent migrants from entering a large range of professions and accessing various social services. Thus, migrants are constrained not only in employment choices (a range of professional jobs are reserved for Beijing residents only), but as most social benefits including access to health or housing are tied to the urban *hukou,* migrants are left at the lowest end of the social scale (see Wu 2002). Nonetheless, migrants from China's countryside have made a significant impact on and contribution to all aspects of everyday Beijing. They have become intrinsically linked with the changes to China's urban landscape: they are the backbone of the construction industry and have filled gaps in the service sector by taking on jobs shunned by wealthier urban residents, such as manual work. Within this context, migrant workers across the urban centres are an essential part of China's economic growth and modernisation drive. Yet, they are often regarded as a necessary evil by local authorities and urban residents. Migrants are perceived as major contributing factors to all things negative in their new urban environments, from rising crime rates to stress on infrastructure. Without legal status, the needs of migrants and their families, including the health and education of their children, are largely left unmet. With government inaction to resolve these issues, a number of migrant-initiated civil society organisations (CSOs)[4] have emerged. Some of these migrant CSOs are also attempting to redress the current state–society relationship within accepted boundaries through engagement strategies with the state.

It is imperative to note that as China is still dominated by the state, the methods used by CSOs to convey their discontent are different from those utilised in most Western and non-Western environments, as is evident in many of the case studies outlined in this volume. The explicit vocalising of dissent by CSOs will be seen as a challenge to the state and will only result in severe punishment. Consequently, cooperation and engagement with the government allows CSOs to generate change needed for migrant workers. Although such strategies of CSOs may be seen as complying with the government's agenda at one level, their existence alone is indicative of their discontent with the current state of affairs. The central government has shown that it is withdrawing from the realms of social welfare such as healthcare (Kaufman, Kleinman and Saich 2006) and this has impacted on its response to migrants. This is where migrant CSOs have stepped in to bridge the gap and thus offer migrants a small but growing voice. Strategies of dissent as adopted by migrant CSOs are framed within tolerated boundaries of the state. Simultaneously, CSOs are renegotiating the relationship between Chinese society and the state. Successful changes to the state–society relationship are not and should not only be interpreted within a conflict-driven mode.

The emergence of migrant CSOs in Beijing suggests that urban change is clearly taking place and that these organisations are exploring ways to challenge the dominant state structure in its dealings with not only migrants, but civil society as a whole. The social and spatial transformation that is occurring in Beijing can best be comprehended within a state–society framework. Such an approach involves an understanding of how the state relates to society, where the state is the dominant factor in social change, but we must realise that change within Beijing does not occur in a purely adversarial nature. The chapter will begin with an introduction to the city of Beijing in the context of economic development and migration. The second section will consider some of the theories that underline this study, particularly the idea of civil society and state–society relationship in China. As CSOs across China are managed and controlled by the state, section three will outline these restrictions, but also assess the general importance of CSOs in China's current state of transition. Section four will examine the range of migrant CSOs in Beijing and explore the strategies employed to promote change for migrant workers. The final section will discuss the possibilities of migrant CSOs in generating effective changes for migrant workers as well as at a wider societal level. Migrants and their CSOs are not passive victims of the state or the process of economic development. This chapter shows that everyday strategies employed to alter and negotiate the terrains of the existing power structure need not be understood within the conflict-driven or politically active model.

Beijing in the context of economic development and migration

Despite being the seat of the government, Beijing has not escaped the process of rural–urban labour migration. The growth of China's economy as a whole, fuelled in part by foreign direct investment (FDI) has accelerated the migration process. FDI has increased from US$276.96 million in 1990 to US$1,792.57 million in 2002 (Wei and Yu 2006: 381). In Beijing, FDI has created new industries and reinvigorated old ones, all needing a substantial workforce of mostly low-skilled and low-waged personnel. As the nation's capital and seat of the government, Beijing has had its economic growth and development take on a political role. These factors have impacted on the flexibility and innovativeness of Beijing's municipal authorities in economic policies, to ensure that 'local initiatives are prudent and consistent with overall national interests' (Ma and Delios 2007: 212). To enhance economic development and increase FDI into Beijing, the central government initiated the creation of development zones, where investors are given preferential treatment, such as tax breaks. By 2000, Beijing had 30 development zones and industrial parks, with approximately US$9 billion of registered capital (Wei and Yu 2006: 383).

As a result of liberalisation, the population make-up and size have changed significantly. Beijing's population in 2007 stood at 17.4 million with approximately 5.4 million migrant workers (Juan 2007) compared to 0.2 million in 1984 (Gu and Shen 2003: 112). The inflow of rural migrants coupled with varying degrees of investment across Beijing's districts[5] has created visible inequalities within the city. The Haidian and Chaoyang districts have become dynamic commercial and service centres which have attracted large amounts of FDI, whereas the Xuanwu and Chongwen districts are old manufacturing zones that have received less investment. The Chaoyang district has become the focus of municipal government efforts to create a central business district (CBD)[6] located only five kilometres from Tiananmen Square. This move to facilitate capital flows is also emblematic of Beijing becoming a global city. Thus, such districts have a high concentration of migrants working and living within the area, particularly during periods of major construction as in the Chaoyang CBD case. In such areas there are disparities between Beijing's urban residents and migrant workers living in self-created settlements lacking adequate basic services (Figure 3.1). Migrants from the same

Figure 3.1 Migrant housing in Beijing (photograph by author, 2006).

provinces congregate, as habits, customs, dialects vary greatly between regions. Consequently, migrant villages have emerged across Beijing's districts, creating new social spaces within the city.

For example, migrants from the Zhejiang province (mainly from Wenzhou) have received considerable attention due to their attempts to create a social space where they are able to gather together and seek out support. The Zhejiang village emerged in the 1990s in the area of Dahongmen located in the Fengtai district south of the city centre. It became Beijing's largest migrant enclave in the mid 1990s, accommodating 70,000–80,000 migrants. The establishment of the village[7] was a response to the lack of services available to Zhejiangnese migrants working in Beijing. The growth of the village from a simple congregation of Wenzhou migrants to a full-fledged residential compound offering clinics, restaurants and child-minding services among many other services can be seen as contesting the existing urban institutional structures. While Fengtai district authorities benefited from substantial revenues of the private enterprises set up by migrants in the district, rising crime rates and the self-governing style of the village with self-appointed authorities, ultimately threatened local and municipal authorities. It was unacceptable that the village could exist and be outside the legal boundaries of the state. The ultimate destruction of the village in late 1995 and early 1996 denotes that the state can withdraw the space offered to social organisations or groups as quickly as it has offered it. This particular example illustrates the potential for migrant CSOs to meet the needs of migrant workers by providing a space for them to live, work and socialise in, but its self-sufficiency threatened the local authorities. Migrant CSOs have therefore emerged as a more recognised and acceptable entity to the state (as they are bound by strict regulations) to undertake the work that is traditionally the state's responsibility. Nevertheless, they are viewed as potential threats to social stability by the authorities, in part due to the constituents that they represent and also because of unfamiliarity with CSOs in general. The Zhejiang village example signifies the complexity of the state–society relationship and that social change in Beijing for migrant workers is one fraught with contradictions. Beijing's migrant CSOs are thus an important component in transforming conditions for migrant workers, but also for civil society as a whole.

Theoretical frameworks

To understand the strategies utilised by Beijing's migrant CSOs in creating change for the urban migrant community and at a broader civil society level, an understanding of the state is indispensable. Social organisations aim to bring about change for their constituents through the expression of dissent and resistance. In the case of migrant CSOs in Beijing, opposition is not an open form of political demonstration but rather a quiet dialogue and, paradoxically, even partnerships with government bodies and institutions. The strategies employed by migrant CSOs to improve conditions for migrants are subtly altering the way in which the Chinese state relates and engages with social actors. The following section will consider state–society and civil–society frameworks within the context of Beijing's migrant groups, allowing for an appreciation of social transformation from a perspective of partnerships.

The state–society relationship

The authority and dominance of the state is the central focus of societal change in the state–society approach. Given that the Chinese state continues to be pervasive in many aspects of society, politics and economy, it is not inappropriate to consider social transformation from the standpoint of the state. Accordingly, the work of Evans, Rueschemeyer and Skocpol (1985) clearly echoes China's current situation. Their work re-centres the pre-eminence of the state in an era where it is no longer fashionable to talk about the state after the failure of communism in Eastern Europe in the late 1980s. The element of history is an important aspect in bringing the state back into our analysis as it shows that the changes and evolution of the state–society relationship are a product of many enduring factors (Skocpol 1985). However, Migdal (2001) seeks to understand the role of the state without overemphasising its importance or ignoring other social factors. Migdal regards the state as an organisation within society and accordingly, sees the state as a dynamic force constantly changing as it interacts with other social forces. From Migdal's perspective, social control is therefore in the hands of many, rather than concentrated in the hands of a few. Migdal's premise is innovative and worth considering, although at this juncture, the Chinese state continues to permeate all levels of society, thus this may be seen as a long-term goal rather than a current interpretation of China's state–society relationship. As a result, the changes that are occurring in China today may well be seen in the light of a corporatist state, whereby it is the state that dictates the process.

The case of the All-China Federation of Trade Unions (ACFTU) indicates how the state has shaped and dictated the role which the ACFTU can play, thereby reasserting its dominance in China's transition period. The liberalisation process presented the ACFTU an opportunity to reshape its image and become more active in representing the workers. However, its efforts were short-lived due to the government crackdown on all dissent in June 1989, following the student protests in Tiananmen. Facing a membership crisis in the late 1990s, the ACFTU tried to restructure itself and re-establish its presence by having branches in private enterprises. The ACFTU has since been accused of sympathising with abusive management practices of private firms. The dual position of the ACFTU, adhering to the Party line and simultaneously representing Chinese workers, presents a dilemma, potentially harming its effectiveness as a representative body for workers.

Although, migrant CSOs in Beijing are not lame ducks, as is the case with the ACFTU, it is useful to employ the corporatist perspective as it illuminates the position of the state. An interventionist state often assists in organising and establishing sectoral association and mediates the relationship between them. The corporatist analysis does explain the rise of associations, in so far as the state is directing and coordinating their development (Gallagher 2004: 420), in line with its goals of managing society. However, while the corporatist model may show the state's control of civil society development, it does not illustrate the aims of the organisations or their functions. Therefore, a civil society perspective may better assist in the endeavour to comprehend horizontal relationships between social groups and the emergence of CSOs.

Chinese civil society

The demise of communism in Eastern Europe in the late 1980s prompted scholars to bring back notions of civil society to understand the socio-political changes which ensued. In the case of China, system change is much more gradual. While the concept of civil society derives its roots from Western/European thought, it is an analytical tool worth using to understand China. To grasp the changes that are occurring within China's urban areas, civil society provides the scholar the opportunity to observe the transformation from a bottom-up perspective, that is, individuals or social groups advocating changes at the grassroots level. In attempting to operationalise the concept of civil society we may consider the United Nations Development Programme's (UNDP) very practical definition of civil society as 'the space between family, the market and the state; it consists of non-profit organizations, and special interest groups, either formal or informal, working to improve the lives of their constituents' (UNDP 2002). Nevertheless, the space between state and society and the discourse that surrounds it is steered by the state (Hampton 2005). This is evident in the unsuccessful attempts by the Uyghur people in Xinjiang to claim their own history and identity within the region. The government dominates and shapes the discourse on ethnic minorities along the lines of national security because of the threat of independent movements in western China (Hampton 2005). Similarly, Zhou (1993) notes state intrusion in mediating conflicts between social groups. Due to a lack of institutional mechanisms to resolve disputes, the state is called upon to arbitrate, thus politicising the process and issues at stake. The state may then seize on the opportunity to initiate action along the lines of its own agenda. Zhou observes that there are opportunities afforded to individuals and groups who participate in state-initiated campaigns, as it provides the space for those groups to pursue their own agenda. Unorganised groups and individuals can be mobilised. Zhou refers to this as *institutionalised collective action*, where the state initiates the action (1993: 61).

Social groups in China are therefore constrained by the state's agenda, reinforcing the idea that the state continues to be pervasive in all areas of society, including civil society (see Gallagher 2004 and Howell 1998). However, this should not discount any attempts to understand social change using civil society as an analytical tool. Using civil society to understand China accentuates the social changes that have occurred since economic liberalisation. Given the shape of Chinese civil society (acknowledging state intervention) it is not surprising that migrant CSOs operate on the one hand within state sanctioned boundaries and on the other seek to work discreetly to address the challenges migrants face, framed within the pursuit of change.

Migrant CSOs and structural obstacles

Rural–urban labour migration has shifted the meaning of state–society relationship in China. There are some 200 million rural migrants working in China's urban areas, the majority in 'bitter, dirty, arduous, and low prestige work denigrated by urban residents' (Solinger 1995: 129). The state has been pressed to engage with CSOs in some form to resolve the challenges posed by migrants to their host cities, such as pressure on existing infrastructure. In general, CSOs across China have garnered enough credibility in the eyes of the government through their social or community development work, to be able to negotiate and advocate social causes. Accordingly, CSOs seeking to represent migrant workers in urban areas have taken the opportunity of the expanded space to improve the plight of their constituents.[8] The state's engagement is attributable to the decline of its ability and resources to exert full control over the society that it governs.[9] Nonetheless, CSOs across China have faced stringent government restrictions.

Under the supervision of the Ministry of Civil Affairs (MCA), CSOs are required to fulfil certain conditions before registration is granted. Following the events in Tiananmen in 1989, the State Council issued the Movement Regulations on Registration of Social Organisations in October 1989. The Regulation required all social organisations to find a willing government department or unit to sponsor the organisation. In effect, the sponsoring government department is responsible for the actions of the CSO and ultimately erodes its independence. This constraint prevents many organisations from completing the registration process with the MCA. To avoid the lengthy bureaucratic process and become registered, many organisations have decided to register as a commercial entity with the Industry and Commerce Bureau (ICB), resulting in confusion as to what exactly constitutes a social organisation.

Documents issued in 1998, while aiming to consolidate the laws regarding CSOs, further restricted their ability to register. Under the Regulations on the Administration of Social Organisations, national associations must have a minimum capital of 100,000 *yuan* (US$13,500) and local organisations 30,000 *yuan* (US$4,050). Furthermore, a minimum membership of 50 individuals is a precondition for both types of organisations. In addition to such restrictions, the long-standing rule of one type of organisation per region continues to hamper the development of new organisations, effectively preventing many from scaling up their services.

The regulations reinforced that the Chinese trajectory of social development is state-directed. The characteristics of Chinese civil society ought to be considered rather than dismissed as not conforming to the standards of a 'Western' civil society. Yet in areas of state control, there is weakening at the same time. Despite the various restrictions on the development of CSOs what is evident is the ability of migrant CSOs to bring about change for migrant workers in Beijing including greater legal representation. The strategies employed by Chinese CSOs are largely non-confrontational and inclusive of the state. Nonetheless, the presence of migrant CSOs denotes that urban and social change is occurring as they endeavour to foster more equitable outcomes for Beijing's migrant population.

From a macro perspective, CSOs provide the space for citizens to engage in the development of their nation. The Chinese state regards CSOs in a more practical manner – they are seen as aiding the state through the delivery of social service; social organisations are gap fillers due to the decreasing ability and capacity of the state to provide welfare to its citizens. According to the MCA representative interviewed, CSOs act as a bridge or *qiaoliang* between the government and the people because of their role in supplementing government policy (Personal communication 21 September 2006). Consequently, the state's interests in CSOs are more attuned to how they can complement the role of the state, rather than taking an interest in the values that these organisations promote. Within this framework, CSOs can be viewed as passive and easily manipulated because of the close nature of their relationship to the state. However, it is precisely this 'passivity' that allows migrant CSOs to produce the conditions needed for change.

Beijing's migrant CSOs and their role in change

Given the current political climate of a dominant one-party state, migrant CSOs have adopted non-threatening strategies such as factoring in the state in all its work in order to advocate change for migrants. Observers may nevertheless charge migrant CSOs as being complicit in maintaining the government's position and hold on society. Yet this does not render them useless in the process of improving conditions for migrant workers in urban areas. Resistance to the dominant state comes in the form of working within the boundary to extend its borders, and therefore change is a gradual process, as opposed to the broad constructs of Western ideals that social change must be rapid. Rapid social transformation is seen by the Chinese state as destabilising and a threat to China's development. A study of the strategies at play in Beijing's migrant CSOs reveals that the effectiveness of the CSO comes from compliance with the government.

Nine Beijing migrant CSOs were studied for the purpose of this research (see Appendix for a list). Interviews were conducted between September and December 2006. As the principal approach, interviews helped to ascertain the relationship between migrant CSOs and the state, as it allowed certain issues to be explored in greater depth. Several migrant CSOs also allowed the researcher to observe the projects and project sites of their work. Such opportunities contributed to the pool of knowledge and information gathered.

Migrant CSOs and the state

Of the nine CSOs studied, each had some connections with different levels of the government. The nine organisations were divided into two categories:[10] organisations working to represent the legal rights of migrants, and organisations focusing on service delivery, providing welfare and activities for the social needs of migrants. It is the first category of organisations that showed the strongest ties to state institutions or Beijing municipal authorities, thus effectively allowing these CSOs to carry out projects at a large scale. I will begin by looking at the first group of CSOs and their tactics to facilitate change for Beijing's migrant workers.

Legal/advocacy-oriented CSOs

The first category of organisations, legal/advocacy-oriented CSOs have shown that they are able to utilise the language and agenda of the government regarding migrants for positive social change. It is their relationship with the government that enables their work. For example, Beijing Legal Aid Office for Migrant Workers (BLAOMW) may perhaps have the strongest connection to the government. BLAOMW was set up under the direction and instruction of the Beijing Municipal Judicial Bureau to represent migrant workers in the judicial system. As such, it has received a total of 1 million *yuan* (US$135,000) in financial support from the China Legal Aid Foundation and the All-China Lawyers' Foundation. These are state-run foundations and therefore the work of the BLAOMW is perhaps reflective of China as a corporate state, where social organisations are coerced into following its direction. BLAOMW's work is to provide legal advice to migrants without challenging the state. To further the cooperation between CSOs and the government, BLAOMW has conducted legal training workshops for migrant members of the ACFTU. Such close cooperation has allowed the organisation to expand its services beyond Beijing. The BLAOMW representative interviewed indicated that the organisation's 'model' will be replicated in Hebei province and the Ningxia Hui autonomous region. This ultimately means that a greater number of migrant workers will be able to access legal advice and representation.

From a macro perspective, BLAOMW and its work have the potential to empower migrant workers in Beijing and other cities with legal rights and the notion of urban citizenship. Only residents with their household registration or *hukou* register in the cities are considered true urban residents and are thus entitled to a range of welfare benefits provided by the government. As the government has focused its efforts on protecting the legal rights of migrant workers in the cities via a number of directives, BLAOMW finds it easier to advance its work precisely because it is in the realm of the government's interest. In pushing for better treatment of migrant workers but also within the larger framework of urban citizenship, BLAOMW is perhaps sowing the seeds of greater institutional change for the future, with its first step of educating migrant workers in their employment rights.

Little Bird is a CSO that has received endorsement from the Beijing Municipal Judicial, and Labour and Social Security bureaux. It has had to register as a commercial entity, whereas BLAOMW has no current need to register because of its establishment under the direction of the state. One of its activities is broadcasting a half hour weekly programme on the Beijing People's Broadcasting Station. The programme provides a space for migrant workers to share their thoughts and experiences. Without the approval of Beijing's authorities, such a programme would not be permitted due to the sensitive nature of the issue. It was reiterated by a representative of Little Bird that their work is supported rather than restricted by the government. Due to this approval by government bodies, Little Bird has also replicated its services beyond Beijing. Offices have been established in other popular migrant destinations such as Shenzhen and Shenyang, where they are able to offer legal advice and basic legal education workshops to migrants.

Facilitators, another organisation located in this first category of CSOs, shows that it is able to push for change at various levels by working with both local and central governments. At the local level, it is encouraged by the *jiedao* or Street Neighbourhood Committee (SNC)[11] to persuade migrant workers of the area to partake in activities such as the celebration of festivals. Before the 2006 Mid-Autumn Festival, the SNC invited facilitators and migrants that it represented to celebrate the Festival through a performance. Such activities, according to the interviewee, occur regularly due to the organisation's aim of integrating migrant workers into local communities. While such methods of integration are helpful at some level, they do denote tokenistic actions. This is best exemplified by another representative of a community development CSO interviewed, who indicated that local levels of government such as the SNC or *juweihui* (local residents' group) are instructed by the central government to conduct several cultural events each year with migrant workers in order to keep them busy and happy, so that they are '[So]exhausted from the singing and dancing that they don't have time to congregate and create trouble' (Personal communication 31 October 2006). Facilitators' cooperation with the state is more in project form, for example, in 2004 its work safety conference attracted several key members of the central government's National Work Safety Administration. More recently, the organisation was approached by the Ministry of Labour and Social Security (MoLSS) to provide input into their training programme for migrant workers. Facilitators' cooperation with the state suggests that the government is willing to be a party to new thoughts and suggestions relating to the well-being of migrant workers as advocated by CSOs. Nonetheless, it is still framed within the government's current agenda as indicated through its policies, notably the May 2005 MoLSS directive that required all employers of migrant workers to adopt labour contracts. Accordingly, to develop relationships with the government, these three organisations have shaped their work whether it be legal rights of migrant workers or work safety issues, within the language and agenda that is set out by the government.

Social service delivery and migrant CSOs

The relationship between the second category of CSOs and the government is much more localised and impromptu. The six CSOs studied were more focused on their immediate community of migrant workers and their needs rather than taking an advocacy-oriented role, to promote change at the macro level. The work of Tongxin Xiwang is located within a migrant community located outside of Beijing's Fifth Ring Road. The majority of its work is dedicated to improving the situation of migrant women living within the community. To this end, Tongxin has established a number of projects including basic health training. The aim of the organisation is to help migrant women improve their skill set and self-confidence level, as many have accompanied their husbands to Beijing and are left with the household carer role. Without much to do during the day, many fill in the time by playing cards or gossiping with other women. In conducting its projects, Tongxin has received some support from the local authorities of the area. Its office space belongs to the local residents' group suggesting some level of cooperation and acceptance. Other than such interactions, Tongxin has no other sustained linkages with other government bodies. This is partly due to its focus on the immediate migrant community, which means it has little to no influence on the government and its policies regarding migrant workers. This service-driven mentality is, to an extent, shared by the other organisations. While the Migrant Women's Club has cooperated with the Beijing branch of the ACFTU and the All-China Women's Federation on various projects, its cooperation is also limited by its service-delivery focus.

The relative passiveness of CSOs Gongyou Zhijia and Worry Assistance Hotline suggests that the impact of their work is contained within their immediate community. Gongyou sees itself as an outlet for migrants to express their experiences in the cities through the performing arts. Thus, it has established a band, which performs on a regular basis. In addition, it has also established a training centre for migrants. The Hotline, on the other hand is essentially a counselling hotline for migrant workers. The level of the Hotline's operations is restricted by its access to funding. While Gongyou has received recognition and an award from Beijing municipal authorities for its work, it is clear that the interviewee, a member of Gongyou, had little patience for talk of the macro issues at hand, namely socio-political change through migrant organisations:

> I don't believe in the concept of civil society or NGOs. We must do the work that is facing us, face the immediate reality. The work of migrants has created most of the cities in China, why must migrants now have to ask for their right? Ask for what is naturally theirs?
>
> (SH, Personal communication 24 November 2006)[12]

His disinterest in the debate on civil society and the impact of Chinese CSOs on the social landscape is clear; instead the emphasis, he believes, should be on the immediate reality of migrant workers. Gongyou uses cultural practices such as singing and performing to assist migrant workers rather than negotiate the politics behind the macro issues affecting them. In this way, Gongyou highlights that it is possible to bring about change to the material conditions of migrants' lives even if they are disengaged or slightly removed from direct government contact. Through their programmes, Gongyou has helped migrants to artistically express their struggles and experience. Such programmes may be viewed sceptically as not addressing the primary issues at hand, namely, inequalities experienced by migrants in Beijing. However, these organisations provide a space for migrant workers to express their experiences (often of frustration). This, in turn, promotes greater awareness among the general population of the plight of migrant workers. At a 2006 book fair in Beijing, Gongyou was given permission to perform its songs and publicise its new book. Having attended this concert in 2006, it was clear that the majority of the audience were Beijingers. Both young and old were sympathetic to the harsh realities of migrant workers including poor working and living conditions, separation from the family, as expressed in the band's lyrics. Events such as the book fair are organised by the Municipal authorities and indicate that there are at least some changes in the government's reception of migrant workers and related issues. This strategy, whether conscious or not, may eventually help migrants to become more aware of their own conditions and, through this, future action will be possible.

The active pursuit of government partnerships can be seen as another strategy towards generating improvements for migrant workers. For example, Shining Stone Community Action (SSCA) is negotiating with the *jiedao* of one particular area in the Haidian district to replicate a community project similar to the one it has implemented in Ningbo. The local officials from Haidian, while receptive to SSCA's work in Ningbo, have generally resisted the implementation of such projects in their own community. Compassion for Migrant Children (CMC) focuses primarily on the children of migrant workers by cooperating with local migrant schools. These schools across Beijing are under constant pressure from the Municipal Government because they operate within a grey area of the law. Many do not meet the regulations as set out by the government and are pressured as a result not to work with CMC for fear of creating difficulties for local authorities. To gain the trust and understanding of the local government, CMC has directly approached the education officials of the Haidian district to explain its projects and plans. The quest to establish government partnerships offers CSOs the possibility to extend their influence in transforming the conditions of migrant workers. However, these CSOs are often seen as a risk by the government as they are regarded to have the capabilities to organise against the government, thus, the process of forging partnerships can be long and difficult.

Discussion and conclusion

Beijing's migrant CSOs demonstrate a range of strategies and tactics employed to improve the situation of migrant workers in the city. Although these may not be overt forms of dissent or resistance such as mass demonstration or protests, what is evident is that these subtle strategies of working with the government are providing results. For example, both BLAOMW and Little Bird have been able to establish offices beyond Beijing resulting in migrants having greater access to legal representation. Although knowledge of the law or access to representation does not necessarily equate with justice, the three organisations of category one are in a position to improve conditions for migrants with their programmes, including education and legal representation. Such changes will take time and it is a negotiated process with the government. For the representative of Facilitators, critique of the government and its failure to appropriately address the challenges faced by migrant workers is certainly a bold step:

> There are some things that the government should not but is doing and as a result is doing very poorly. As we can see from the Sunshine Training Programme, how ineffective it is, yet the government continues. In this situation, we can say that CSOs probably have a better success rate in devising and conducting training programmes.
>
> (LT, personal communication 12 October 2006)

Recognising the state's languishing ability to adequately provide for migrant workers, CSOs across both categories have attempted to bridge this gap. Similarly Gongyou's representative is practical regarding the roles of the state and of CSOs: 'The work we are doing should be the role of the government and *juweihui* but normally they do not have the ability or the resources to do such work therefore it is up to the NGO' (Personal communication 8 October 2008). Thus, discontent towards the state for its failure is vocalised and acknowledged. CSOs believe that change for migrant workers will come from social organisations.

For these three organisations, the state has demonstrated its willingness to engage and these CSOs are prepared to work and communicate in the government-approved realm, namely the protection of migrants' basic legal rights as workers. Change for migrant workers in Beijing will take the form of cooperation between state and society, rather than through adversarial methods. Subtle opposition is framed within the perspective of contrasting the successes of the CSOs against those of the state.

While recognising the inaction of or lack of support from local governments and the state regarding the provision of social support to migrants, CSOs in category two have sought to rectify this by meeting the social needs of their constituents. To further their work with migrants, two of the CSOs in category two are actively seeking government partnerships. Although this can be seen as far from resisting the status quo, what is interesting is their desire to effect change by becoming a player in the game as established by the government. These strategies of resistance are consistent with Thornton's study of dissent in contemporary China. Thornton (2002) focuses on the use of *duilian* or couplets that adorn door frames during festivals or for daily use, as a form of citizens expressing their dissatisfaction with the government. State-approved couplets for various festivals and situations are available for purchase by the general public. However, to show discontent, citizens have carefully altered these state-approved couplets or write their own in often cryptic terms for the passer-by to solve. The subtle adjustment of state couplets (playing on the meaning of words) is often an attempt to rebuke the state for its lack of action against issues such as corruption. By acting in this way, citizens are able to frame their dissent within government-stipulated boundaries but it is also an attempt to impose some sort of moral standard as often such actions are taken when there is seemingly disorder within their society or community (Thornton 2002).

The methods used by migrant CSOs in Beijing demonstrate that individuals or groups can convey their dissatisfaction via subtle ways that are still within established boundaries of the state. It is working within the system that will produce the improvements needed for migrant workers. We are seeing changes in the urban landscape initiated by migrants, as seen in the Zhejiang village example outlined earlier, and a new form of how the urban is conceived by Beijing's local authorities is emerging. As Zhang writes: 'The narrative of urban space in China is largely situated in the narratives of progress, development, and modernity, in which the past is often treated only as a precursor to the future, something ultimately to overcome' (2006:45).

Migrants entering China's cities occupy a complex paradoxical position of being seen as a blemish on the progress of the city as well as making a necessary contribution to the city's economic development. Migrant communities on the city's outskirts often do not conform to building codes or meet hygiene standards, running counter to the government's desire to modernise. They are seen as naïve and backwards by the media, general population and the government because of their rural status and it is considered necessary by government authorities to improve their cultural level or *suzhi* in order for Beijing to continue modernising. The work of category two CSOs in particular may be interpreted within this framework, in that the workshops, training sessions and other 'improvement' programs are shaped by this general idea of modernisation. Strategies of resistance are therefore not overt, which is important to note. The collaboration and negotiation that we see occurring between CSOs and the state, while mundane do reveal that CSOs are slowly pushing the boundaries, altering the way the state comprehends and relates to new social actors.

As mentioned previously, the idea of resistance and change is articulated carefully within established boundaries of the state. However, through the work of the migrant CSOs, migrant workers have had greater opportunities than before to access a wide range of facilities and services offered by these organisations, albeit, on a relatively smaller-scale bearing in mind the sheer number of migrant workers in Beijing (within the vicinity of 5.5 million). The work of Gongyou and Tongxin offer migrants the prospect of becoming part of a wider community, both migrant and non-migrant. For example, Gongyou's dedication to the performing arts has given migrant participants the opportunity to present their work and talents in front of a large and diverse audience. Such opportunities suggest that the notion of resistance is channelled 'constructively' rather than demonstrated in an oppositional form. Tongxin with its female constituents has established a second-hand clothing store where migrant women are volunteering to help staff the store. By initiating such a project, Tongxin has given migrant women the prospect of learning new skills, connecting with other women and establishing a link with their new environment. Nonetheless, challenges for migrants and subsequent discontent amongst this social group will greatly increase in the future, if existing state (or non-state) institutions are not able to address the increasingly complex set of issues. One possible result of this scenario is that resistance and dissent will become increasingly overt.

Despite the challenges ahead for all stakeholders, migrant CSOs are optimistic that more service organisations will emerge in the near future. This optimism is valid if seen in the light of CSOs across China, increasing in a number of fields, including environment organisations. Regardless of this belief, the likelihood of civil society contributing to social change is not solely dependent on their quantity but also the quality of those organisations that operate within civil society (see Chamberlain 1998). Creating the space in which a CSO can negotiate with the state is by no means an easy task, it demands the ability to maintain the balance, or at least the appearance thereof, between government and stakeholder demands.

As discussed earlier, the tactics employed by CSOs are not what we see elsewhere in the world, where vocalisation of dissent may be the norm. The quiet nature of migrant CSOs' work may be perceived as colluding with the state. The desire for some CSOs to partner more closely with the government suggests that both the Chinese state and civil society have the ability to engage constructively, while to openly lobby the government is difficult and potentially dangerous for CSOs. Thus working within set parameters can be, in the short-term at least, equally as effective. Another factor for consideration is that the nature of success of social movements is predominantly understood within terms of achieving policy reform (see Edelman 2001). However, the work of migrant CSOs in Beijing ought to be seen as attempting to alter the way in which the state responds to migrant workers specifically and more generally to civil society. This strengthening of civil society forces in order to effect change on a more equal footing with the state is a process of cultural transformation rather than simply about obtaining policy objectives.

In an era where Beijing is pressing ahead with its modernisation drive and improving its international image, it is particularly important to see that urban transformation is not solely in the hands of the state. Rather, as we have seen with migrant CSOs, social change can be achieved by both the state and CSOs through dialogue and partnerships. Even though the state controls the space in which social organisations operate, migrant CSOs have shown their ability to provide for migrant workers where the state cannot. The civil society framework highlights the ability of stakeholders such as CSOs and their capacity to be more than passive entities of the state. What appear to be complicit acts on the part of the CSOs should be seen as maximising their position with the state to push for further change, demonstrating that the nature of discontent manifests itself in different forms.

The action of migrant CSOs to transform the conditions affecting Beijing's migrant workers is a subtle art of mastering relationships with the government. By framing their work within the language of the state, migrant CSOs are able to pursue their goals. Through dialogue and partnerships CSOs have pushed the state's limits further in its engagement with social groups. In order for the state to avoid urban conflict, it is necessary for this space in which CSOs operate to be expanded. Tactics currently utilised by migrant CSOs suggest that the pace at which this is occurring is slow and can be time consuming. However, for CSOs to openly criticise and oppose the state would be a dangerous path to take, resulting in harsh rebuke. The quiet nature of migrant CSOs' work and their engagement with the state has produced improved conditions for migrant workers, particularly in the area of legal rights. Whether this pace of change can continue in the face of rapid economic upheaval and urbanisation is an area for future concern.

Acknowledgements

Financial support for the fieldwork was provided by Cambridge Commonwealth Trust, Hong Kong Research Grant, Suzy Paine Fund and Universities' China Committee in London. I would like to thank the two anonymous reviewers for their helpful comments, and also Shailaja Fennell and Reza Hasmath for their suggestions and support.

Notes

1 Each individual is registered in their place of birth, otherwise known as the *hukou* or household registration system. The transferring of one's *hukou* to another place, particularly to cities such as Beijing is especially difficult for those registered with rural status.
2 The central government has experimented with *hukou* reforms in certain cities across China, usually in small to medium size cities, to better integrate migrants into the urban community. For example, Shijiazhuang, capital of the Hebei province has allowed migrant workers to apply for temporary residence.
3 Beijing suspended its *hukou* reform project in mid-2002 after eight months, claiming that it did not have enough finances to meet the social needs of migrants.
4 The term CSOs is applied to a wide range of civil society actors including non-state, non-profit, voluntary organisations and non-governmental organisations (NGOs).
5 Beijing is divided into sixteen districts and two counties (Beijing Government website).
6 Prior to the 1990s, Beijing did not have a discernible CBD due to its status as the political centre and thus restrictions were placed on the business sector, land was publicly owned until the mid-1980s and the historical heritage of Beijing limited building heights within the Second Ring Road (Wei and Yu 2006: 386).
7 The emergence and demolition of the Zhejiang village has been well documented by China scholars. For an in-depth study see Li Zhang's *Strangers in the City: Reconfigurations of Space, Power, and Social Networks within China's Floating Population*. Stanford: Stanford University Press, 2001.
8 The sheer numbers and unorganised nature of migrant workers means that to assess their relationship with the government and their potential in generating change will result in vast generalisations. Hence, migrant CSOs serve as a better point of analysis and as many are registered in some form with the government, they carry more legitimacy.
9 The decline of state control is in one part accredited to the state giving local and regional governments greater power or decentralisation. The other part is the redistribution of resources to areas such as the economy and military, and less on social welfare.
10 The organisations studied may be registered in some form with local or municipal departments.
11 Approximately 2000 people are under each neighbourhood committee's jurisdiction. This level of governance once known for its interference in people's everyday lives has been professionalised in the last few years with many displaced state employees staffing these committees. These committees are responsible for a range of issues from

cleanliness of the community to birth control. At the lowest level, is the *juweihui* or local residents' group, where some of the roles of the Street Neighbourhood Committee are delegated to the residents.

12 Names of interviewees have been abbreviated to ensure their privacy.

References

Chamberlain, H.B. (1998) 'Civil Society with Chinese Characteristics?', *The China Journal* 39: 69–81.

Edelman, M. (2001) 'Social Movements: Changing Paradigms and Forms of Politics', *Annual Review Anthropology*, 30 (1): 285–317.

Evans, P., Rueschemeyer, D. and Skocpol, T. (eds) (1985) *Bringing the State Back In*, Cambridge: Cambridge University Press.

Gallagher, M.E. (2004) 'China: The Limits of Civil Society in Late Leninist State', in M. Alagappa (ed.) *Civil Society and Political Change in Asia*, Stanford: Stanford University Press.

Gu, C. and Shen, J. (2003) 'Transformation of urban socio-spatial structure in socialist market economies: The case of Beijing', *Habitat International*, 27 (1): 107–122.

Hampton, A.F. (2005) 'Unlocking the Hegemonic Power of "The People's Democratic Dictatorship": An Analysis of Civil Society and the State in the PRC', *China Report*, 41 (3): 255–266.

Howell, J. (1998) 'An Unholy Trinity? Civil Society, Economic Liberalization, Democratization in post-Mao China', *Government and Opposition*, 33 (1): 56–80.

Juan, S. (2007) 'Migrant population swelling in Beijing', *China Daily*, 5 December.

Kaufman, J., Kleinman, A. and Saich, T. (2006) 'Introduction: Social Policy and HIV/AIDS in China', in J. Kaufman, A. Kleinman and T. Saich (eds), *AIDS and Social Policy in China*, Cambridge, MA: Harvard University Asia Center

Ma, X. and Delios, A. (2007) 'A Tale of Two Cities: Japanese FDIs in Shanghai and Beijing, 1979–2003', *International Business Review*, 16 (2): 207–228.

Migdal, J. (2001) *State in Society: Studying How States and Societies Transform and Constitute One Another*, Cambridge: Cambridge University Press.

Skocpol, T. (1985) 'Bringing the State Back In: Current Research', in P. Evans, D. Rueschemeyer and T. Skocpol (eds) (1985).

Solinger, D.J. (1995) 'China's Urban Transients in the Transition from Socialism and the Collapse of the Communist Urban Public Goods Regime', *Comparative Politics*, 27 (2): 127–146.

Thornton, P.M. (2002) 'Framing Dissent in Contemporary China: Irony, Ambiguity and Metonymy', *The China Quarterly*, 171: 661–681.

UNDP (2002) 'Essentials UNDP Practice Area: Democratic Governance Synthesis of Lessons Learned', Available http://www.undp.org/eo/documents/essentials/CivicEngagement-Final31October2002.pdf (accessed 3 July 2007).

Wei, D.Y. and Yu, D. (2006) 'State Policy and the Globalization of Beijing: Emerging Themes', *Habitat International*, 30 (3): 377–395.

Wu, W. (2002) 'Migrant Housing in Urban China: Choices and Constraints', *Urban Affairs Review*, 38 (1): 90–119.

Zhang, L. (2006) 'Contesting Spatial Modernity in Late-Socialist China', *Current Anthropology*, 47 (3): 461–484.

Zhou, X. (1993) 'Unorganised Interests and Collective Action in Communist China', *American Sociological Review*, 58 (1): 54–73.

Appendix

Migrant Civil Society Organisations studied and Summary of their Major Activities

Organisation Name	Major Activities	Registration and Funding Status
Beijing Legal Aid Office for Migrant Workers	• Provides legal service and advice to migrant workers • Works with ACFTU in training programmes and workshops	• Established under the guidance of Beijing Municipal Judicial Bureau • Financially supported by China Legal Aid Foundation and All-China Lawyers' Foundation
Little Bird	• Provides legal service and advice to migrant workers • Conducts training programmes such as computer skills	• Local organisation registered with the local Commerce and Industry Bureau
Facilitators	• Undertakes advocacy work • Conducts research into and produces case studies on various issues (e.g. Factory working conditions, labour laws) • Publishes its own materials, journals and books	• Local organisation registered with the local Commerce and Industry Bureau • Support from international organisations
Tongxin Xiwang	• Works with migrant women of a community within Beijing • Has established a second-hand clothing store, where migrant women of the local community are in charge • Is exploring options of opening a day care centre	• Local organisation registered with the local Commerce and Industry Bureau • Has some partnerships with other local organisations – can share resources • Support from international organisations • Money raised from second-hand store also goes back into the organisation
Migrant Women's Club	• Has conducted health training, provides some legal advice • Publishes newsletters and magazines to connect migrant women in the city • Holds major events such as group weddings	• Local organisation registered with the local Commerce and Industry Bureau • Support from international organisations • Events are sometimes sponsored by local businesses
Gongyou Zhijia	• Works with migrant workers through the medium of art and music • Undertakes performance-based projects • Runs a training school for migrants • Has opened a school for migrant children	• Local organisation registered with the local Commerce and Industry Bureau • Support from international organisations
Worry Assistance Hotline	• Offers a hotline for migrant workers to call and receive advice on a range of matters	• Local organisation registered with the local Commerce and Industry Bureau

	• Holds regular meetings for migrant workers within the community – provides space to share stories • Provides basic sexual health training	• Has some partnerships with other local organisations – can share resources • Seeking international funding to extend projects
Shining Stone Community Action	• Has no current active projects in Beijing as yet. But works with Tongxin Xiwang and provides skill and capacity training	• Local organisation registered with the local Commerce and Industry Bureau • Support from international organisations
Compassion for Migrant Children	• Works with several migrant schools to run weekend programmes for students including English lessons, arts and crafts • Is building a community centre in a community on the outskirts of Beijing to accommodate its projects	• Currently registered in Hong Kong but seeking local registration • Support from individual international donors • In kind and financial support from businesses

4   Singapore's public housing spaces

Alter-'native' spaces in transition

Limin Hee

Introduction

> The heartland implies by its name that it is the core of Singapore.
> Geographically the heartland is spread out all over Singapore, but in its rep-
> resentations it is a space that denotes national and local identity beyond
> coordinates. It is an exclusionary space ... it is a myth of origins, of a belief
> that history and landscape that are exclusively Singaporean exist. They are
> nationalist narratives, taking on 'the naiveté of nativity: the pure, true
> national story that is pure and true because it is native'.
>
> (Yeo, 2004:27)

Although the form of public housing adopted by Singapore from the 1950s
onwards was not unique at that time, the way spatial practices have developed
within the new environment, the so-called Singaporean 'heartland,' took on a
unique shape – a condition the earlier excerpt terms as 'native.' The mass 'migration' of the hitherto variously housed migrant population in the 1960s into the rigid
framework presented by the modernist new towns presented fertile grounds for
social and cultural transformations.

A review of the history of Singapore's public housing and the development of
public spaces within this framework would reveal a history of experimentation
with new spatial typologies – or the construction of the alter-'*native*.' These alter-
native spaces may or may not have become animated as public spaces, but nevertheless form part of an armature of potential spaces of resistance. As public housing
spaces had been cumulatively built, they exist in contemporary Singapore simultaneously, irrespective of their vintage, and as a collective present a rich spatial field
for investigating spatial practice in contemporary Singaporean society. These collective spaces also form the armature of the spaces of resistance, made potent
through the practices of everyday life played out in space.

The iterations of these hybrid spaces constituted through social and cultural
adaptations and transformations will be discussed first within their macro-context
and historical development, and then within specific instances of forms, space and
spatial practice. While the spaces of public housing in the early days were

functional in nature and served to provide light and air rather than act as social spaces, later spaces in the form of neighborhood clusters and precincts were devised with some kind of social agenda (such as 'building communities'). In the latter, urban design politics is dominated by the hegemony of planned spaces. The hierarchical progression of spaces in the new towns, their even distribution and their increasingly bounded nature might be read as concrete manifestations of the Confucian ethics and paternalistic nature of government in Singapore, where a predominantly Chinese sense of authority and control still persists. These spaces nevertheless mark the basis of experience of public spaces for many Singaporeans, as almost nine out of ten in the population find homes in public housing.

The discussion of public housing spaces will be approached first from its macro-context and historical development, and then within specific instances of spatial practice. The study will begin by tracing interrelationships between the political agenda and choices made by the state, and the ensuing design choices in public housing in the Singaporean context. In the planning of new town spaces, urban design politics is dominated by the hegemony of planned spaces. However, at the level of spatial practice, the design politics of the macro-level is not always translated to prescribed use or desired social outcomes. The space of public housing makes manifest the interpretive nature of spatial practice within the designed environment. This article examines in particular the roles and forms of spaces of resistance or alter-*native* spaces in these instances:

1. Space where social practices have persisted, with these practices sometimes taking on new shapes, but often easily adapted to the new spaces in public housing.[1]
2. Space where new social practices have occurred, where new forms of spatial practices have been created through the interaction of people and the built environment, as well as instances where altogether new spaces and new practices have sprung up.
3. Space where subtle forms of defiance have occurred in spite of efforts to reinforce the status quo, and cumulatively provide some form of resistance to an idealized picture of the public realm and of the notion of 'native space.'

The spaces of public housing shaped from both above, through planning and design, and below, through spatial practices, capture alter-*native* constructions of Singapore (public) space in transition, and in many ways exemplify migration from one form of traditional society into the constructed notion of the 'native heartland,' albeit in a rapidly globalizing city.

One of the functions of Singaporean public space is in the forging of a national identity. While the state constructs the dominant rhetoric with regard to the Singapore identity, the very constructed-ness of this identity, conceived and manipulated throughout the short history of Singapore's independence, makes this subject to negotiation and contestation by different groups or individuals (Kong and Yeoh, 2003: 2). Instead of overt confrontational events in public, these situations and negotiations often take place in ordinary public life, through the bodies that

inhabit public space and the recurring practices of these. It is through spatial practices that the notions of 'national' and 'identity' are constructed, both by the state,
and through lived experiences, in public space by the Singapore people. This chapter discusses how spaces of everyday life have the capacity to act as a decentralized
democratic resource, forming a constellation of public spaces that ultimately serves
to shape the developing public sphere.

By looking at the microcosm of everyday space in everyday life in the heart of
the 'native' state, acts of resistance in space can be seen as forms of an ongoing
negotiation in the development of the relations between society and state, and
constitute a reading of cultural resistance in the context of Singapore.

Singapore public housing – A brief history

Each decade of public housing, from the colonial attempts at public housing proto-
types through to the inception of a massive public housing program from the 1960s
to the present, relates the role of state politics, through planning and urban design
choices, in attempting to socialize the population towards the desired social and
political goals.[2] The role of public space had not always been of prime concern in
the history of Singapore's public housing, but its importance had emerged in recent
years in tandem with its current emphasis on 'building communities.' The trajectory of the development of public space in this context is itself illustrative of the
changing mode of thinking of the polity with regards to space as a social resource.

The public housing of today is a far cry from the early days of cramped, low-cost
housing, when the call of the day had been to 'break the backbone of the housing
shortage.' (Liu, 1992). To date, the Housing and Development Board (HDB) has
built 21 new towns with a total housing stock of more than 800,000 flats. Public
housing in Singapore is widely accepted as the form of housing for the lifetime of a
lower-to-middle class Singaporean. Currently, about nine in ten Singaporeans live
in public housing.

However, with growing affluence, there are higher expectations of the quality of
the housing environment. The spaces of public housing have shifted in function
from pragmatic spacing between buildings and left over spaces, to become the
focus of planning for 'cohesive communities' and also as tangible images of an
improved quality of life.[3] The transformation of spaces in the design of new towns
impacts most at the level of small residential public spaces, as these are the most
immediate public spaces for the everyday life of many flat dwellers.

The decades for which we trace the development of public housing are themati-
cally articulated in Figure 4.1 to reflect the political agenda embedded within the
design and planning of each decade:

Shelter (1952–1960)

The policy to resettle families away from the central area, which was to be developed for commercial purposes, and the systematic acquisition of parcels of
land for new housing, favored the building of high-rise flats. The high-rise option

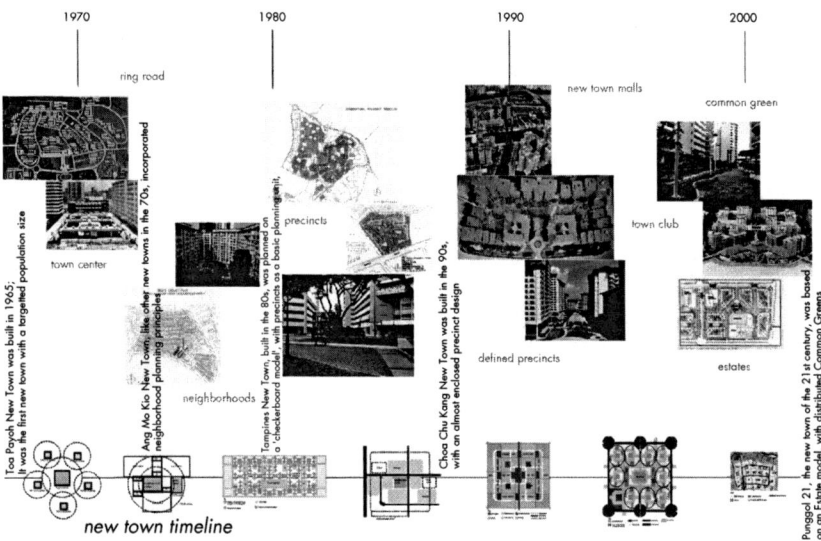

Figure 4.1 Timeline depicting development of new towns in Singapore (photograph by author).

also provided a viable symbol of progress and improvement with the new self-government.

Many of the ideas about housing being implemented in Europe in general and Britain in particular found suitable testing ground in Queenstown, where the high-rise model was first adopted, initiated by the Singapore Improvement Trust (SIT) in 1952 and completed by the HDB, the local housing authority in the 1970s.[4] The urban fabric of Queenstown broke away from the street-based city blocks of the shophouse-type, which was the predominant urban form of the city center at that time, to being primarily oriented in the north–south direction with green space in between blocks to fulfill light and ventilation requirements.

Consolidation (1961–1970)

During this period, public housing was seen as a means to allow for hollowing out the central areas of Singapore for commercial development, with the resulting need to cater for the massive resettlement of the population. Toa Payoh New Town, initiated in 1965, was the first new town planned with a target population of 180,000 and was in fact HDB's flagship project for public housing – very much based on the *Congrès Internationaux d'Architecture Moderne* (CIAM) model of functional mass housing, with its integrated life, transport, work and recreation components.[5] Spaces between buildings simply served pragmatic functions of allowing light and ventilation, with the occasional playground being provided where space allowed.

Social disintegration and re-integration (1971–1980)

Although public housing presented a superior living environment compared to what it replaced, there was an undercurrent of dissatisfaction with the failure of the HDB to protect a sense of community, neighborliness and identity, and the breaking up of the traditional extended family structure (Yeh and HDB, 1972). On a more insidious level, there were criticisms of new public housing as an attempt to atomize already existing racial enclaves, which in Singapore's history had initiated strong communal lobbies, protests and even inter-racial conflicts.

Throughout the 1970s, as the public housing programs were consolidated and housing provisions brought up to an adequate level, the political will turned to the planning of new towns with neighborhoods of convenience as a functional model of distribution of infrastructure and facilities, as well as some means of social integration for a society dislocated from its vernacular and ethnic origins – addressing the perceived need for some form of re-integration and notion of neighborliness. Neighborhoods were conceived of as self-contained 'communities' defined as 'total living environments' of about 6,000 dwelling units, sufficient to support a primary school as well as shopping and community activity nodes within a walking distance of 400 m.[6]

The early neighborhoods were planned as centers of convenience, not centers of community building (Liu, 1975), and executed at a very pragmatic and functional level. The blocks were typically arranged in a north–south orientation, which was one of the important layout criteria for flats with the emphasis on functional planning. Since the spaces were laid out as functional spacing and as car parks, there was little hierarchy in the scale and types of spaces. The presence of void decks (the space below the flats which are raised by *piloti*) also made the space at ground level even less defined.

Building communities (1981–1990)

In the late 1970s and early 1980s, the abstract notions of 'building communities' and optimization of land took concrete form through the implementation of the precinct concept, which created opportunities to foster a sense of identity and belonging through the inward focusing and compact precincts that form the interlocking lattice for the new town.

In parallel to the development of the precinct, the building of new towns was the perfect opportunity to encourage an even greater extent of inter-racial mixing (or of greater racial distribution). Explicit controls in the form of racial quotas in each new town, even at the level of each block of flats, based on the current demographic profile of the nation were introduced in 1989. This was combined with deliberate mixing of classes through the mix of flat types within neighborhoods, precincts and even within each block of flats.

The New Town Structural Model made its first appearance in the late 1970s and formed the basis of the 'checkerboard' model of town planning (Tan *et al.*, 1985), characterized by the use of the precinct as a basic unit of planning. It repeated itself in clusters of 4 ha or sometimes half the size, serving 400–800 families housed in four to eight blocks of flats. Each precinct had a precinct center, which could include small games courts, children's playgrounds or landscaped gardens. Six to eight precincts would share a neighborhood center, which was usually within a 400 m radius or five-minute walking distance from the precinct.

The idea behind the creation of the precinct was to try to encourage meaningful social interaction among residents (now deemed lacking in neighborliness) through the shared use of this focal point of activity at a scale that residents could recognize and understand. The precinct space and facilities were planned with the

> expectation that residents using them will come into social contact with each other, and in so doing, develop a sense of belonging to their individual precincts. Unlike the other physical planning elements, the precinct is a spatial engineering strategy to effect the achievement of social goals.
>
> (Teo, 1996: 279–294)

Imaging public housing (1991–2000)

While the early new towns reflected pragmatic planning to meet housing quantities and were the cornerstones of the growth and economic development of Singapore by housing the disciplined workforce, the new towns of the 1990s were to embody the aesthetics of progress and of a global city. Quality of housing and perceived choices of lifestyle were carefully packaged in imaging the new town of the 21st century, such as Punggol New Town, marketed as 'A Waterfront Town of the 21st century.'

In the Punggol 21 blueprint, two of the stated planning objectives of the Urban Redevelopment Authority (URA) indicated the intention to 'create a high quality residential town which will serve as a model for the 21st century,' as well as to 'create an environment which fosters a sense of community bonding.' (URA, 1998) The new paradigm sought to integrate the components of housing, education, shopping and recreation into compact, pedestrian-friendly, mixed-use developments served by light rail transport nodes within a walking distance of 300–350 m.

Within an 'estate,' the precinct open space surrounded by the precinct buildings were often raised on a podium level above 2–4 stories of car parks. Such a layout, effectively a 'precinct on a plinth,' was quite efficient in maximizing land use and afforded a high degree of privacy. The emphasis on privacy and exclusivity in construing public housing in the image of private condominium housing in Singapore tended to undermine the continuity of the network of public spaces in the new town.

Urban design politics vs spatial practice

This history of public housing recounted in terms of urban design politics shows first a pragmatic layout of spaces, initially with blocks laid out in functional arrangements for light and ventilation, progressively partitioned to create notions of neighborhoods; then smaller communities or precincts, then estates or common greens, with an accompanying re-allocation of shared amenities to each of these individualized communities rather than on a shared neighborhood basis; and subsequently the packaging of these spaces into semi-private domains, suggesting the notion of private properties. Such a reading suggests that design was increasingly manipulated towards political ends such as forging communities, creating identity and notions of privacy, and garnering political legitimacy, but these have not always created successful spaces or environments meeting planned intentions.[7]

However, it is only at the level of spatial practice that one can begin to understand the meaning of these spaces in the everyday life of public housing dwellers, how these spaces form part of the notion of resistance in everyday life to the hegemonic discourses of Singapore society, and whether they form a meaningful notion of public space. As such, the discussion shifts from the macro-scale of planning and urban design to the scale of spatial practice: how do people inhabit and move through public space, what are their interactions therein, how do these become a part of their everyday lives, and do these practices lead to transgressions and transformations of space? These instances of the delimiting of spatial boundaries or spatial practices are treated discursively as forms of resistance against the embodied dominant political discourse that has been translated into space.

Persistent spatial practices

The design of HDB apartment blocks, elevated off the ground on *piloti* to create a sense of flowing space (at least at ground level) and to alleviate the feeling of oppressive density, leaves a blank space interrupted by columns and piers on the ground floor. This space, simply called the 'void deck,' plays an important role in structuring the spatial practices of the everyday life of residents. For many, it is the point of arrival and departure from their homes, part of the system of void decks, lift lobbies, corridors and landings in the transition from home to the outside world. It is the point of sending schoolchildren off, waiting for them on the way home, and of informal social encounters, as embodied in selected excerpts of the poem, *Void Deck* by Singaporean poet Alfian Sa'at:

> Where the neighborhood wives,
> After a morning at the wet market,
> Sit facing the breeze
> To trade snatches of gossip …

Naturally, the inhabitants of void decks include children, who engage in wanton play:

> And children orbit around them
> Laugh without diction –
> Their games of tag a reassurance
> That there has been no hothousing
> Of who is unclean, unwashed,
> Untouchable …

And the older inhabitants of the void decks, who:

> ... sit like sages
> To deploy chess pieces with ancient strategies.
> In a corner, a caged bird bursts
> With the song of its master's pride
> (Alfian Sa'at, *Void Decks* 1998)

The system of spatial transitions of corridors and void decks appealed to the cultural habit of the Singaporean dweller of public housing in extending personal and cultural space outside the threshold of the home. The extensions in question take the form of the physical extension of personal artifacts, like footwear, plants, religious paraphernalia, including altars, incense burners and graphic representations of the Hindu *Mandala* drawn in chalk outside of the home; furniture, including benches, seats, umbrellas, bicycles and other paraphernalia.

Cultural extensions of space also include the 'exteriorizing' of family events such as weddings, funerals and birthdays, bringing these to public space. It is already an HDB estate tradition in its history of just over 40 years, that Malay weddings were held in the void decks of flats. The extension of cultural practice to public space had, in my observation, been the strongest in the Malay ethnic group.

Despite the efforts by the government throughout the history of Singapore public housing to effectively disperse the ethnic groups, the Malays had maintained a sense of community and ethnic identity in several ways. Through the buying of re-sale flats, the Malays had generally been able to acquire as a preference, most of the lower level flats, which the Chinese majority of flat dwellers, when given a choice, did not prefer.[8] Living on the lower floors gave the Malays greater accessibility to the ground floor space and to have other Malay neighbors. A representative 'headman' is also informally selected within each block to resolve any matters involving the Malays. The void deck acts – not by drawing a simple vernacular parallel but more alluding to a persistent spatial practice in new spaces – like a *kampong* (village) compound and the corridors as elongated common *serambi* (verandahs). The Malay wedding in the void deck is very much a communal affair, with neighbors and friends helping to cook, wash and even host the event.

The void deck is quite often used for Chinese funerals, the wake for which lasts between three to seven days, and the proceedings range from visits by friends and relatives to pay their last respects to elaborate Taoist rituals involving musical accompaniment and the burning of paper offerings, for example, a large *papier maché* model of a condominium block.[9] Temporary tents, mobile toilets, sound systems, lighting, seating and tables, as well as an elaborate backdrop for the coffin form the paraphernalia of the Chinese funeral, filling up the void deck. The whole set-up of the funeral temporarily transforms the void deck into an extension of the Chinese family home, and strangers who pass through the space are treated with mild suspicion; the public space is temporarily transposed to private realm. The

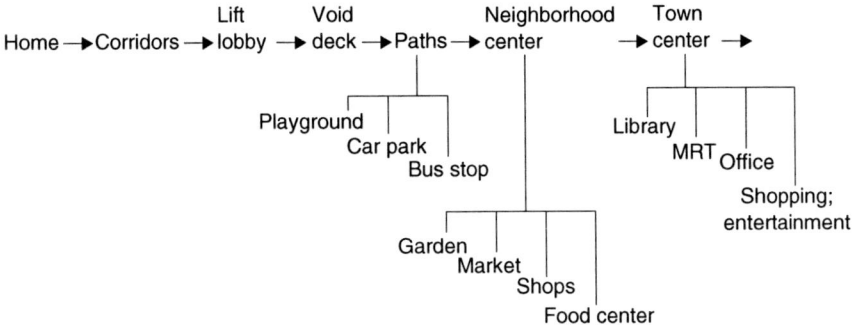

Figure 4.2 Movement sequence in a typical HDB new town.

the precinct towards the town center. A mapping of incidental routes for different types of people is shown in Figure 4.3.

An interpretive reading of this simulated graph of different routes taken during the day by different subjects show that the places nearer home are where people would most likely run into each other. Such places, including void decks, paths, neighborhood coffeeshops, the food center and market, form channels of activities, interspersed with nodes, constituting a spatial system in which recurring spatial practices, re-enacted on an everyday basis, become embedded (Ooi and Tan, 1992).

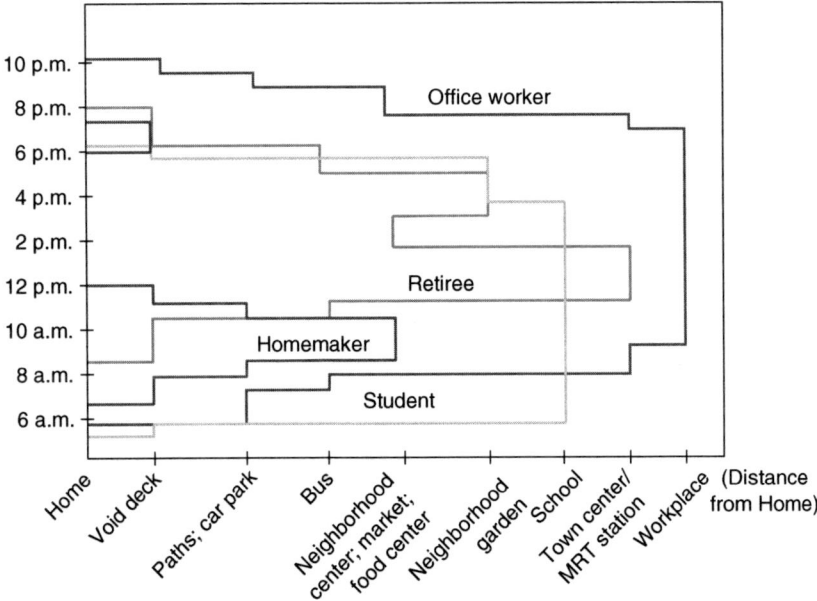

Figure 4.3 The concept of 'public time,' as illustrated by the overlapping of space and schedules.

Coffeeshops within the neighborhood and town centers often play the role of the new village squares or commons, with residents often meeting neighbors and friends from within the estate or neighborhood, exchanging greetings, news or even watching important sports events together over the coffeeshop TV set. During political campaigns, coffeeshops are important campaign stops for the politicians who are keen to win the 'heartland' vote.

Hawker centers and markets are also places where one is most likely to meet with neighbors: groups of women are often seen chatting at the market as most of them have a routine that is likely to coincide with that of their neighbors. It is a Sunday morning breakfast routine at the coffeeshop in Tiong Bahru, when elderly men place their songbirds on their perches and spend the morning listening to their melodic songs. A prominent void deck space near the new town library in Toa Payoh, is the favorite spot for a group of regular, older, male chess players who sit informally around the space to indulge in their pastime.

The configuration of new town centers often has routes converging along the shop fronts, creating intensely used paths narrowed even further by the spilling of goods along the arcaded fronts of the shops, such that an intermediate zone between the shop and the external spaces is created. The channels formed through the orchestrated routes in the town center again increase the chance encounters of neighbors and friends in these spaces, enriching the prospects of these spaces as social spaces. The spatial practice of shopping in the town center is an adaptation from that imagined by planners and architects. At the level of spatial practice, shop fronts are often blurred zones of public and semi-private spaces, evoking again a cultural habit of claiming public space for private use. Plastic canopies extend beyond the neat rows of terracotta-tiled canopies provided by the HDB. Mobile carts and kiosks animate the space, and in some places such as the Kreta Ayer HDB development, vendors occasionally lay plastic ponchos on the ground to display their wares.

Town centers and the areas around Mass Rapid Transit (MRT) Stations are the new 'hang-outs' for groups of young people, who meet and while away time chatting or, as in the case of the space around the Bishan MRT station on Saturday afternoons, schoolboys meet to exchange coveted trading cards. Instead of the coffeeshops, teenagers hang out at the new town Starbucks or meet around the new town shopping mall, where the occasional mini-amphitheatre or seating ledges are provided for waiting.

The elderly too, find their own niches in the new towns. Early mornings at an Ang Mo Kio precinct, a group of feisty older women meet to do pre-dawn tai-chi, to finish in time for their daily market shopping. Groups of Indian women meet round a landscaped garden in a Bishan precinct to chat every evening. Groups of foreign domestic helpers, such as the Filipinos, also meet in the new town centers, as an alternative to the crowded Orchard Road rendezvous spot. At the town centers, food and shopping are also likely to cost less.

Re-visiting the daily routines, it is possible to draw out temporal zones of the day when the greatest likelihood of meeting in public places take place, and consider these as collective 'public time.' Such a concept helps to explain the rhythmic flux in the liveliness of these spaces, which may be quiet at certain times of the day, but become lively animated spaces in 'public time.' Within the macro gestures embedded in planned new town structures, the emergent, temporal spatial practices of everyday life enacted by flat dwellers reproduce space in the image of the Singaporean communality. These are the emergent new practices that inform the re-contextualization of new town culture and social systems, situating spatial practice in concrete spaces, bringing to real terms the generalizations of use conceived in the town-planner's eye.

Defiant spatial practices

Spatial practices that defy rules and regulations of public housing spaces, or transcribe trajectories within space not anticipated or sanctioned for these contexts, it could be argued, are an attempt to leave a personal mark within space regarded as anonymous or alienating. These may include acts of claiming space; leaving personal items or furniture in public space – such as groups of elderly men who assemble their own 'living room' within void decks; leaving traces in public space – such as graffiti, vandalism and littering.

Just as social spaces and niches are found by new town dwellers, there are many for whom living in public housing has been an alienating experience. Filmic, poetic and fictional narratives set in public housing tend to offer the following perspective:

> (T)he displacement of individuals and their rootedness in Singapore, in personal histories, circumstances and the environment … crops up again and again … its presence seems to be intended to alert readers and audiences to the gritty and sometimes disturbing reality behind the façade of uniform housing.
>
> (Yeo, 2004:24)

These aspects of public housing seldom get an airing in the official discourse of public housing success, or even in local, mainstream television sitcoms such as the happy, multi-racial neighbors portrayed in 'Under One Roof.'

Portrayal of HDB living often takes place in generic HDB spaces such as void decks, corridors, or flat interiors, which give a sense of placeless-ness, and also represent the alternative of the global city, as exemplified by places like Orchard Road or the Central Business District. Discomfort and a sense of alienation can be read in another of Sa'at's pieces, about something as innocuous as railings in an HDB block of flats:

> As a child, I was always warned by my mother not to touch the railings that zigzag vertically on the medial side of HDB staircases. Her rationale was that 'people spit from above', and consequently, the metal railings are coated with saliva, contaminated and thus stripped of its supportive function. They become, instead, sites of danger, where initially they would provide some safety, especially if the stairs are slippery.

Another site which represents a potential space of hazard is the threshold at the periphery of the block, where one walks from the void deck into 'open air'. This is a space of vulnerability, where one is exposed to infelicitous weather: a rain of tissue paper, cotton buds, sweet wrappers, cigarette ash, and if of sufficient mass, what has been called 'killer litter'. Thus HDB existence is characterized by aerial threats, where a mouth expels its contents, a hand dispatches its cargo, before withdrawing back into a planar anonymity (which one hides the culprit, one wonders, looking up), where a primary accomplice to misfortune is gravity.

(Sa'at, 2004)[11]

Cases of killer litter, as the potentially deadly aerial projectiles are called, are frequent in the everyday life of HDB living and impact on the perception of public space 'downstairs' as dangerous places. The deviant behavior of the spreaders of killer litter show up the sub-altern culture of HDB dwelling, in these instances of deliberate flouting of rules and vandalism of public space. Other instances of what is deemed anti-social behavior by the authorities, punishable by the law, include urinating in lifts and public spaces, scrawling on public surfaces, etc.[12] The feeling of alienation and emptiness is effectively captured in the last part of Sa'at's poem *Void Decks*:

Eyes reveal a meeting-point
For loners and loiterers:

A sense of things reduced–
Conversations that trickle through
Brief noddings at lift landings,
Teenage rhetoric scrawled, in liquid paper,
On the stone-table chessboard,
(Where the king used to sit)
The grandiose house-selling dreams of residents
Compacted in anonymous letterboxes;
As an afterthought, an old man pees
Under a public phone.

A place to be avoided, this,
How in its vastness it devours hours.
Little wonder then,
Why residents rush through void decks
Back to the cramped comforts of home
As if in fear of what such open space might do
To cozy minds.

(Alfian Sa'at, *Void Decks* 1998)

Spatial practices that defy rules and regulations of public housing spaces, or transcribe trajectories within space not anticipated or sanctioned for these contexts are sometimes attempts to leave a personal mark within space regarded as anonymous or alienating. Acts of defiance against the rules of living in public housing are also enacted by children who unwittingly play in void decks, ignoring signs prohibiting football, in-line skates and so on in these places. One town council, in its zealous bid to stop children from playing ball in void decks, actually nailed barbed wire to the walls. Although such drastic measures are laughable, serious punishment had been considered time and again by the authorities to deter these practices in public housing.

A more subtle defiant practice, in fact only becoming obvious when practiced over recurring time and space, is the act of walking. Making one's own way through a new town is a kind of *tactic*, such as de Certeau would describe: 'The act of walking is to the urban system what the speech act is to language or to the statements uttered' (1984: 97). De Certeau has painted a vivid picture of how a walker in the city is in the act of becoming rather than being, actualizing possibilities, improvising, transforming and abandoning spatial elements, and through these choices, creating a unique set of spatial experiences through the city.

Indeed, investigating the act of walking through new town spaces already helps us to deconstruct the broad strategies laid out for such an activity and how these have been observed or subverted in the practice of walking. As explained earlier, blocks of flats in new towns are laid out with void decks at the ground level to create the impression of openness. Open footpaths link these blocks to other spaces in the new towns and are the prescribed pedestrian thoroughfares. Often, the walker takes a serendipitous route through the new town to get to his destination, ignoring footpaths and cutting through grassed areas, under void decks, and across open, hard-paved car parks, in other words, often transcribing an almost straight line between where he started and where he was going.

As new towns developed, concepts of separating people from traffic became more concrete, and covered footpaths linked blocks of flats and led to common amenities like bus-shelters, markets and other places. However, the traces of the walker through the new town can still be discerned: it is not uncommon to see well-worn paths cut through grassed areas, diagonally transgressing prescribed covered foot paths. While some of these informal routes are eventually paved over to create new paths, the insistent re-turfing of such worn out patches of grass also takes place, with new barricades placed alongside footpaths to prevent straying off onto the grass. At the same time, crossing the street at undesignated spots was deemed 'jaywalking' and punishable by a small fine if the transgressor is caught in the act. Such conflicts between walkers and the managers of new towns occur on a daily basis, and produce creative 'walking rhetorics' encompassing unprescribed experiences of the new town.

The range of defiant spatial practices exhibit creativity, a need for identity, inconsiderate behavior, venting of frustrations, or criminal behavior. The most recent phenomenon in new town public spaces is the practice of *le parcour* or parkour (free-running) in which perpetrators of the activity move quickly and fluidly through space without pauses, including vaulting and jumping over obstacles like railings and walls.[13] The practice caught on in Singapore rapidly,

Figure 4.4 Defiant practices, (clockwise from top left): outdoor 'sitting room'; walking as rhetoric; 'parkour' (i) and (ii); peddlers; leaving traces; blurring boundaries (i) and (ii); doing the 'do nots'; (i), (ii) and (iii) graffiti; ad-hoc gathering and displaying 'identity'.

perhaps due to the challenge it gives adolescents over the banal new town landscape.

Spatial practices in transition

Such an overlaying of practices in space, accompanied by spatial narratives and anecdotes help us to conceive of the dense texture within which public space is used and experienced. The layering of routines and commentaries, capturing the points of view of those who inhabit (or choose not to inhabit) public space provides some notions of the meanings of public space. The spaces of the new town, although prescribed as the public space of the community, tend often to merely accommodate isolated groups who appear within the space but have very little interaction. Such a space seems to suggest the appearance of a community, but this remains on a symbolic level as individual bodies that inhabit this space mainly perceive others rather than coming into actual social contact or friction.

The public spaces of the precincts represent the community, and their value lies perhaps in that they are a concretization of the territorial space of those who live within their confines, making visible their members, and thus imparting knowledge and information about others. The playing out of cultural differences within such a space is not always welcome, such as the instances of the Chinese sometimes burning paper offerings in the space, or the Malay tradition of cooking in public, but is nevertheless tolerated. However, the layering of individual narratives over space and time creates texture invisible in the space. Many of the everyday spatial practices of residents leave no trace but add to the meaning and constructions of public space.

Within the larger context of the new town, the system of channels and nodes constituting its spatial movement system and public spaces creates ample opportunities for the invention of new spatial practices as forms of resistance while leaving room for the adaptation of persistent spatial practices within its framework. Although the hierarchical system[14] of the new town structure tends to be rigid and disperses rather than assembles communities, the increasingly coherent movement system tends to bring people into more concentrated channels and nodes, allowing an overlapping of routines and space in 'public time.'[15]

When there is a temporary interrogation of established rules and accepted spatial practices, the space could be described as having been transgressed. 'Transgressive' spatial practices may have the effect of a catalyst for change over time and repeated acts of transgression.[16] The transgressions may take a 'polite' form, a de Certeau-esque tactic of the weak, of which the only strength is that over time these may have transformative effects. Defiant spatial practices may be instances of ignorance, overt flouting of laws, creative resistance or destructive, criminal behavior. The transgressed 'space' exists in time rather than in space, for example, in the case of vandalism, or children ignoring rules regarding playing games in particular places; or as an experiential realm, for example, when a group of teenagers indulge in *le parcour*, disregarding prescribed footpaths and routes as a sort of creative resistance to a rigid spatial environment.

Acts of transgression on a recurring basis define a realm of spatial practice signaling emerging sociabilities in space. The often harmless, polite acts of resistance, defiance or expression of difference in public space may lead to transformations in public space, or serve to bring to the surface sub-altern groups and spatial practices, as in the case of youths practicing *parkour*. Transgressed space may not always have political content although some of the examples in the previous section may be considered critical spatial practice.

The display of defiance or dissent in public space suggests that a narrative of loss exists, drawing from a time and place when and where people were better grounded in society and in space. This has been replaced by the feeling of rootlessness, from moving from one new town to another whenever there is a change of circumstances: a young couple marry and move to a new flat in a new estate, or in the effort to upgrade, a family moves out from their flat into a bigger, newer flat in a new estate. The lack of memories about place and the lack of distinctive difference in many of the new town public spaces contribute to the abstract nature of their perception and representation. Without psychoanalyzing this phenomenon, what is clear is the divide between representations of public spaces in this global city and public spaces in public housing. There is little middle ground in the transition of these spaces, but rather an abrupt and mutually exclusive division. HDB spaces are indeed exclusionary, where a belief that a truly Singaporean vernacular exists, and where national identity is cultivated.

New spatialities: Cultural resistance in the creation of
Singapore's public space

The notion of public space discussed in this chapter is that it is more than just a physical space, constructed through embodied spatial practices, that is, recurring actions of bodies in space. The emphasis on spatial practice puts bodies in space as the transformative subjects through their actions and engagement with space. The recurrent spatial practice shapes the embedded structures of public space such that these produce the space just as they are shaped, facilitated or constrained by it.

Modern discourses on public space are based on democracy as a precondition of the existence of a true public sphere.[17] However, the political milieu in which public space and the public sphere exist in Singapore does not fall under the ideal western, liberal definitions of democracy. Democracy is arguably decentralized within the Singapore context such that it exists at local levels of practice. Within each micro-cosmic system of public space, physical space itself acts as a functional democratic resource, not just as a stage for the enacting of social structures and cultural practices, but also exposing tensions and conflicts, so that public space participates in the shaping of democracy and the notion of public sphere.

As a democratic resource, microcosms of public space enable the reinforcement of identities, representation, the establishment of boundaries and the negotiations of these. Microcosmic public space, as the physical locus of interaction, allows for the mixing of races, even under the condition of weak people-to-people relationships, so that it is as a 'thing in the making,' that is, a larger Singaporean identity that may be constituted, ironically, by discrete cultural practices. Like speech, the media and the Internet, public space is not just the space of communication but is itself a communicative medium embodying knowledge and difference. And as there is communication through public space there is a potentiality for action that may lead to consequence and transformation. In Singapore, the local-level public spaces as an aggregate serve as a testing ground for an adaptive model of public-space-in-the-making, more so than the civic spaces in the city.

The form of public space described in this study does not depend on talk as the communicative medium, as spatial practice is the *modus operandi* here. As such, 'discursive public space' within this context has to be defined more broadly than the mode of communicative action in the Habermasian model. The form of negotiation through practice situated within public space in everyday life, supplemented by discussions in the media such as the forum page of the local dailies, potentially generate change over time. Negotiations through spatial practice may not be in the form of a dialogue in which channels of communication are open between two parties, but take place in public space.

More often than not, spatial practice may influence public opinion or create awareness on the part of the state of the needs of certain groups, trends, resistance, or other forms of knowledge regarding its citizenry. Spatial practice is not only the mode of communication between the people and the state, but also in people-to-people relations. As different groups exist in proximity in space, or share public space, some form of communication or exchange of information, achieved through spatial and visual means, occurs between them, who may or may not engage in actual dialogue.

The formation of a national identity also involves the formation of a palpable sense of being 'one people.' However, Singapore can be considered a low-trust society as a result of social capital of culturally disparate groups, which makes it difficult to develop natural wellsprings of cooperation (Barr, 2000:117–118). The challenges of a multi-racial, multi-cultural society are made apparent in public space, especially in the context of high-density living in public housing. Public space shows up the antagonistic aspects of Singapore society, especially in the lack of trust between fellow citizens, and the reliance on the state as the arbiter of socially accepted behavior. The widely held notion of the 'Singaporean Dream,' embodied within the notion and physical space of public housing, is really about aspiring to flee from a life in public housing, to own private property, to play in the private playgrounds of exclusive clubs, to travel with one's own transport, not public transportation, and to achieve status and means beyond one's fellow men.[18] The role of public space in public housing thus offers an alter-*native* view of the 'Singaporean Dream,' one in which community, consensus and conflict may play a part in the constitution of care and (multi)culturalism than in purely personal material gains.

It is particularly in the quotidian landscapes such as in public housing that the concept of public space is taken for granted and is thus ideal for 'ideological appropriation' by the state (Kong *et al.*, 2003:3).[19] The notion of the Singaporean heartland and the Singaporean Dream are constructed within these spaces, especially within those spaces that remain defiant and resistant to such notions. The understanding by Singaporeans of public housing space as the 'exclusionary space of national narratives' (Yeo, 2004:27), and the state's use of public housing to materially nurture ideal Singaporean communities, already make these spaces heavily invested with function. However, it is clear that a close reading of public housing spaces goes beyond interpreting these as the reification of power relations between the state and the people. These spaces allow for the insertions of negotiation through forms of resistance, collusion, translations of meanings and transformations within the sphere of everyday life.

Notes

1 Singapore's first generation of public housing dwellers brought with them various social practices originating from ethnic practices in vernacular environments like Chinese and Malay villages or *kampongs*.
2 The desired social goals stipulated by the Singapore government change through time, as outlined in the history segment of the article.
3 This is the term used in the current corporate vision of the HDB. It is also pertinent to note that the ethnic composition of Singapore to date (of the 3.6 million Singapore citizens and permanent residents) is 75.2 percent Chinese, 13.6 percent Malays, 8.8 percent Indians, while Eurasians and other groups form 2.4 percent (Singapore Department of Statistics 2006). See also http://www.singstat.gov.sg/pubn/reference/mds.pdf
4 The HDB was set up in 1960, after Singapore's self-rule, to oversee the task of housing the growing population.
5 The proposal of the CIAM at its 4th Congress in 1933 produced 'The Athens Charter', a document that remained controversial in its commitment to the planning of functional cities, high-rise housing, zoning and green belts.

publicizing of private grief alerts the flat dwelling community of a death in the family, performing the role of communication and at the same time re-enacting shared cultural identity.

The enacting of weddings and funerals in the public space of the void decks not only causes neighbors to lose the use of the void deck temporarily, but also imposes on the private realms of other flat dwellers through the presence of crowds, pollution of the air through burnt offerings and cooking in public, not to mention the noise levels these events generate. However, fellow flat dwellers have demonstrated extraordinary tolerance honed through years of dwelling in close proximity to neighbors whom one hardly knows. The tolerance of the extension of cultural practices in public space, though passive, is itself a form of spatial practice.[10]

Through the imposition of rules of behavior, charges and temporal boundaries to the events, the authorities maintain a form of control over when, where and how these take place. In other words, within the boundaries of sanctioned behaviors these activities and events are deemed benign and are seen from above to promote a sense of community life.

Persistent spatial practices as outlined earlier continue to thrive in the system of transition spaces from the home to the public realm, with flat dwellers and the government regarding these practices as benign, to be tolerated and as contributing to a sense of community. These practices may no longer take place in the vernacular space of the past but are transposed to spaces of new configurations in public housing. However, the forms of the practices persist, sometimes within a diluted but still intact social structure, and have similar meaning and content as the original.

New spatial practices

The new spatial configurations of the new towns have resulted in entirely new forms of spatial practices within the new spaces, or at least led to changes and adaptations of practices to these new environments such that they are of a different form. However, this does not mean that the social meanings of these practices have changed, although entirely new practices may occur in the new configurations of spaces, how people move through them, interact, and inhabit them. A simple but significant spatial configuration in this instance is the movement system of the flat dweller in transition from his flat to the spaces outside his home. We have seen that the corridors and void decks espouse the persistent spatial practices transferred from a spatial vernacular. In the large scheme of the movement system leading from the apartment blocks to the neighborhood center and town center, a pattern changing from linear progression from precinct, through neighborhood and then to town centre spaces to a more distributed system of spaces is experienced, as shown in Figure 4.2.

One encounters more spatial choices as one moves further away from the flat. As many of the new towns built in the 1970s and 1980s followed a hierarchical system of containment of spaces, one moves outwards into expanding spatial systems from

6 As detailed by Tony Tan, Chief Architect of the HDB, in his public lecture at the Department of Architecture, National University of Singapore in September 1999.
7 As discussed in depth by Beng Huat Chua (1997).
8 Chinese flat dwellers consider views and breeziness from high floors a premium over lower floors that are exposed to traffic noise and smells from rubbish chutes serviced from the ground level.
9 Burnt paper offerings in the form of material properties and 'Hell' currency are rooted in Chinese beliefs in which earthly provisions from the pious could help make the after-life in the Hades much more tolerable.
10 See Lai Ah Eng's work *Meanings of Multi-ethnicity* (1995).
11 Sourced from the author's private blog, which is no longer available for public viewing.
12 Surveillance cameras have been installed by the HDB in lifts where cases of urinating are recurrent.
13 The French word 'parkour' comes from the word parcour, which loosely translates to mean an obstacle race. Parkour was invented in 1988 by a group of Parisian teenagers, including David Belle and Sebastien Foucan who are now recognized as the founders of the sport. The practice caught on in Singapore recently after French director, Luc Besson's film, *Yamakasi – Les samouraï des temps modernes* (2001) became a cult film for urban youth. The film depicted a group of disenfranchised youths from housing estates in France, perhaps stirring a chord of empathy from the highly confined lives of Singapore adolescents.
14 A new town, based on the structural models used by the HDB, is planned hierarchically, with the town Center at the top of the hierarchy, and centrally located, to the neighborhood Centers, which surround the town center, and finally, the precincts, a few of which constitute a neighborhood.
15 Public time is used here to denote time spent in public spaces.
16 Here I use the term in the sense of Stallybrass and White in their book, *The Politics and Poetics of Transgression* (1986).
17 Democracy is indeed a problematic term as there are many forms of democracies, and the discourse within this realm is plentiful. As I do not intend to engage in a prolonged discourse on democratic forms, Habermas' deliberative form of democracy is referred to here.
18 To have the five Cs – condo, club, car, credit card and career. These are the explicit material gains that a Singaporean could possibly wear as the badges of success in a society often defined by 'conspicuous consumption.'
19 The precinct spaces, void decks, neighborhood centers and other spaces are so embedded in everyday existence, that they do not enjoy the same level of awareness as, for example, celebrated public squares in cities.

Reference

Barr, M.D. (2000) *Lee Kuan Yew: The Beliefs Behind the Man*, Curzon Press, Richmond.

Chua, B.H. (1997) *Political Legitimacy and Housing: Stakeholding in Singapore*, Routledge, New York.

de Certeau, M. (1984) *The Practice of Everyday Life*, University of California Press, Berkeley.

Kong, L. and Yeoh, B.S.A. (2003) 'Reconstructing the Nation' in Kong, L. and Yeoh, B.S.A. (eds) *The Politics of Landscapes in Singapore: Constructions of 'Nation,'* Syracuse University Press, Syracuse.

Lai, A.E. (1995) *Meanings of Multiethnicity – A Case Study of Ethnicity and Ethnic Relations in Singapore*, Oxford University Press, Kuala Lumpur.

Liu, T.K. (1975) 'Design for Better Living Conditions' in Yeh, S.H.K. (ed.) *Public Housing in Singapore – A Multi-Disciplinary Study*, Singapore University Press for HDB, Singapore.

Liu, T.K. (1992) 'Public Housing in Singapore: An Architectural Portrait' in *Proceedings of Housing Design 2000 Conference*, Housing Development Board and Real Estate Developers' Association of Singapore, Singapore.

Ooi, G.L. and Tan, T.W. (1992) 'The Social Significance of Public Spaces in Public Housing Estates' in Chua, B.H. and Edwards, N. (eds) *Public Space: Design, Use and Management*, Singapore University Press, Singapore.

Sa'at, A. (1998) 'Void Decks' in *One Fierce Hour,* Landmark Books, Singapore.

Straits Times (2005) 'Void Deck Daredevils,' *Straits Times*, 20 February.

Stallybrass, P. and White, A. (1986) *The Politics and Poetics of Transgression*, Cornell University Press, Ithaca.

Tan, T.K.J., Loh, C.T., Tan, S.A., Lau, W.C. and Kwok, K. (1985) 'Physical Planning and Design' in Wong, A. and Yeh, S.H.K. (eds) *Housing a Nation: 25 years of Public Housing in Singapore*, Maruzen Asia for HDB, Singapore.

Teo, S.E. (1996) 'Character and Identity in Singapore New Towns: Planner and Resident Perspectives', *Habitat International*, vol. 20 no. 2, pp. 279–294.

Today (2004) 'The nails-and-barbed-wire mentality,' *Today*, 30 September.

Urban Redevelopment Authority (URA) (1998) *Punggol Planning Area – Planning Report 1998*. URA, Singapore.

Yeh, S.H.K. and Statistics and Research Department, HDB (1972) *Homes for the People: A Study of Tenants' Views on Public Housing in Singapore*, Government Printing Office, Singapore.

Yeo, W.W. (2004) 'Of Trees and the Heartland' in Bishop, R., Phillips, J. and Yeo, W. (eds) *Beyond Description: Singapore Space Historicity*, Routledge, London.

5 'Talking cock'

Everyday dissent through complaint and humour in Singapore

Selvaraj Velayutham

Exercise free speech – keep talking cock![1]

At the end of 2007, the founders of the Complaints Choir Project announced that they would bring the project to Singapore. Established in Helsinki, Finland, the movement had become immensely successful right around the world in teaching people to sing about their displeasures to fellow citizens. The Complaints Choir of Singapore was formed and it began rehearsing to perform in the Singapore Fringe Arts Festival 2008. A song listing some common complaints about life in Singapore was composed. However, a few days before the scheduled performance, Singapore authorities banned the choir from performing. They cited that the choir had two foreign members (non Singapore citizens) and as the lyrics touched on 'domestic affairs', they preferred that only Singaporeans take part in the performance. The Choir members refused to accept the conditions and eventually the performance was abandoned. However, a video and the lyrics of the Complaints Choir of Singapore is circulating on the internet.[2]

*   *   *

Singapore is one of Asia's most globalised cities and according to some scholars it is regarded as one of the Alpha (top ten) cities in the world along with New York, London and Tokyo (Beaverstock *et al.* 2000). Singapore's People's Action Party (PAP) government came to power in 1959 and has governed the country continuously ever since. In that time the PAP has achieved remarkable success in transforming Singapore into a prosperous modern nation and in the process has cemented its position as the dominant political force there. The PAP dominance of the political scene is compounded by the economic and social pressures that exist in this highly globalised city. There are two contradictory images of Singapore that circulate widely in academic and popular discourses: one is that of a bustling, modern, efficient, clean, green and thoroughly modernised Asian metropolis, and the other is one of authoritarianism and boring cultural sterility. A deep division remains between those who advance these opposing views. Singapore is held up as a model for cities in the rest of the developing world to emulate at the same time as it is criticised for being a highly regulated and oppressive police state. The preoccupation with Singapore's modernity and state power has produced a rather predictable analysis of its social conditions and the changes it has undergone. While state intervention and management of every aspect of Singaporean life have supposedly brought about social order, stability and economic progress, they have also curtailed the development of spontaneous social formations and movements. In particular, civil society and oppositional voices against the ruling government are relatively limited (see Ho 2000). Within this context, Singaporeans are often portrayed as either acquiescent or powerless subjects under constant official scrutiny and control.

While these observations may hold true, they do miss a significant point. I want to suggest that it is incorrect to argue that Singaporeans are totally subservient to the government, that is, state power is never absolute. While there has been some attention paid to Singapore's emerging civil society and grassroots movements, very little research has explored everyday forms of informal and non-structured dissent in Singapore (but see Rodan 1993, 1996; Chua 2000; Lee 2002; Koh and Ooi 2004). In this article, I want to explore two such forms: a culture of complaint, and humour. These fairly ubiquitous practices when examined closely offer an insight into how Singaporeans deal with the economic and social pressures of living in a global city that is also an autocratic state. Drawing on my fieldwork in Singapore and internet sources, I will highlight examples of these forms of everyday dissent. Shared widely, these practices act not only as a coping mechanism – an outlet for Singaporeans to vent their disaffection, frustration and resignation – but also serve to express their dissent. In the words of James Scott (1990: xii) they work as a 'hidden transcript' that 'represents a critique of power spoken behind the back of the dominant'. I argue that both a culture of complaint and humour represent modes of creative everyday resistance in a city which otherwise provides little space for expressions of opposition to the state. I am juxtaposing a culture of complaint and humour in this instance simply because in Singapore the act of complaining in informal situations – as is evidently the case in England also (Fox 2004) – always has an undercurrent of humour, and vice versa.

State power, authority and control

The rise of Singapore from its beginnings as a small fishing village to a global city has been well documented. For the most part, this success has been attributed to the island's British colonial legacy and the economic pragmatism of the ruling PAP government. Postcolonial Singapore brands itself as representing the New Asia – thoroughly modern and westernised as well as rooted in eastern traditions and cultures. It is a leading financial, business, transportation and communication hub in the Asia Pacific region. Singapore's developmental drive and economic prosperity have been carefully managed by the PAP government. It is swift to respond and adapt to global economic changes and conditions. The economic imperative has always been a central theme of the government strategy to gain legitimacy and control the population. The PAP has continuously relied on its economic track record, good governance and performance for its political campaigns. Although Singaporeans have benefited enormously from Singapore's economic success, they are frequently reminded not to take it for granted and told to work hard and keep up with the demands of a changing global economy.

In part this economic imperative is driven by Singapore's lack of natural resources and dependence on its geographical position and people for economic survival. In addition, geopolitical insecurity and racial fragility have added to the question of 'national survival'. Much of the political legitimacy enjoyed by the PAP government derives not only from the rhetoric of the 'uncertainty of Singapore's future' but also from the internalisation of such fears by Singaporeans themselves (Velayutham 2004). Furthermore, through coercion and repressive social policies the state has produced consent or acquiescence to its political rule. This system of social control has enabled the PAP to remain in power unopposed (see, for instance, Tremewan 1994; Chua 1995; Lingle 1996; Trocki 2006). For example, the term 'OB' marker (short for 'out-of-bounds' markers) is often used by politicians to refer to the limits of political discussion in Singapore. Though there are no clear written rules around what issues are permissible for public discussion, the term is frequently used by the government to silence agitators and repudiate their causes. However, when an open challenge to the PAP government and its authority arises, the dissenters are censured and dealt with immediately. According to Rodan the government applies blatantly repressive and political laws such as the Internal Security Act (which allows for detention without trial) and 'increasingly administrative law to restrict the political activities of organisations' and in addi-tion, 'defamation, libel and contempt of court actions by government Members of Parliament are deployed against individual political adversaries and critics' (2003: 506). The Catherine Lim Affair, in which a prominent local writer who published a critical commentary in the *Straits Times* on the PAP's so-called consultative style of government was admonished by the government (a good example of the use of OB markers to restrict public criticism levelled at the government), defamation suits against opposition politicians, and restrictions imposed on circulation of foreign publications such as *Newsweek, Time, Far Eastern Economic Review* and *International Herald Tribune* because of their supposedly biased coverage of Singapore, are a few examples of how the government has responded to dissent (Chua 1998; Velayutham 2007).

Within this stifling micro-management of public comment which considerably restricts opportunity to express dissent, how do Singaporeans respond to the pres-sures of socio-economic changes and daily living? According to Chua Beng Huat (1998) national identity construction in Singapore has been largely predetermined by the hegemony of economic discourse. Excluded from this identity construction are the cultural, social and political consequences of capitalist economic develop-ment, namely, the anxieties of living under the demands generated by a highly mar-ket-driven yet highly state-managed capitalist regime. He argues that:

> Without irony, these anxieties are mixed with the measures of pride in being part of an incorruptible system which is efficacious in generating economic growth, in improving material consumption for all, [in] maintaining a clean and efficient city and, finally, in maintaining social stability and public secu-rity. This pride is reinforced by constant comparison with the 'decadence', 'chaos' and 'irrationalities' that apparently surround this island of 'rational

planning'. These comparisons are repeated in the speeches of national leaders, circulated widely by the national media, and in the popular sphere, directly 'experienced in their travels'. Indeed, it is with these comparisons that a 'Singaporean' differentiates himself/herself from Others (for instance from neighbouring countries like Malaysia and Indonesia) in terms of level of economic development, and difference in the levels of corruption of public officials and even level of public cleanliness.

(Chua 1998: 42)

Consequently, as Yao argues, this ideological climate has produced:

A tendency among Singaporeans to believe that whatever the social problems – from air pollution and delinquent teenagers hanging out in shopping malls, to aging parents abandoned by their children – the government is able to do something. The government becomes the reference point in which people cast their hopes and personal wishes. Moreover, the government 'should be able to "fix things", even those which normally lie outside its responsibility'.

(Yao 1996: 350)

The intermeshing of personal concerns and national destiny, I would argue, is a key factor that has given impetus to the development of a culture of complaint and humour in Singapore. In other words, as Singaporeans rely on the government to address their personal needs and aspirations – which are inextricably tied to the survivability of nation, its material provision and social modernity – its perceived failure to do so becomes the basis for Singaporeans' complaints. What is particularly interesting about the nature of complaints and humour, as I will elaborate later, is that they are mostly about mundane everyday issues and not about freedom of expression, speech, democracy and individual rights. However, while complaints and humour are not politically motivated, they are certainly highly charged and politicised. This is not to suggest that dissenting political voices do not exist but rather, as Yao discovered among his fieldwork participants in Singapore, 'while many complain of the limitations imposed by the state, these are talked about with a gentle resignation' (1996: 351). Nonetheless, the disquiet and disaffection that manifest in a culture of complaint and humour are potent responses to demands of everyday living in Singapore as pointed out by Chua and Yao earlier. In my view, they are an indirect and ambiguous means of expressing dissatisfaction or what Scott (1990) terms 'thinly veiled dissent', in that, while they do not directly challenge authority or the social order, their persistence constantly calls into question the status quo. In a recent publication, Yao (2007) observes that the bantering and complaining, while they seemingly engage with the state, do not necessarily have a formal quality denoted by clear organisation and intent. Such conversations, as Yao argues, 'air nagging concerns and mock the grandiose pretensions of the State. An event of the everyday, it is a kind of politics without form, a freewheeling account of state power without thought' (2007:131).

Complaining and humour as dissent

Complaining is a universal and ubiquitous social phenomenon, with connotations, as North (2000) observes, of both selfishness and righteousness. He adds:

> Complaining is synonymous with protesting, grumbling, whining, and accusing. To complain is to be ill natured, surly, mean-spirited, objectionable, or spoiled. Complaining can also imply standing up for what is right, defending the weak, and speaking the truth in difficult circumstances.
>
> (North 2000:1)

The practice of complaining, that is an outcry against injustice suffered, occurs daily, about almost anything. The legitimacy and power of complaining arises from a conviction that one's self-interest or that of others is at stake as a result of a real or perceived unjust encounter. Thus, when one complains it is expected that the act will potentially benefit the person or others. But of course, it can also lead to negative consequences such as abuse and physical violence. Further to this, North argues that complaining and griping are 'functionally comparable' (2000: 2). He states:

> Both are plaintive speech that requires an audience. They have, however, different audiences and goals. Griping is ritualistic, repetitive, plaintive speech aimed at reaffirming group solidarity. In contrast to gripes, the object of complaint is not group solidarity, but the reaffirmation of the relationship of a person or people to culturally sacred objects.
>
> (North 2000: 2)

Of course, there are different modes of complaining, scales of complaint, and structured processes and mechanisms in place to deal with them. Attending to complaints, or feedback euphemistically speaking, is a serious business and is not taken lightly in our late modern consumer-driven society. Even governments are involved in collecting and addressing complaints.

The role and effects of humour have been well theorised by scholars who generally agree that it plays a significant function in everyday life, particularly in the lubrication of social relationships (Freud 1905; Bergson 1911; Apte 1985; Billig 2005). Humour is a loaded concept and its consequences may vary from situation to situation. The most popular and revered aspect of humour is its goodness – 'the ability to have a laugh' or 'just having fun' is a good thing. According to Billig, having a sense of humour has historically been viewed as a positive attribute and 'a way of telling people to make the most of things, to cope with dissatisfactions that might not be [of] their own making' (2005: 11). In this sense, humour serves as a panacea or momentary relief from the difficulties, social tensions and challenges we face in our lives. Another aspect of humour is that it can potentially produce negative and unintentional consequences resulting in hurt and embarrassment (in the case of sexist and racist jokes). Humour has also been theorised in the context of dominant–subordinate relationships. Disciplinary humour is employed by those in

power to 'mock those who break social rules and thus can be seen to aid the maintenance of those rules' (Billig 2005: 202). Conversely, oppositional humour is used
by subordinates and the powerless to challenge authority – a kind of bottom-up
resistance. As Billig points out 'if the social world is full of codes that restrict what
can be said and done, then delight can be taken in breaking the rules that constrain
social actors' (2005: 207). The 'safety-valve' theory of humour suggests that it is
used in a non-threatening way by subordinates to 'let off steam' (Rodrigues and
Collinson 1995). In other words, the powerless express their disaffections through
humour which in turn signals a resignation to their fate. Such form of humour is
sanctioned by the authorities as it is not seen as threatening the social order. As
Rodrigues and Collinson (1995) observe, from antiquity onwards court jesters,
clowns and comics with licensed criticism and freedom of speech under the guise
of stupidity, tomfoolery or madness, have served royalty and the ruling classes.
Sanctioned humour helps to release social tension and reduce hostility, while the
existence of jesters and clowns appears to symbolise the tolerance, openness and
liberality of their rulers (Powell 1988:101). A more radical perspective of oppositional humour would argue that it can function as a form of resistance. As Paletz
points out, 'humour is anarchic and subversive because it heaps scorn and abuse on
respected figures, cherished institutions; and does so in a way that, were it not presented as humour, would be unacceptable' (1990: 484). While humour and dis-
sent/resistance are by no means synonymous, it can be argued that in practice it
might be difficult to classify unambiguously a particular piece of humour (Billig
2005). In this article, I take the view put forward by Rodrigues and Collinson that
'elements of resistance, compliance and consent may be inextricably linked in
complex ways' within specific instances of humour (1995: 745). That is to say, the
ambivalent quality of subordinate humour is potentially a weapon of the weak
(Scott 1990).

While a culture of complaint and humour can be regarded as practices that are
common to all societies, they are by no means homogeneous. These practices often
convey different characteristics and culturally specific meanings according to the
context of production. In this sense, complaint and humour produced in Singapore
reflect the cultural idiosyncrasies of the Singaporean way of life and social context.
They are also given a distinctively Singaporean quality through the use of Singlish,
a widely spoken local version of English that is infused with Chinese dialects and
other languages, such as Hokkien, Cantonese, Mandarin, Malay and Tamil. In recent
times, however, the Singapore government has criticised the use of Singlish, especially in the media, as it regards it as not 'good' and 'proper' English. The government also launched an annual Speak Good English Movement in 2000 to cultivate
the use of standard English and discourage the use of Singlish. Despite the ban on the
use of Singlish in the media, it continues to be used widely in Singapore in everyday
situations. Its popularity is testimony to cultural practices that evade the 'civilising'
and disciplining efforts of the government. Thus Singlish expressions give additional weight and context to a culture of complaint and humour in Singapore.

The ritual of complaining and ridiculing Singaporean life and society
(always with reference to the state) takes place right across Singapore in homes,

neighbourhoods, coffee shops, hawker centres, offices, in the media and the Internet. Singaporeans complain about almost everything – the hot and humid weather, high cost of living, high cost of owning a car, government fees and taxes, crowded public transport, poor customer service, the PAP government, rules and regulations, migrant workers and expatriates, stressful life, and so forth. Such complaints are raised through formal channels and in informal settings like newspaper forums, online discussion and bulletin boards, blogs and websites. Complaints expressed through formal channels are restrained and never openly critical of politicians, the government and its agencies. This includes letters to the editor and official internet websites and forums. In fact the Singapore government established a Feedback Unit in 1985 to gather public views and suggestions on government policies and national issues. This unit is still in operation and in 2006 was renamed REACH (Reach Everyone for Active Citizenry @ Home). It now also has a dedicated website, online forum and blog page to encourage young and computer-savvy Singaporeans to express views online on issues concerning Singapore. However, in informal settings such as hawker centres, homes, neighbourhoods, the workplace, personal websites, bulletin boards, and blogs where anonymity can be maintained, a culture of complaint especially critical of the state and its leaders is widespread. As Lee points out:

> Alternative online media providers in Singapore tend to feature commentaries and stories that have been reported by the mainstream media. [But] their innovations lie neither in breaking news nor on-site reporting, but in the publication of unadulterated letters and articles from readers, or the use of satirical or subversive humour, to outwit the conventionality of the mainstream media.
>
> (2005: 25)

While some scholars view these practices as a sign of an emerging civil society, this is by no means an organised movement. Complaints and satires are often individually articulated. Though others may share similar sentiments, they are not always anti-government or oppositional per se but express deep dissatisfaction and mistrust of the government and its policies.

A culture of complaint

The ritual of complaining has a unique place in the cultural politics of Singaporean everyday life. Complaining is often regarded as one of Singaporeans' favourite pastimes. As there are an infinite number of complaints, for the purpose of this article I shall highlight the more common ones directed at the government and that also illustrate the pressures of living in Singapore. Singaporeans constantly complain about the high cost of living, as this widely circulated anecdote on the Internet suggests:

> In Singapore, the majority of us live in *Highly Dangerous Buildings ...* *[Housing and Development Board]*. And most people have already got used to *Paying and Paying ... [People's Action Party]*. Not only do you have to pay,

you *Pay Until Bankrupt ... [Public Utilities Board]*. If that's not enough, somebody still *Purposely Wants to Dig ... [Public Works Department]* and get more from you.

So what more can you do when you are in the *Money Only Environment ... [Ministry of Environment]*? With the current *Mad Accounting System ... [Monetary Authority of Singapore]*, you are forced to *Pay the Sum Ahead ... [Port of Singapore Authority]*, which left some people *Permanently Owe Some Banks ... [Post Office Savings Banks]* and live on *Loan Techniques Always ... [Land Transport Authority]* system.

When you fall sick and happen to be admitted to a *Money Operating Hospital ... [Ministry of Health]*, you might be able to use your *Cash Prior to Funeral Fund ... (Central Provident Fund)*. If you are out of luck, you may meet doctors who *Never Use Heart ... (National University Hospital)* to treat you and you will be *Sure to Give up Hope ... (Singapore General Hospital)*.

To help ease the traffic, motorists have to pay *Cash On Expressway ... (Certificate of Entitlement)*. If that doesn't help, they can always *Eternally Raise Prices ... (Electronic Road Pricing)* on the roads. If you don't own a car, you can always make a *Mad Rush to the Train ... (Mass Rapid Transit)*, OR get squashed in a bus *Side By Side ... (Singapore Bus Service)*.

Lastly, under all these pressures, there are not many places we can relax, not even the good old place we used to go because it has become *So Expensive and Nothing To See Actually (SENTOSA)*!

(Talkingcock.com 2000b; italics added)

The PAP, variously referred to as the 'Pay and Pay' party, 'Papa' (in reference to its paternalism) and 'gahmen' (Singlish spelling of 'government'), is always a primary reference point of most complaints. It is not uncommon to hear Singaporeans endlessly complaining about the difficulties of making a living and leading a comfortable life and about government services as being money driven. Singapore is caricatured as a society consumed by monetary exploitation. In this quite popular complaint, the various government ministries, statutory boards and institutions in charge of public infrastructure, health, retirement funds, transport and even recreation have been renamed and portrayed as uncaring, unreliable and greedy organisations not interested in the welfare of Singaporeans but only in 'profiting' from them. This is not to suggest that Singaporeans distrust these institutions or they offer poor services. Rather, there is a prevailing attitude that government ministries and public bureaucracy lack compassion and a sense of caring and only manage to exacerbate the cost of living in Singapore. The complaint arises precisely because of a disequilibrium in the expectations that Singaporeans have about the role of the government which has always tended to be highly interventionist in every aspect of private Singaporean life but less so when providing social welfare. The pervasiveness of the Singapore government has created a mindset among Singaporeans that it is responsible for everything, even things it has nothing to do with. As has been well documented, this attitude develops as a result of the government's emphasis on developmentalism and material prosperity (Chua 1995; Hill and Lian 1995;

Trocki 2006; Velayutham 2007). Such an economic-oriented nation-building process has meant that Singaporeans are expected to work hard and never slack off. In turn, the government is expected to provide good governance, public infrastructure, education, housing, health and so forth. However, when the cost of these services goes up for whatever reasons, Singaporeans are up in arms about it because they feel that the government is not doing enough to ease the situation and has failed them.

Another common complaint is based on the government's high expectations of Singaporeans to perform and contribute to the national economy. As this online correspondent argues:

> We have seen the continuous efforts from the government telling Singaporeans they need to get their skills upgraded in this ever competitive landscape. On one hand, we have been told that when we upgrade our skill-sets, opportunities will be plentiful. On the other hand, the government opens the flood gate in issuing work permits and PR [permanent residence] status, thus creating competition for Singaporeans. I think the agencies in question need to sit down to look into this seriously. What are the priorities? What is more important? Getting more 'would be Singaporeans' to join us to boost our GDP or helping real 'authentic' Singaporeans find jobs? It seems that the government is interested in getting quick fixes. I have seen reports saying we need to have foreign talents so that MNCs would be more interested in setting up operations and investing in Singapore. Let's not forget that the Government's responsibility is to take care of its people first. What's the point of having investments in the pipeline when there are real Singaporeans suffering and can't wait to end their lives ...
>
> (Ng 2006)

As a nation with limited resources, Singapore's position within the competitive global capitalist economy has made it both a necessity and a legitimising tool for the government to continuously explore new opportunities to sustain the city-state's economic standing. As a consequence, Singaporeans are told to re-train themselves to meet the challenges of the new economy. In addition, since the 1990s, the Singapore government has been seeking to attract talented people from abroad to work and live in Singapore in order to tackle a 'brain-drain' problem, the fall in fertility rates and to keep up with the demands of the new economy. A two tier migrant employment category was developed. 'Foreign workers' are recruited on short-term contracts to do low skilled, dirty, dangerous and difficult jobs mainly from South India, Bangladesh, Thailand, Burma and China. Expatriates or 'foreign talents' from Australia, Britain, Europe, India and China fill positions that require expertise and high skill levels. Foreign talent is also encouraged to take up permanent residency and citizenship in Singapore. The policy has not been well received by educated Singaporeans who feel threatened by the special privilege given to foreign talent, considering them potential competitors in the job market, as suggested by the earlier response (Velayutham 2007). Essentially then, the feeling that migrants have an unfair advantage and that the government is not putting the inter-est of its citizens first are the points of contention. It is clear that the correspondent quoted earlier is resentful towards government policies of attracting skilled and unskilled migrants, and moreover doubts the national loyalty of these new permanent residents.

Recently, the government decided to raise the retirement age of Singaporeans from 62 to 65 by 2012 and eventually to 67 so as to better deal with the higher life expectancy of its ageing population. The government was concerned about the long-term implications of an ageing population and its attendant impact of higher social cost, a shrinking workforce and slower economic growth. A blogger responded:

> During the last election, while campaigning PM Lee saw an 80 year old woman still working hard for a living, his response was one of delight that old folks here are working ... wonderful!! Instead of wasting their time idling at home or looking after grandchildren, it is best to have our old folks working. Self-help is the best, our govt has often told us. We should be prepared to work longer and harder. Singapore govt cannot afford to give welfare or public assistance that is sufficient for more than 2 meals a day.
>
> [...] Many of our elites are hired into GIC [Government of Singapore Investment Corporation] & Temasek to manage this money that technically belongs to the people of Singapore. While they are unable to help our elderly who work to support themselves, the govt is able to invest in troubled banks and losing a few billion here and there. You might think that in your time of sickness and poverty, this wealth to which you have contributed is there to take away some of the financial pain ... but let's get real here, helping Singaporeans is a waste of money when you can use the money to invest for higher returns e.g. Citibank, UBS, Shin Corp.[3]
>
> (Tan 2008)

This kind of direct criticism of the government is never allowed in the public media but circulates widely on the Internet. In particular, blog websites set up by Singaporeans are fast becoming an important space for airing complaints.[4] However, it should be noted that the Singapore government has been closely mon-itoring and on some occasions have closed down Internet sites which it deemed were contentious or subversive to public order (see Lee 2005). The previous blog entry again highlights how the economy and social welfare issues emerge as a com-mon theme of complaints. The PAP government has consistently opposed estab-lishing any kind of safety net or social assistance package for struggling Singaporeans. This is not to say that such programmes do not exist; however, they are not formalised and only offer minimal support to underprivileged Singaporeans. In this instance, the raising of the retirement age as a way of main-taining a productive workforce and reducing the burden of caring for an ageing population is seen as strikingly economically driven. Rather than providing welfare benefits to its ageing population who have worked hard and contributed to the economy, they are told to return to work again. The respondent sarcastically remarks that the government would rather invest tax payer dollars and revenues than care for Singaporeans who are unable to work, poor and old.

In November 2006, a Member of Parliament, Dr Mohamad Maliki Osman, told Parliament that 'Singapore is a nation of complainers' and a 'society increasingly reliant on the Government for help'. He called on Singaporeans to take more responsibility and be less dependent on the government to address social problems. It is not surprising that this statement attracted criticism and prompted many responses on the Internet. A contributor to the *commentarysingapore.blogspot.com* forum wrote:

> Maybe the MPs are indirectly asking for a pay rise as the 'complaints' are getting too much for them to handle. The $13K per month part-time work cannot do the job of several departments in the government. Seems like the MPs are overworked by the tons of 'complaints'.
>
> (Layman 2006)

And another respondent wrote:

> I'd rather migrate to a country that is not as 'rich' but where the spirit is strong amongst the people, there is a sense of identity.
> Here, the media is self-congratulatory of its success (where is the competition? looks more like a monopoly! the #1 tag is a bloody joke) and so does the govt.
> They pronounce the nation rich and successful, people would think these damned Singaporeans must be pretty darn happy …
> But I see soul-less zombies everywhere, every day … In the morning, they march like the death army to work and then home ...
> There is no life in this place at all.
>
> (Anonymous 2006)

These comments clearly highlight the level of cynicism and resentment and to some extent resignation that Singaporeans feel about politics, politicians and life in Singapore in general. It is interesting to note that while these views have always circulated privately among the circles of family and friends, the Internet has created an even greater opportunity for Singaporeans to express their discontentment and establish a sense of solidarity with likeminded online users.

Complaints are part and parcel of Singaporean everyday life. In his comparative study of cultures of complaint in Japan and America, North makes two points: one, 'complaints arise in the context of exchange: people complain when they think they have been shorted, when someone is not holding up his or her end of a deal', and two, 'the person complaining must perceive the risk of complaining to be worthwhile' (2000: 33). In some sense, the weight of social expectation that is asserted by the state becomes an embodied experience as it is internalised by Singaporeans. As the demands of economic growth and global competitiveness intensify, Singaporeans are expected to re-skill themselves, embrace foreign talent coming to the country, and retire at a later age. While the city-state has enjoyed steady economic growth, modern living conditions and way of life, these have come at a cost. In particular, a lack of concern for the well-being of Singaporeans and the privileging of the economy above all other social issues by the government have created a disenchanted citizenry. Most of their complaints are aimed at the government for not being more supportive and sympathetic to the needs of Singaporeans. At the same time, these complaints are rarely expressed through official channels, circulating in the informal sphere precisely because the complainant can escape scrutiny and persecution by the state and as such they remain informal, ineffectual and potentially lacking in credibility as far as the government is concerned. Nevertheless, insofar as complaints continue to circulate, they remain a popular form of dissent that is both subversive and defiant against the discourse of the state.

A Singaporean sense of humour

A distinctively Singaporean brand of humour in the form of satire, nitpicking, ridicule, mockery and cynicism flourishes in daily conversations and in the media and Internet. Humour is also largely present in the most of the complaints that Singaporeans make. Expressed in these various settings, humour serves as a way of dealing with the paternalistic state and its highly regulated social order. To illustrate these points, I would like to highlight two sites where humour is produced. One is a popular satirical and humorous website called *Talkingcock.com* (there are numerous other websites)[5] and the other the burgeoning Singapore film industry. *Talkingcock.com* was created by Colin Goh, a Singaporean lawyer turned cartoonist in August 2000, and the website explicitly states that:

> *Talkingcock.com* is a satirical feature site for Singaporeans.
>
> WE MAKE STUFF UP. We do not engage in rumour, we indulge in humour and fiction. Do not believe or rely on what we write! If you do, you're even more cock than us! WE ARE NOT A POLITICAL SITE. For all the *kaypohs* [nosy] and muckrakers out there, we have completely no political agenda whatsoever. Our main aim is to celebrate all the nonsensical parts of Singaporean life. We make fun of people in every sector, strata and profession in a completely democratic way. (If you feel that you or people you know have not been made fun of, please let us know so that we can address the oversight.) Anyway, the good people in Parliament have already deemed us to be a non-political site.

> (Talkingcock.com 2000)

Talkingcock.com features news (local and international), editorial columns, features, forums and a Singlish dictionary. The articles and stories produced on the website are written in Singlish and are generally based on daily events. The humour is created by a play on words using Singlish expressions and local knowledge, for example, the following snippets from the website:

NEWS IN BRIEFS Weekly Roundup
Posted on Thursday, April 03, 2008

Hard to Swallow

Singaporeans should not panic if rice supplies run out, says the Gahmen. 'They can always just eat cake,' said Mdm Marie Ang Tua Net, Permanent Secretary of the Ministry of Elitism.

It's a Wrap

After concluding the Singapore-Egypt Cultural Pact, the Gahmen denied allegations that the agreement was all just one big pyramid scheme. However, the Ministry of Foreign Affairs refused to confirm or deny rumours that an Egyptian archaeological team would be coming to Singapore to teach us how to mummify a certain father figure.

Waiting for the Son to Rise?

The Prime Minister's Orifice has been denying suggestions that the reason why PM Lee will only be stepping down after 13 years is that the Gahmen is waiting for one of his sons to grow up. 'This is just malicious and not true. We're not waiting for any of PM Lee's sons to grow up and take over from him. Rather, we're waiting for his dad's clone to be developed.'

(Talkingcock.com 2008)

The first story is a slightly cynical take on the government's efforts to calm anxiety after recent rises in the price of rice in Singapore. Quite deliberately, the fictional 'Ministry of Elitism' signals the class divide between the ruling elite and ordinary Singaporeans, and that Singaporeans 'can always just eat cake' further reinforces how out of touch the government is. The second item ridicules the government's grand nation-building schemes that are rolled out every so often. The 'father figure' here refers to Lee Kuan Yew, the nation's first Prime Minister and who still remains active in politics although he retired in 1990. The third news item pokes fun at the continuity of the Lee dynasty in Singapore politics. 'PM Lee' here refers to Lee Hsien Loong, the son of Lee Kuan Yew and current prime minister of Singapore. It would appear that Lee Kuan Yew is not likely to leave political life and that his longevity will be protected by his clone replacing his son. These tongue-in-cheek remarks about the government and politicians convey a sense of rebelliousness that is otherwise not found in other contexts of the well-ordered Singaporean city life.

In March 2008, Mas Selamat bin Kastari, an alleged leader of the Singapore wing of the militant Islamic group Jemaah Islamiyah, escaped from a highly secure detention centre in Singapore. This was a huge embarrassment for the government as it dented the country's reputation for airtight security. People on the streets and others especially on the internet were having a field day seeing the funny side of this incident. *Talkingcock.com* released this story:

Terrorist Escapes, So Ministers' Pay to Go Up
Posted on Sunday, March 02, 2008

by Pak Cham Kai

According to the Gahmen, Ministers should get another salary raise because of the escape of terrorist Mat Alamak [a Malay expression of surprise] Kastari.

'We need to equip our Mini-stars with everything they can to deal with this crisis,' said Ministry of Enrichment spokesman Mr. Ho Wah Looi. 'And as we know in Singapore, public service and legislative influence are all not sufficient incentives. Only the highest salaries in the world will do.'

Mr. Ho said that the raise was not only an incentive, it was necessary.

'Are you kidding?' he said. 'With this terrorist still on the loose after so many days, our Mini-stars need to have more security than just one police pondok [Malay word for hut/house] outside their house. They need a whole SWAT team each. And they have to get their cars bullet-proofed. And security detail to accompany their spouses and children. I mean, what if the Mini-star has a daughter in SCGS [Singapore Chinese Girls' School], and Mat Alamak is cleverly disguised as a SCGS girl? We need undercover special ops officers in there to protect them! All these things cost money, mah!'

Mr. Ho also said that they have reason to believe that Ministers were under threat from more than just Mat Alamak.

'We are very concerned about reports that citizens are angry that this kind of cockup could happen in Singapore, with the highest paid government in the world,' he said. 'We need to beef up security at all their meet the peasa ... I mean, people sessions in case some crazy buay song [Hokkien for 'not satisfied'] peasa ... sorry, sorry, person comes and throw rotten eggs or donno what at the Mini-star.'

(Pak 2008)

The Singapore government has regularly raised the salary scale of top bureaucrats and politicians in a bid to retain them in the public sector – often bringing them on a par with the corporate sector. In this instance, the escape of a terrorist is being used to justify another ministers' pay rise. This story is humorous and at the same time critical of the often pragmatic problem solving and justification strategies that the government employs to strengthen its own position. What is interesting here as with the previous examples is the level of cynicism that is expressed through the telling of a joke.

The licence accorded to humour and satire is fairly ambiguous. As I noted earlier, the OB markers remain an arbitrary terrain and subject to government whim. A case in point is that a number of alternative online media sites have come under government scrutiny and some of them have been forced to shut down as they were deemed to be politically motivated and interfering with government affairs[6]. But as Terence Lee observes, 'by adding humour, fictitious characters and fabricated events, *Talkingcock.com* delivers commentaries that are concomitantly ludicrous and cynical, a category that is grey enough to sidestep the shackles of media codes and political censorship' (2005: 25–26). The sort of commentary, cynicism and ridicule expressed in *Talkingcock.com* is very much reflective of the sentiments that most Singaporeans would display in their daily lives. They also reveal a different side of Singapore that is often overlooked – where people are challenging the authority of the state.

The same kind of humour can also be found in Singapore TV sitcoms and films. The most prominent sitcom, titled PCK (Phua Chu Kang) and based on a building contractor, creates an archetypal working class Chinese character, Chinese educated but prone to conversing in Singlish. Many of his throw away lines poke fun at Singaporean life, culture norms and attitudes. Unfortunately, in 2000, the then Prime Minister Goh Chok Tong singled out PCK as 'doing disservice to Singapore by promoting the use of Singlish'. Since then PCK has refined its English quality. Perhaps the most fascinating development in recent years is the rejuvenation of the Singapore film industry and in particular, the films by actor and director Jack Neo. His comedy films are centred around Singaporeans complaining about government policies. Jack Neo's *12 Storeys* (1997), *Money No Enough* (1998), in the wake of the Asian Financial Crisis, *I Am Not Stupid* (2002) and *Just Follow Law* (2007), through the use of humour offer critical commentary on various social issues concerning Singaporean way of life. The film *I Am Not Stupid* depicts the lives and struggles of three primary school students in a special academic stream.[7] This satirical comedy is highly critical of the Singaporean education system and social attitudes, including the competitive mentality (fear of losing out) and over-obedience to authority. As one punch line from the film suggests, 'Why can't anybody catch any fish in Singapore?', 'Because the fishes, like Singaporeans would rather die than to open their mouth!' Nevertheless, perhaps indicating that strategies of resistance such as the use of subversive humour can create change, this film with its light hearted highlighting of the problem of streaming at primary school level subsequently generated public debate and revamping of the education process. In the comedy film *Just Follow Law* (a pun on the Singlish phrase 'just follow lor', which means to comply with orders without questioning why), Neo took a satirical look at the inflexibility of the civil servants and their blind adherence to outdated government regulations.

Singaporean humour with a liberal use of Singlish – a form of thinly veiled criticism – is doubly transgressive but is not entirely free from government scrutiny. The cynicism and mockery of Singaporean urban life and government expressed through humour has the potential to overstep the rather arbitrary out-of-bound markers of permissible criticism as sanctioned by the state in Singapore. Similarly, the government has already expressed concern about the use of Singlish in public broadcasting. Nevertheless, I would argue that the use of humour in film and on the Internet smooths the 'contentious' and subversive edges of dissenting expressions and allows Singaporeans to 'live' and 'laugh' at themselves (Lee 2005).

Conclusion

As Neo's films demonstrated, a culture of complaint and humour directed against the PAP government and everyday life in Singapore has the capacity to transform social conditions in one way or another, that is, through providing a release valve for frustration, stress and economic difficulty, and potentially undermining the positive global image of Singapore. Beneath the efficiency, orderliness, and prosperity that are characteristic of Singapore, a culture of complaint highlights the frustrations and difficulties that people experience in this well-oiled Asian metropolitan machine. Beneath the boring and regulated image of Singapore lies, at least from this perspective, a spontaneous and vibrant civil society that is actively seeking to negotiate the consequences of living in a global city.

Without overly exaggerating and mindful of the obvious and real limits to such practices, there are several intersecting issues that make complaining and humour interesting and viable forms of dissent. In the first instance, being a highly regulated and rigid society – driven by a disciplinary and modernistic rationality where the emphasis is on efficiency, cleanliness, orderliness, civility, conformity and obedience – the practices of complaint and humour disrupt the monopoly that the government has over its citizens' lives. Through complaining and humour Singaporeans are engaging with policies and government decision-making processes. They are not a docile citizenry. When they complain, they are able to vent their anger and dissatisfaction. The use of Singlish puns and idioms adds colour and depth to the dissenting voices and allows for potential elisions of meaning through deliberate ambiguity that challenges government definitions of order and rationality. While they are not always taken seriously – which in Singapore can be a good thing given the restrictions on freedom of speech – at times they have the potential to effect change. A culture of complaint and humour are concrete examples of the everyday forms of dissent that exist in Singapore. They are strategies employed by ordinary Singaporeans that challenge the state's top-down approach to governance and deal with the anxieties of living in a globalised city.

Notes

1 Cited in Singapore's satirical humour website www.talkingcock.com. 'Talking cock' is a colloquial term commonly used in Singapore to refer to either nonsensical or idle bantering. See Yao (2007) for an interesting analysis of the art of talking cock.
2 This is the author's own anecdote.
3 The Government of Singapore Investment Corporation and Temasek Holdings are Singapore State owned global corporations.
4 As a cursory remark, it should be noted that while the Internet is fast becoming a key site for expressions of dissent in Singapore, it nonetheless remains under the close watchful eye of the state. As such, criticisms levelled against the government are not often direct or explicit out of fear of persecution except in the case of Singaporeans who have emigrated overseas. The Tomorrow – Bulletin of Singapore Bloggers at http://tomorrow.sg is one such website that offers a daily digest of all major blogs devoted to Singaporean issues.
5 Other satirical websites include: http://www.mrbrown.com, www.thevoiddeck.org and www.yawningbread.org.

6 These websites include www.thevoiddeck.org, www.samboy.com, www.thinkcentre. org, www.yawningbread.org and www.singapore-window.org. For further readings on electronic media and civil society, see for instance, Rodan (2003) and Lee (2005).
7 In Singapore, upper primary pupils are streamed into three different academic streams: EM1, EM2 and EM3. The first stream is for the brightest and the last is for pupils with learning difficulties (and thus popularly regarded as inferior).

References

Anonymous. 2006. Kopi-tiam-talk-parliamentary-debate. Online posting. Available http://commentarysingapore.blogspot.com/2006/11/kopi-tiam-talk-parliamentary-debate. html (accessed 5 May 2008).

Apte, M. 1985. *Humour and Laughter: An Anthropological Approach.* New York: Cornell University Press.

Bergson, H. 1911. *Laughter: An Essay on the Meaning of the Comic.* London: Macmillan and Co.

Beaverstock, J.V., Smith, R.G., Taylor, P.J., Walker, D.F.R. and Lorimer, H.N. 2000. 'Globalisation and World Cities: Some Measurement Methodologies'. *Applied Geography* 20: 43–63.

Billig, M. 2005. *Laughter and Ridicule: Towards a Social Critique of Humour.* London: Sage.

Chua, B.H. 1995. *Communitarian Ideology and Democracy in Singapore.* London: Routledge.

Chua, B.H. 1998. 'Culture, Multiculturalism, and National Identity in Singapore', in K.H. Chen (ed.) *Trajectories: Inter-Asia Cultural Studies.* London: Routledge.

Chua, B.H. 2000. 'The Relative Autonomies of the State and Civil Society', in G. Koh and Ooi, G.L. (eds) *State–Society Relations.* Oxford: Oxford University Press.

Fox, K. 2004. *Watching the English: The Hidden Rules of English Behaviour.* London: Hodder & Stoughton.

Freud, S. 1905. *Jokes and their Relations to the Unconsciousness.* Harmondsworth: Penguin.

Hill, M. and Lian, K.F. 1995. *The Politics of Nation Building and Citizenship in Singapore.* London: Routledge.

Ho, Khai L. 2000. 'Citizen Participation and Policy Making in Singapore: Conditions and Predicaments', *Asian Survey* 40(3): 436–455.

Koh, G. and Ooi, G.L. 2004. 'Relationship between State and Civil Society in Singapore', in L.H. Guan (ed.) *Civil Society in Southeast Asia.* Singapore: Institute of Southeast Asian Studies Publishing.

Layman. 2006. Kopi-tiam-talk-parliamentary-debate. Online posting. Available http:// commentarysingapore.blogspot.com/2006/11/kopi-tiam-talk-parliamentary-debate.html (accessed 5 May 2008).

Lee, T. 2002. 'The Politics of Civil Society in Singapore', *Asian Studies Review* 26(1): 97–117.

Lee, T. 2005. 'Going Online: Journalism and Civil Society in Singapore', in A. Romano and Bromley, M.(eds) *Journalism and Democracy in Asia.* Abingdon, Oxon: Routledge.

Lingle, C. 1996. *Singapore's Authoritarian Capitalism: Asian Values, Free Market Illusions, and Political Dependency.* Fairfax, VA: The Locke Institute.

Ng, E. 2006. 'Double Standards from the Government?', Available http://edmund-ng. blogspot.com/ (accessed 4 March 2008).

North, S. 2000. 'Cultures of Complaint in Japan and the United States', Centre for Working Families – Working Paper No. 17. Berkeley: University of California.

Pak, C.K. 2008. 'Terrorist Escapes, So Ministers' Pay to Go Up', Available http://www.talk-ingcock.com/html/article.php?sid=2489 (accessed 5 May 2008).

Paletz, D. 1990. 'Political Humour and Authority: From Support to Subversion', *International Political Science Review* 11(4): 483–493.

Powell, C. 1988. 'A Phenomenological analysis of Humour in Society' in C. Powell and G. Paton (eds) *Humour in Society: Resistance and Control*. New York: St Martin's Press.

Rodan, G. 1993. 'Preserving the One-Party State in Contemporary Singapore', in K. Hewison, Robison. R. and Rodan, G. (eds) *Southeast Asia in the 1990s: Authoritarianism, Democracy & Capitalism*. St Leonards, New South Wales: Allen & Unwin.

Rodan, G. 1996. 'State–Society Relations and Political Opposition in Singapore', in G. Rodan (ed.) *Political Opposition in Industrialising Asia*. London: Routledge.

Rodan, G. 2003. 'Embracing Electronic Media but Suppressing Civil Society: Authoritarian Consolidation in Singapore', *The Pacific Review* 16(4): 503–524.

Rodrigues, S.B. and Collinson, D.L. (1995) '"Having Fun?" Humour as Resistance in Brazil', *Organisation Studies* 16(5): pp. 739–768.

Scott, J.C. 1990. *Domination and the Arts of Resistance: Hidden Transcripts*. New Haven and London: Yale University Press.

Talkingcock.com (2000a) 'Homepage', Available http://www.talkingcock.com/ (accessed 4 March 2008).

Talkingcock.com (2000b) 'Singapore Acronyms', Available http://www.talkingcock.com/html/jokexec.php?op=JokeView&lexicon=jokes&jcat=Acronym (accessed 4 March 2008).

Talkingcock.com (2008) 'News in Briefs Weekly Roundup April 03', Available http://www.talkingcock.com/ (accessed 5 May 2008).

Tan, L. (2008) 'Elderly Cleaners in Singapore', Available http://singaporemind.blogspot.com/ (accessed 5 May 2008).

Tremewan, C. (1994). *The Political Economy of Social Control in Singapore*. New York: St. Martin's Press.

Trocki, C.A. (2006). *Singapore: Wealth, Power and the Culture of Control*. Abingdon, Oxon: Routledge.

Velayutham, S. (2004). 'Affect, Materiality and the Gift of Social Life in Singapore', *SOJOURN: Journal of Social Issues in Southeast Asia* 19(1): 1–27.

Velayutham, S. (2007). *Responding to Globalisation: Nation, Culture and Identity in Singapore*. Singapore: Institute of Southeast Asian Studies Press.

Yao, S. (1996). 'Consumption and Social Aspirations of the Middle Class in Singapore', *Southeast Asian Affairs*. Singapore: Institute of Southeast Asian Studies.

Yao, S. (2007). *Singapore: The State and the Culture of Excess*. Abingdon, Oxon: Routledge.

6 Negotiating urban activism

Women, vending and the
transformation of streetscapes
in the urban Philippines

B. Lynne Milgram

Introduction

In the mid-1980s, Carol Esteban,[1] at 22 years old, began to look for work in Baguio City, Philippines to augment her husband's irregular earnings in periodic wage labor. Given the lack of formal sector employment opportunities for men and women throughout the Philippines, Carol, even with two years of college educa-tion, found herself with little choice but to carve out a particularized space in which to earn a living. Carol, now 45 years old, explains that in order to financially support her three children, she took up work as a street vendor joining her mother, Nancy Balbao who sells seasonal fruits. Nancy, who had started her street sales in the early 1970s after arriving from Mountain Province north of Baguio City, is currently accompanied in business by Carol as well as by her two other daughters who sell peanut products and local vegetables. As start-up capital for vending, Carol borrowed 1,500 Philippine pesos (US$33.00)[2] from family members and fellow vendors using these funds to purchase her stock of cooked rice and cassava cakes. Street traders like Carol foster such interconnected livelihood relationships because they must continually negotiate Baguio City Tax Ordinance Number 2000–001 (City of Baguio 2000–2001: 50–51) that, in accordance with past laws, prohibits "any person to sell merchandise" in public places "outside of the market premises." In on-the-ground practice, however, city officials charged with enforcing this law, implement its restrictions on some days while turning a blind eye to its violations on others, citing compassion for vendors' situation.

Thus, Carol, like her fellow sellers, started her trade by displaying her goods in one *bilao* – a basket or plastic container. As street vendors in the 1980s lacked the right to conduct business on the city's public streets, this portable carrier enabled them to quickly pick up their goods and run when police appeared. In the late 1990s, to obtain a somewhat more secure place to conduct their trade, Carol and her five neighboring vendors requested and received permission from the centrally located Baguio City Supermarket to display their products outside the store. These vendors explain, however, that although they have obtained a place in which to conduct business, they remain acutely aware of the tenuousness of their positions. Their right to sell in this location is secured only through the good will of the supermarket's verbal agreement that is itself vulnerable to the municipal government's ongoing debates about how to manage the city's growing street vendor population.

While structural adjustment and international development policies have encouraged foreign investment in Southeast Asian economies since the 1970s, they have simultaneously constrained livelihood opportunities for the majority of urban residents such as Carol Esteban (Balisacan 1995; Chant 1996; Ofreneo and Habana 1987). This occurs in the midst of growing rural to urban migration and a decrease in urban formal sector jobs. In the northern Philippines, such emergent shifts in labor distribution are particularly visible in Baguio City, the region's most highly industrialized, administrative and education center. The ongoing tension in Baguio between street vendors, large retailers and agents of the state regarding who has rights over and access to the city's streets for commerce "touch at the core of the changing interrelationship between local people, their state and global forces" (Hansen 2008: 213–214). These global forces are frequently linked to northern-based development plans aiming to restructure southern economies in ways that more often meet the former's vision and needs (Broad 1988; Morton 1996). Such agendas intersect with local socioeconomic and political dynamics with regard to the channels men and women pursue, depending upon age, gender, ethnicity and class, to operationalize urban livelihood options as countries move to modernize and globalize (Hansen 2008: 214–218).

Throughout the Philippines, within this political-economic context, women, in particular, have made city streets their business venue for selling fresh produce, cooked food or dry goods. Women's predominance as street vendors is consistent with their historical role as the foremost public market traders throughout the Philippines as in much of Southeast Asia (Brenner 1998; Milgram 2001, 2004). That the number of their small-scale enterprises continues to increase, moreover, evidences a rise in other-than-formal sector economic activity accompanied by fundamental shifts in the organization of social relations, the spatial and socioeconomic reconfiguration of urban streetscapes and understandings of legal/illegal activities.

In this chapter, I use Philippine women's engagement in street vending in Baguio City to suggest that such micro-traders, by persisting with their right to livelihood and resisting constraints on this right, unsettle essentialist categories of work, space and legal/illegal practice. Street vendors, many of who are unskilled and have migrated to the city from rural provinces may appear to be poorly qualified to undertake such labor organizing. As Mary Beth Mills (2005: 118) points out, however, scholarship on labor worldwide identifies that "the question is not whether women can organize, but rather what are the conditions that enable them to mobilize" resources despite the constraints they face. Few immigrant or informal sector workers generally, may have the information they need about their rights, labor laws or how to organize, and few have the financial resources to challenge employers or government systems (Mills 2005: 117–118; Mills 2008). That many of their new businesses take place on urban public streets where private commerce is prohibited, further challenges the very existence of these enterprises.

I suggest then, that Filipina street vendors capture their place in an increasingly contested urban terrain by working across household and market, and across economic and political sectors; they simultaneously draw on customary practices such as favored or *suki* relations, on kinship and community networks as well as on formal sector institutions (NGOs, legal counsel). Individually and in collectives, women's activism in vending thus engages what Mary Beth Mills terms, "a distinctly gendered politics of place" (2005: 121). By utilizing such multiply-rooted channels, vendors' initiatives call into question the taken-for-granted goals of many development programs that seek to "modernize" cities in accordance with a global normative, usually northern-based, standard. That Filipina vendors have moved their livelihoods into mainstream arenas where city residents across classes consistently use their services, thus suggests new ways of thinking about how cities can materialize good governance within the changing parameters of urbanization.

The street vending activities that I consider here include selling goods such as cooked food, fresh produce and manufactured products as well as offering services such as shoe cleaning and cosmetic grooming. I do not include activities considered to be organised illegal businesses such as those of drug dealing and prostitution although these are often street-based enterprises (see Cross 1998). To situate the debates about the legality or illegality of street vending in Baguio City, I first discuss the concepts of informal and street economies, urban public space and women's activism. By exploring vendors' specific street trades, I then analyze the extent to which women's locally based actions can, in fact, transform globally rooted urban policies at the same time as they respond to them.

Informalizing the economy

In Asia, "informal" work accounts for approximately 45–60 percent of urban employment with these numbers increasing after the 1997–1998 Asian financial crisis and again with the economic slowdown in 2008 (Brown 2006: 7; Ordoñez 2008; Remo 2008). This growing informalization of economies is part of the broader context in which confrontations over street vending space take place and it emphasizes the need to reconsider how informality is understood and performed (Hansen 2008: 217–228). Current research problematizes any singular understanding of informal economic activities. Informalized work is characterized as unregulated production, distribution and service provision differing by size, type of actors and location (Hansen 2001), and often straddling legal/illegal spheres (Abraham and van Schendel 2005). Informal economic enterprises encompass non-wage workers, owners and owner-operators, roles for kin and community members and, in circumstances involving home-based work and street vending, they are dominated by women (Castells and Portes 1989: 12; Chen *et al.* 1999). Within this context then, street vendors operate in the interstices of global systems managing to take advantage of the way the world economy works, but without fully playing by its rules (MacGaffey and Bazenguissa-Ganga 2000: 3).

Informal economic activities, closely connected to urban growth, were often uncounted and ignored or viewed by city planners and developers as undermining the healthy functioning formal economy and thus as a practice to be eliminated, often hostilely (Mitullah 2004; Palangchao 2006b; Rillorta 2008). In the 1990s, in an about-face policy shift, development practitioners reclassified the informal economy as a source of growth and flexibility recognizing that pro-poor policies such as support for microenterprises can stimulate economic development (Bromley 1997, 2000). While this new approach acknowledges the limitations of the formal economy to accommodate the growing numbers of unemployed (Seligmann 2004: 92), it does not consider the consequences of differently-rooted economic activities competing for limited urban space and policy agendas at the local level that still discriminate against street vending. Failing to recognize the importance of this realm as a key source of income for increasing numbers of people, is relevant to Baguio City where the growth of the "street economy" (Brown 2006: 7)[3] continues to develop its own economic momentum and spatial organization amid government policy vacillations and irregularities (see Cross and Morales 2007).

Rethinking urban public space

Scholarship on the organization of cities demonstrates that urban planners often privilege a northern normative vision of public order and tidiness when they design urban spaces (Anjaria 2006: 2140; City of Marikina 2002; Edensor 1998; Miao 2001). But, as economic liberalization policies of the 1980s forced more urban residents into other-than-formal-sector jobs, competition for city space and questions about rights over its use grew (Drummond 2000; Lund *et al.* 2000).

The concept of "urban public space" is useful to apply here as it identifies all types of physical space to which people have access or use rights whether in public, private, communal or unknown ownership, including vacant private land (Brown 2006: 10; Douglass *et al.* 2002). As private space for the urban poor is restricted, urban public space becomes an essential resource that is often ignored in development programs that more often focus on housing (Zlolniski 2006). To maximize business, street traders commonly occupy sites with high pedestrian flows (e.g., transportation terminals, main shopping streets). Since these sites may be limited-access or conflict zones where street trading is legally barred, vendors may ensure their access to these locations in informal, sometimes illegal ways (Kusakabe 2006a, 2006b). The paradox is that while governments seek to clear city streets from congestion, they simultaneously develop policies to reduce poverty by supporting microenterprises that often rely on inexpensive street locations for their operations (Milgram 2005). This is evident in Baguio City where local government initiatives to control the growing number of street vendors have resulted in a confusing mix of directives advocating persecution, tolerance and regulation (Opiña 2006c, 2007). The challenge for rapidly urbanizing cities then is to reconcile competing claims for space through a rights-based approach that enables vendors' livelihoods while providing services urban residents, across classes, request.

Gender and personalized resistance

In the northern Philippines, as in much of island Southeast Asia, women as small-scale producers and traders, draw on customary values and practices that support women's parity within households and their right and access to extra-household social and economic opportunities. Although women more often assume the major role for domestic and childcare responsibilities, the Philippine customs of bilateral inheritance, primogeniture and women's long-standing positions as intra- and extra-household financial managers, enable them to pursue potential work and education options. As Wazir Karim argues for Southeast Asia, women secure a "continuous chain of productive enterprises" for family and personal well-being by establishing "a repertoire of social units" linked to household, market and environmental resources; and they "unlink" themselves in an "open-ended" and "multi-focal" system when situations change (1995: 28). Particular socioeconomic circumstances, however, facilitate some women's emergence as more effective advocates for new work opportunities.

Beyond vendors' small earning differentials, which certainly occurs, other-than-economic factors are more crucial in determining which vendors assume leadership roles. Women who have completed some college education, like Carol Esteban, tend to be better equipped to publicly represent their groups. Equally important is the knowledge and experience that women gain from their long-term work in street vending as well as their ability to communicate across socioeconomic sectors – to grasp how government policies will affect their practice, and to effectively articulate and redistribute this information to fellow vendors. Philippine customary practice supports leadership roles for women, but those who assume such positions tend to build on personal assertive entrepreneurial personalities and on strong social and economic networks (see also Gibson-Graham et al. 2000).

Contemporary development initiatives, as noted, tend to position street vendors, and women, in particular, who comprise the majority of sellers, against the state's modernizing vision for cities, leaving vendors with limited options for physically relocating their trade (Babb 2001; Bhowmik 2005). Recent studies identify the multiple strategies that women use to organize street space as their "weapon," such as using their bodies as resistance by maintaining an ongoing physical presence in their vending sites (Seligmann 2004: 207–208). Other forms of everyday resistance include constantly switching locations, paying people to hide goods and adjusting the commodities being sold. Vendors also use mainstream channels through which to voice their concerns, such as voting, lobbying, founding associations, using legal counsel, the popular media and NGO assistance (Laking 2006; Scott 1985). However, although women have access to resources and can challenge particular ideologies, they may be unable to realize livelihood options because of the individual nature of street-based work, their limited power over infrastructure change, the constraints of community obligations and because class-based positions may divide them (Freeman 2007; Ong 1999: 19).

Resituating legal/illegal practice

The scale of women's engagement in street vending in Baguio City, as in other southern cities worldwide, continues to grow as vendors' sophistication increases and despite the vigilant policing to control such trade. I suggest then, like Abraham and van Schendel, that rather than taking the state as the primary point of departure with regard to assessing a trade as being either legal or illegal, "we build upon a distinction between what states consider to be legitimate ('legal') and what people involved in such work consider to be legitimate ('licit')" (2005: 4). Activities such as street vending are considered illegal because they operate outside formal political rules, but these actions may be regarded as "acceptable or licit" in the opinion of participants because they enable people to earn a living within what they feel are just circumstances (Abraham and van Schendel 2005: 4; Browne 2008; Seligmann 2004: 220).

Research exploring such legal/illegal spheres argues that, "there is a qualitative difference of scale and intent between the activities of internationally organized" crime and "micro-practices that, while often illegal in a formal sense" do not set out with the "unified purpose" to break national laws (Abraham and van Schendel 2005: 4). Small-scale sellers such as Carol Esteban defend their work by explaining that vending requires their personal labor, capital and ingenuity and enables their right to livelihood. Not unquestionably accepting state, or in this case city government policy, as the only yardstick by which to determine what constitutes legal or illegal practice, opens alternative avenues through which to assess local rationales for marginal, and often, "(il)licit" microenterprises that continue to persist over time and space (Abraham and van Schendel 2005: 4).

Mapping street vending in Baguio City

In the early twentieth century, the American colonial government in the Philippines established Baguio City – a pine-tree alpine location – as its mountain summer resort to escape the hotter lowland climate. Built to accommodate 25,000 people, today Baguio City's renowned hills are barely visible under its current population of 300,000. The city is the northern Philippines' government, education and administration center for the five mountain or Cordillera provinces. Its cooler temperatures ensure Baguio's ongoing attraction as a summer vacation destination for lowland visitors and the city's extensive Marbay and Maharlika markets that offer fresh produce, cut flowers and crafts support retail and wholesale businesses throughout the Cordillera and lowland provinces (Reed 1976). Baguio's first shopping complex, Baguio Center Mall, opened in 1999 and similar shopping centers began operations soon afterwards – Porta Vaga Mall opened in 2002 and the well-known chain, Shoemart City Mall, opened in 2004. Baguio's universities, government services, retail stores and extensive markets thus provide the customer base that those establishing new businesses seek.

Since the 1986 restoration of democratic government in the Philippines, however, successive national leaders have failed to institute economic and political reforms that effectively act "on behalf of the public interest"; instead, state policies continue to initiate anti-poverty programs that rarely come to fruition and to support a "logic of patronage" (Hutchcroft and Rocamora 2003: 260, 281; *Philippine Daily Inquirer* 2008). While the Philippine government agenda, liberalization, deregulation and privatization, succeeded in opening up to greater competition and efficiency economic sectors previously accessed primarily by the politically privileged, Philippine government leaders, to date, have not constructed the basic economic-political infrastructures required even by a minimalist role of the state in economic transformation (Hutchcroft and Rocamora 2003: 279). Growing migration into cities throughout the Philippines amid a corresponding decline in formal sector jobs leaves few viable livelihood options for many new urban residents. Both long-term Baguio City urbanites and new immigrants have thus established vending enterprises on the city's public streets, sidestepping local government policies that prohibit such practice.

Street vendors, as noted, often establish their businesses in those areas of the city with the highest pedestrian traffic. Along the east side of Session Road, Baguio City's main commercial shopping street, for example, vendors sell manufactured goods such as cell phones and phone accessories, sunglasses, jewelry and pop art posters that they have purchased from wholesalers in Manila. On the vacant blocks of Session Road where buildings have not been reconstructed since the 1990 earthquake, the city has erected walls to protect residents from the building rubble beyond. Vendors have claimed sections of these walls – measuring approximately one meter wide by two meters high – on which to display their wares to the constant flow of pedestrians. Vendors selling fresh produce and cooked food stake out positions in the streets that provide jeepney (small open-backed trucks) and bus transportation for residents. These transportation-hub locations for vending enable people to conveniently purchase food for their trips. The streets that border the city's centrally located green belt, Burnham Park, provide opportune sites for vendors selling cooked food and souvenirs, as residents and visitors use the park's large person-made lake and picnic and playground areas for recreation activities throughout the year. Both periodic and permanent vendors also assemble along the streets surrounding the central Marbay and Maharlika markets as this area is consistently crowded with local shoppers and tourists.

The illegal status of street vending, however, means that micro-traders must strategize to maintain the spaces in which they work and navigate business uncertainties characterized by fierce competition and fluctuating sales. Most vendors thus nurture linkages with family and fellow traders – personalized networks that facilitate access to stock on consignment, credit, loyal clients and employees. Such ties, grounded in customary rights and obligations and bolstered by mutual trust, are also common among street vendors facing similar challenges in other cities (Lazer 2007). Traders use this "intimate" (Wilson 2004) or "personal culture of trade" (Stoller 2002: 44) to create multiply-sited networks of support that can overcome situations in which formal financial or legal infrastructures are not well developed or, as in street vending, simply not available.

Figure 6.1 Women sell secondhand clothing on a Baguio City street during their allotted 12.00 noon to 1.00 p.m. time period for vending, 2008 (photograph by the author).

Carol Esteban, who has worked for over 20 years as a prepared-food vendor, as noted earlier, secured her selling location through an informal agreement with the Baguio City Supermarket and borrowed her business capital from family and friends. Carol preorders her cooked rice and cassava cakes from lowland women vendors and pays her suppliers promptly to ensure their loyalty. By ordering in advance, Carol can receive her goods at 6.00 a.m. rather than having to meet the lowland vendors at 4.00 a.m. on a first-come-first-serve basis. These prepared foods are more abundantly produced in lowland areas where the warmer climate supports higher agricultural yields. Women vendors from the neighboring lowland provinces of Pangasinan and La Union make the one-hour road trip to Baguio City seven days a week to sell their products to their regular *suki* customers; they usually return home by mid-day once they have sold their goods.

Although some vendors such as Carol have secured informal selling arrangements with selected retailers, the majority of vendors are subject to Baguio City's Tax Ordinance 2000–001 that prohibits street vending in all urban public or non-market-zone areas. Thus, police regularly pursue street sellers especially during city-wide clean-up campaigns (Opiña 2007). While some vendors escape losing only a few products that police pluck from their baskets, others may have their entire stock confiscated. I have accompanied different vendors to local police headquarters where women have had to pay the 1,000-peso fine (US$22.00) to retrieve their goods. If the value of their products is less than the fine, vendors, quite logically, do not reclaim their wares forfeiting their capital investment.

To obtain the right to continue their street-based livelihoods, in late 1998, Carol Esteban and Patricia Tayad, an established vegetable street vendor in her late 50s, obtained the assistance of their community leader or *barangay* captain to lobby Baguio City counselors for access to downtown spaces for their trade. Equipped with an extensive petition identifying hundreds of vendors who supported this action, Carol and Patricia repeatedly visited city counselors' offices to argue their case. In response to their persistent actions, the then Baguio City mayor issued an informal directive from his office granting street vendors permission to sell their goods in specific street locations, at specified times. Within this "maximum tolerance" initiative, street vending is not legal, but it is tolerated within prescribed conditions.[4]

Many established sellers such as Carol and her neighboring vendors had secured regular vending locations simply by being the first players to physically claim these spots. Indeed, such urban public spaces emerge both as possessions that can be passed down to family members and as commodities that may be traded, albeit in customary but not legal practice. The new maximum tolerance agreement confirmed vendors' rights to occupy their respective positions for the duration of the shopping day that for most sellers extends from 6.00 a.m. to 7.00 p.m.

Since the mid-1990s, however, new residents arriving in the city with few work options have increasingly claimed whatever feasible edge space they could occupy to work as street sellers. *Barangay* captains thus worked with local vendor groups, as they continue to do, to identify locations in which these new players can sell part-time from 4.00 a.m. to 8.00 a.m., 12.00 noon to 1.00 p.m. and 5.00 p.m. onwards. These periods correspond to those before the permanent shops open in the morning, the lunch break and the busy evening shopping period. Under maximum tolerance, all sanctioned street traders, depending on the size of their display area, must daily purchase 10- to 20-peso (25–50 cents) vending permits in order to sell in their assigned locations.

Upon achieving maximum tolerance, most street vendors organized themselves into associations if they had not done so beforehand. Baguio City Hall currently records over 100 registered street vendor associations whose memberships range from 15 to 60 members. Membership in a vendor association is determined first by the neighborhood in which one works. Carol Esteban, Nancy Balbao and Patricia Tayad, for example, belong to one of the largest vendor federations called SEDCO – each letter is the first letter of a street included in their central location. Within SEDCO, there are ten associations based on the type of products vendors sell. The Hilltop Vendors' Association is readily identified by its upper-market site. Smaller organizations such as the Secondhand Clothing Night Vendors' Association, identified by the product members sell as well as by the time during which they conduct business, is affiliated within SEDCO's umbrella organization.

Each association drafts by-laws, elects officials and contributes a small yearly dues payment. To visually formalize members' rights to conduct their businesses in allotted street locations, some associations purchased specially colored uniforms bearing the group's name. These garments, usually sleeveless vests, physically distinguish group members from the itinerant lowland vendors who regularly compete for street space. Association members also designate one day a week to clean their neighborhood streets to support both the national government's "Clean and Green" campaign and the municipal counselors who supported the maximum tolerance initiative.

Contesting spaces, controlling streetscapes

The arrangement of maximum tolerance, however, continues to fuel protests by large-scale retailers and permanent market stall owners whose rents exceed the token amount street hawkers pay and who complain of losing potential sales to vendors (Opiña 2006a). In May 2005, municipal counselors suspended the maximum tolerance initiative and introduced a series of Proposed Ordinances (by-laws) to dramatically reorganize the city's street trade (City of Baguio 2005). The ordinances suggested that: (1) All daytime street vendors will be assigned stall locations (one per family) in a newly constructed building outside the city centre; (2) The different night markets will be combined into one location with shorter night vending hours to extend from 7.00 p.m to 10.00 p.m. rather than from 4.00 p.m. onwards; (3) Anyone purchasing goods from illegal street vendors will be fined 500 pesos (US$11.00); (4) A *balsakan* or distribution area for lowland goods – those not sold by Baguio City resident vendors – will be established outside the city center. The introduction of these measures met with determined protest from street vendors (Olson 2005).

Evelyn Balbun, 37 years old and the president of the Baguio Vegetable Vendors' Association, outlines some of the arguments against these ordinances: "The new daytime vending area," she explains, "cannot accommodate all of the city's current street vendors as the municipal census identifying 3,000 sellers underestimates the number of businesses. In addition, the proposed building cannot give all vendors selling times that most benefit individual schedules." Many consumers confirm that since the new vending location will not be located in the heart of the city, they would need to make separate trips to find their *suki* rather than coordinating their daily food purchases with their transportation to and from work and home as is their current practice. Evelyn adds that, "As traders sell similar goods, each of us depends upon keeping our well-located sites to best serve our *sukis*. What will happen when we move and itinerant vendors start to sell in our former spots?"

Cecille Dala-an, a veteran street vendor, 47 years old, who prepares boiled and fried fish and who is president of the Park Cooked Food Vendors' Association, is particularly concerned with the proposed out-of-the-way locations and new hours for the night market. Cecille's members set up their cooking carts every afternoon along a well-used street that borders one edge of Burnham Park, a dedicated green space that is consistently used by residents and tourists. Evening hours for cooked food street sales, in accordance with the maximum tolerance agreement, begin at 4.00 p.m., but vendors often start selling by 3.00 p.m. to 3.30 p.m. to catch students and shoppers who are returning home. Cecille explains:

> I see sales decreasing for my members if they are relocated to the proposed night-selling area where pedestrians do not usually congregate and if we

cannot start to sell until after 7.00 p.m. Our central park location encourages our clients to sit and eat, and often return for a second order of hamburgers, soup, fried noodles, fish balls or boiled corn.

The most accessible of the proposed sites for the new night market is on Harrison Road, a major street that also borders the park. Some food sellers explain, however, that Harrison Road is not long enough to accommodate all of the night food vendors and that the exhaust fumes from the street's heavy bus and jeepney traffic will discourage their customers from patronizing the varied stalls for their meals.

Katharine Talango, president of the Secondhand Clothing Night Vendors' Association, wants to protect her group's claim to their well-positioned vending sites – an L-shaped strip of road along two sides of the Marbay Market building as well as generous sidewalk displays on two side streets off upper Session Road. Both locations give vendors access to late night diners and club goers. The proposal to designate vendors as either day or night sellers, but not both, also concerns

Figure 6.2 A Baguio City street vendor sells boiled peanuts and cooked rice cakes wrapped in banana leaves, 2008 (photograph by the author).

Katharine as this means that women vendors who continue to juggle income-generating work with domestic and childcare responsibilities lose the work flexibility they need. Some members sell during the allotted daytime slots if domestic responsibilities preclude them from selling in the evenings or if they want to work additional hours to earn extra income.

During the 2004 election campaign, many city counselors supported issues specific to the concerns of women and the urban poor. To preclude undermining their electorate support following the protest their vending measures met, throughout late 2005, counselors held a series of meetings with vendors to review the city's proposals. Throughout these meetings, however, counselors continued to justify their initiatives, as one official explains:

> The 2001 anti-peddling law prohibiting street vending is not the solution to our challenge of ever-increasing numbers of street sellers. I have seen fruit, vegetables and cooked food confiscated by the police who patrol our streets, and I realize the hardship of this loss in capital and in labor for vendors. But our proposals will educate buyers and standardize vending practices.

During these early meetings between city officials and vendors, it became clear that counselors would not move much beyond giving lip service to vendors' concerns (Refuerzo 2006c).

Activating street vending access and rights

To protest Baguio City's new ordinances then, some of the more prominent vendor association leaders secured legal assistance from locally-based NGOs – the Cordillera People's Alliance (CPA), a pan-Cordilleran NGO, and ORNUS, a grassroots organization whose social welfare mandate addresses issues of women's and children's health care and violence against women. Following a series of informational meetings with NGO facilitators, presidents representing the majority of vendor associations, submitted member-signed response letters to City Hall outlining association objections to the municipal measures and offering suggestions for alternative initiatives. To sustain pressure on Baguio City officials, association leaders and members repeatedly visited counselors' offices and attended the weekly, public Monday afternoon City Hall meetings. Whether or not vendors had opportunities to publicly speak about their case, their ongoing presence at meetings served as a physical reminder of the concerns they advocated.

Between mid-2005 and mid-2006, the city demolition crews from the POSD (Public Order and Safety Division), continually harassed vendors by demolishing their displays and confiscating their goods (Opiña 2006b; Palangchao 2006a). Indeed, this prompted some Baguio City residents to point out that such actions disrupted the daily consumption services on which they had come to rely while threatening public safety (Opiña 2006c). In December 2005, approximately 500 vendors participated in a rally at the Baguio City Hall to publicly protest the proposed ordinances.

By late-2006, municipal counselors had placed on hold the ordinances they had proposed to reorganize Baguio City's street vendors (Liporada 2006). In interviews, counselors confirmed that it might have been more prudent to introduce their initiatives one at a time, moving to the next by-law only after implementation measures for the previous initiative had been resolved: "Presenting these ordinances together proved to be too much, too fast for both vendors and consumers." Indeed, this adversarial situation continues to be regularly fed by media coverage that casts these proposed changes in the guise of "anti-vending" rather than as reorganization measures (Opiña 2006d). In early 2006, the mayor created an appointed municipal position, that of the City Administrator, whose mandate it is to advise on interim policies that can accommodate the needs of Baguio's increasing street vendor population and the concerns of city residents and retailers. The appointed, rather than elected, status of the City Administrator, however, means that meetings between his office and vendors often prove frustrating as placating reassurances for settlement obtained during repeated discussions are often contradicted on the street by continuing police harassment. The City Administrator explains that although his recommendations to the mayor's office consistently include some form of tolerance for street vendors, the former and the current mayors, in juggling the divergent interests of their constituents, have failed to develop and implement viable policies on this issue. Since municipal elections were scheduled for May 2007, the then current city counselors hesitated to introduce new vendor by-laws that might arouse the displeasure of their constituents and thus threaten their chances for re-election (Opiña 2006c).

To mitigate the tension among vendors, city officials and large-scale retailers at this time, Patricia Tayad, president of SEDCO and Cecille Dala-an, president of the Park Cooked Food Vendors' Association, initiated a series of meetings with the then head of the POSD to discuss how they might collaborate in this interim period. In one effort, for example, POSD officers worked with vendor association presidents to limit the physical street presence of each vending enterprise by reducing maximum size dimensions for sellers' displays and the distance their goods extend into the street. The smaller size structures have noticeably increased space for pedestrian traffic.

The failure of Baguio City counselors to develop workable street vending policies has meant that vendors' businesses remain subject to a patchwork of temporary and often contradictory band-aid measures that, as noted, swing between tolerance and persecution (Agoot 2008; Palangchao 2008; Refuerzo 2006a, 2006b; Rillorta 2008). Restricting vendors' access to this viable employment option and limiting urban residents' right to services they actually demand, primarily serves the modernizing vision of city planners, but fails to respond to people's on-the-ground livelihood needs.

Conclusion

At the same time that urbanization and structural adjustment policies in the Philippines have constrained formal-sector work opportunities for many urban residents, they have facilitated the growth of informalizing economic sector options (Stoller 2002: 18). Throughout the Philippines, people's dependence on street economy enterprises and their integration of these services into their daily lives evidence that such alternative practices are, in fact, already workable parts of the wider urban economy. Urban development policies that do not make room for such activities in their vision of "modern" cities hold limited applicability for the livelihood needs of residents across classes. Baguio City's current development plan that supports the construction of shopping mall complexes while banishing street vending to the city margins, privileges a northern-based notion of appropriate urban public land use rather than promoting realistic subsistence options for the urban poor that can correspondingly enrich the texture of city streetscapes (see also Hansen 2008: 216).

Baguio City street vendors have managed to operationalize the streets as captured economic, social and political spaces that can enable their livelihoods. By protesting the exclusion of their voices from urban planning schemes, these vendors demonstrate how actors at the margins can reconfigure, to some extent, formal city power relations in localized ways through struggle and personalized resistance. Female vendors' current advocacy thus evidences the new modes of "embodied practice and vocal expression" that they have adopted to fight for their right for fair treatment (Mills 2005: 138). They garner the resources they need to take on unfamiliar positions of leadership, learn their legal rights, develop the confidence to speak out and effectively organize actions that can meet oppressive measures instituted by those who find their presence "a constant reminder of the failure of modernity" (Seligmann 2004: 219). In so doing, they negotiate limits on their entrepreneurial flexibility to realize active roles in processes that have otherwise been used to identify them as passive recipients of northern initiatives.

Within such circumstances, however, street vendors cannot unilaterally surmount challenges to their already tenuous positions. Among vendors themselves, the different personalities that usually occur within one group mean that disagreements may arise over the best course of action to take for specific challenges; conflicts also occur from ongoing competition for limited resources and from vendors' undetermined rights. Vendors' small-scale and informal economy work, moreover, also means that sellers may find themselves in ambiguous legal positions – where the law no longer applies or is not fully respected – even when they are involved in legal or sanctioned activities such as when street trading was deemed "tolerated" in Baguio City. In cases where vendors' legal position remains under debate, they are particularly vulnerable to crime, violence and other forms of harassment, both on the part of official and unofficial bodies.[5] These might include under-the-table payments to police or to neighborhood leaders to occupy certain locations or to retrieve confiscated goods (Seligmann 2004: 202–219).

In an ongoing yearly pattern that vendors describe as playing "cat and mouse" with city police and officials, Baguio City's street sellers are chased from their business locations or have their goods seized depending upon the government's agenda. Continually confronting such threats to their livelihoods means that vendors, and women in particular, garner the information and develop the tactics they need to better resist "the next time around" which inevitably occurs (Seligmann 2004: 202). Despite the risks in street vending, women vendors continue to craft pragmatic sideroads fashioning particularized spacial and cultural domains that can enable their right to make a living, as tenuous as it may be.

Acknowledgements

Field research for this paper has been conducted in the Philippines during June to August 2003, 2005, 2006 and 2008. Financial support has been provided by the Social Sciences and Humanities Research Council of Canada (SSHRC) through Standard Research Grants (2000–2003; 2004–2007; 2008–2011) and by the Ontario College of Art & Design, Faculty Research Grants. In the Philippines, I am affiliated with the Cordillera Studies Center (CSC), University of the Philippines Baguio, Baguio City. I thank my colleagues at CSC for their generous support of my research. I also thank Judith Bangaan for keeping me up to date with street vending and city-wide developments in Baguio City. To the street vendors who have responded to my many questions, I owe a debt of gratitude.

Notes

1 All personal names of individuals are pseudonyms.
2 During this research the exchange rate varied between, US$1.00 = 55 PHP to US$1.00 = 42 PHP. The exchange rate I use here is US$1.00 = 45 PHP.
3 Allison Brown (2006:7) suggests substituting the term, "street economy" for street trade as the former concept captures the multiple commercial activities that profit from street businesses.
4 John Cross (1998: 120) identities a similar arrangement of "tolerance" between street vendors and the municipal government in Mexico City.
5 In Baguio City, between 2001and 2006, one vendor association president, having gained power through successful money-lending practices, required members to submit weekly payments to her to secure their selling locations (see also Singh 2000).

References

Abraham, I. and van Schendel, W. (2005) 'Introduction: The Making of Illicitness', in W. van Schendel and I. Abraham (eds) *Illicit Flows and Criminal Things: States, Borders, and the Other Side of Globalization*, Bloomington and Indianapolis: University of Indiana Press, pp. 1–37.
Agoot, L. (2008) 'Mayor asked to locate vending place in city', *Baguio Midland Courier* (February 10): 20, 39.
Anjaria, J.S. (2006) 'Street Hawkers and Public Space in Mumbai', *Economic and Political Weekly* (May 27): 2140–2146.
Babb, F.E. (2001) 'Market/places and Gendered Spaces: Market/women's Studies over Two Decades', in L.J. Seligmann (ed.) *Women Traders in Cross-Cultural Perspective: Mediating Identities, Marketing Wares,* Stanford, CA: Stanford University Press, pp. 229–239.
Balisacan, A.M. (1995) 'Anatomy of Poverty during Adjustment: The Case of the Philippines', *Economic Development and Cultural Change* 44(1): 33–62.

Bhowmik, S.K. (2005) 'Street Vendors in Asia: A Review', *Economic and Political Weekly* (May 28–June 4): 2256–2264.

Brenner, S.A. (1998) *The Domestication of Desire: Women, Wealth, and Modernity in Java*, Princeton, NJ: Princeton University Press.

Broad, R. (1988) *Unequal Alliance: The World Bank, the International Monetary Fund, and the Philippines*, Berkeley and LA: University of California Press.

Bromley, R. (1997) 'Working the streets of Cali, Columbia: Survival Strategy, Necessity, or Unavoidable Evil?', in J. Gugler (ed.) *Cities in the Developing World: Issues, Theory and Policy*, Oxford: Oxford University Press, pp. 33–62.

—— (2000) 'Street vending and public policy: A Global Review', *International Journal of Sociology and Social Policy* 20(1): 1–29.

Brown, A. (2006) *Contested Space: Street Trading, Public Space, and Livelihoods in Developing Cities*, Warwickshire, UK: ITDG Publishing.

Browne, K.E. (2008) 'Economics and Morality: Introduction', in K.E. Browne and B.L. Milgram (eds) *Economics and Morality: Anthropological Approaches*, Walnut Creek: CA: Altamira Press, pp. 1–40.

Castells, M. and Portes, A. (1989) 'World Underneath: The Origins, Dynamics and Effects of the Informal Economy', in A. Portes, M. Castells and L. A. Benton (eds) *The Informal Economy: Studies in Advanced and Less Developed Countries*, Baltimore and London: Johns Hopkins University Press, pp. 11–40.

Chant, S. (1996) 'Women's Roles in Recession and Economic Restructuring in Mexico and the Philippines', *Geoforum* 27(3): 297–327.

Chen, M., Sebstad, J. and O'Connell, L. (1999) 'Counting the Invisible Workforce: The Case of Home-based Workers', *World Development* 27(3): 603–610.

City of Baguio (2000–2001) *City Tax Ordinance Number 2000–001* (Sections 143, 153), Baguio City, Philippines: Office of the City Treasurer, City of Baguio.

City of Baguio (municipal counselors) (2005) *Proposed Ordinances Nr. PO 050–05, 058–05, 128–05*. Baguio City, Philippines: City of Baguio.

City of Marikina (2002) *Marikina Public Market*, Marikina City, Philippines: Marikina Public Market Office.

Cross, J.C. (1998) *Informal Politics: Street Vendors and the State in Mexico City*, Stanford, CA: Stanford University Press.

Cross, J. C. and Morales, A. (eds) (2007) *Street Entrepreneurs: People, Place and Politics in Local and Global Perspectives*, New York: Routledge.

Douglass, M., Ho, K.C. and Ling, O.G. (2002) 'Civic Spaces, Globalization and Pacific Asia Cities', *IDPR* (International Development and Planning Review) 24(4): 345–363.

Drummond, L.B. (2000) 'Street Scenes: Practices of Public and Private Space in Urban Vietnam', *Urban Studies* 37 (12): 2377–2391.

Edensor, T. (1998) 'The Culture of the Indian Street', in N. R. Fyfe (ed.) *Images of the Street: Planning, Identity and Control in Public Space*, London: Routledge, pp. 205–221.

Freeman, C. (2007) 'The "Reputation" of Neoliberalism', *American Ethnologist* 34 (2): 252–267.

Gibson-Graham, J.K., Resnick, S. and Wolff, R. (2000) 'Class in a Poststructuralist Frame', in J.K. Gibson-Graham, S. Resnick and R. Wolff (eds), *Class and Its Others*, Minneapolis, MN: University of Minnesota Press, pp. 1–22.

Hansen, K.T. (2001) 'Informal Sector', in *International Encyclopedia of the Social and Behavioral Sciences*, Amsterdam, The Netherlands: Elsevier, pp. 7450–7452.

—— (2008) 'The Informalization of Lusaka's Economy: Regime Change, Ultra Modern Markets, and Street Vending, 1972–2004', in J.B. Gewald, M. Hinfelaar and G. Macola (eds) *One Zambia, Many Histories: Towards a History of Postcolonial Zambia*, Leiden: Brill, pp. 213–239.

Hutchcroft, P.D. and Rocamora J. (2003) Strong Demands and Weak Institutions: The Origins and Evolution of the Democratic Deficit in the Philippines. *Journal of East Asian Studies* 3: 259–292.

Karim, W.J. (1995) 'Introduction: Genderizing Anthropology in Southeast Asia', in W.J. Karim (ed.), *"Male" and "Female" in Developing Southeast Asia*, Oxford and Washington: Berg, pp. 11–35.

Kusakabe, K. (2006a) *On the Borders of Legality: A Review of Studies of Street Vending in Phnom Penh, Cambodia. Informal Economy Poverty and Employment*, Cambodia Series #4, Bangkok, Thailand: International Labor Office.

—— (2006b) *Policy Issues in Street Vending: An Overview of Studies in Thailand, Cambodia and Mongolia. Informal Economy Poverty and Employment*. Bangkok, Thailand: International Labor Office.

Laking, J. (2006) 'Vendors Battle for Role in City Market Development', *Baguio Midland Courier* November 15: 1, 3.

Lazer, S. (2007) '"In-betweenness" on the Margins: Collective Organisation, Ethnicity and Political Agency among Bolivian Street Traders', in J. Staples (ed.) *Livelihoods at the Margins: Surviving the City*, Walnut Creek, CA: Left Coast Press, pp. 237–256.

Liporada, I.S. (2006) 'Flea and Night Market Proposals Impossible', *Baguio Midland Courier* December 10:1, 20.

Lund, F., Nicolson, J. and Skinner, C. (2000) *Street Trading*. Durban: School of Development Studies, University of Natal.

MacGaffey, J. and Bazenguissa-Ganga, R. (2000) *Congo-Paris: Transnational Traders on the Margins of the Law*. Bloomington; Indianapolis: University of Indiana Press.

Miao, P. (2001) 'Introduction', in P. Miao (ed.) *Public Places in Asia Pacific Cities: Current Issues and Strategies*, Dordrecht; Boston: Kluwer Academic Publishers, pp. 1–48.

Milgram, B.L. (2001) 'Situating Handicraft Market Women in Ifugao, Upland Philippines: A Case for Multiplicity', in L.J. Seligmann (ed.) *Women Traders in Cross-Cultural Perspective: Mediating Identities, Marketing Wares*, Stanford, CA: Stanford University Press, pp. 129–159.

—— (2004) 'Refashioning Commodities: Women and the Sourcing and Circulation of Secondhand Clothing in the Philippines', *Anthropologica* 46(2): 123–136.

—— (2005) 'From Margin to Mainstream: Microfinance, Women's Work and Social Change in the Philippines', *Urban Anthropology and Studies of Cultural Systems and World Economic Development* 34(4): 341–383.

Mills, M.B. (2005) 'From Nimble Fingers to Raised Fists: Women and Labor Activism in Globalizing Thailand', *Signs: Journal of Women in Culture and Society* 31(1): 117–144.

—— (2008) Claiming Space: Navigating Landscapes Of Power and Citizenship in Thai Labor Activism, *Urban Anthropology and Studies of Cultural Systems and World Economic Development* 37(1): 89–128.

Mitullah, W.V. (2004) *A Review of Street Trade in Africa. Report: Women in Informal Employment Globalizing and Organising*, Boston: WIEGO and Kennedy School of Government, Harvard University.

Morton, A. (1996) 'Assessing Policy Implementation Success: Observations from the Philippines', *World Development* 24(9): 1441–1451.

Ofreneo, R.E. and Habana, E.P. (1987) *The Employment Crisis and the World Bank's Adjustment Program*, Quezon City: University of the Philippines Press.

Olson, E. (2005) 'Vendor Killed, Another Hurt in Hilltop Accident', *Sun Star Baguio*, (December 2): 1, 3, 9.

Ong, A. (1999) *Flexible Citizenship: The Cultural Logics of Transnationality*, Durham, NC: Duke University Press.

Opiña, R. (2006a) 'Vending Along City Streets Alarms Dad', *Sun Star Baguio* (January 16): 1, 9.

—— (2006b) 'City Exec Explains Side on Illegal Vending', *Sun Star Baguio* (February 7): 1, 11.

—— (2006c) 'Yaranon Turns Down Request for More Anti-peddling Men', *Sun Star Baguio* (February 10): 2.

—— (2006d) 'Anti-peddling Czar Hits Vendors' "Abuse" of Tolerance Permit', *Sun Star Baguio* (August 25): 1, 9.

—— (2007) 'Weed out of Illegal Stalls Starts Today', *Sun Star Baguio* (January 15): 1, 9.

Ordoñez, M. (2008) 'Who's Afraid of a Food Crisis?', *Philippine Daily Inquirer* (July 6): A11.

Palangchao, H. (2006a) 'Lady Councilor Seeks Probe on Illegal Traders' Increase', *Baguio Midland Courier* (June 4): 1, 39.

—— (2006b) 'Park Body Seeks Demolition of Illegal Stalls at Burnham', *Baguio Midland Courier* (October 15): 2.

—— (2008) 'Dad Seeks Probe on Flaws of Anti-vending Program', *Baguio Midland Courier* (May 18): 22, 42.

Philippine Daily Inquirer (editorial) (2008) 'Worsening Corruption', *Philippine Daily Inquirer* (July 1): A10.

Reed, R. (1976) *City of Pines: The Origins of Baguio as a Colonial Hill Station and Regional Capital*. Baguio, Philippines: A-Seven Publishing.

Refuerzo, A. (2006a) 'City gets Tough with Illegal Vendors', *The Baguio Reporter* (June 11): 3.

——(2006b) 'Night, Flea Markets Proposal Okayed', *Sun Star Baguio* (June 24): 2, 9.

——(2006c) 'Solution to Vendors' Clamor for More Selling Space Still Elusive', *Sun Star Baguio* (August 5): 1–2.

Remo, M. (2008) 'Inflation hit 11.4% in June', *Philippine Daily Inquirer* (July 5): A1, A15.

Rillorta, P. (2008) 'Illegal Vending, Who's to Blame? The City's Slaughterhouse', *Baguio Midland Courier* (May 18): 2, 42.

Scott, J.C. (1985) *Weapons of the Weak. Everyday Forms of Peasant Resistance*, New Haven: Yale University Press.

Seligmann, L.J. (2004) *Peruvian Street Lives: Culture, Power, and Economy among Market Women of Cuzco*, Urbana; Chicago: University of Illinois Press.

Singh, A. (2000) 'Organizing Street Vendors'. Paper presented at, Street Vendors: A Symposium on Reconciling People's Livelihood and Urban Governance. India, July 2000. http://www.india-seminar.com/2000/491.htm, accessed May 2007.

Stoller, P. (2002) *Money Has No Smell: The Africanization of New York City*, Chicago, IL: University of Chicago Press.

Wilson, A. (2004) *The Intimate Economies of Bangkok: Tomboys, Tycoons, and Avon Ladies in the Global City*, Berkeley; Los Angeles, CA: University of California Press.

Zlolniski, C. (2006) *Janitors, Street Vendors, and Activists: The Lives of Mexican Immigrants in Silicon Valley*, Berkeley; Los Angeles, CA: University of California Press.

7 The streets of Kuala Lumpur

City-space, 'race' and civil disobedience

Yeoh Seng Guan

Introduction

In early March 2008, a 'political tsunami' swept throughout Malaysia.[1] The twelfth General Elections churned out polling results that jolted both sides of the political divide, confounded all predictions, and are now touted as historic and epochal in transforming the manner in which political contestation along racialized lines in Malaysia is currently constituted. The promise of a 'new politics' originally heralded by the large-scale street protests in Kuala Lumpur (*Reformasi* movement) in the late 1990s when Mahathir Mohamad unceremoniously deposed his deputy premier Anwar Ibrahim has now come to fruition. Barisan Nasional lost its political stranglehold of two-thirds parliamentary majority held for nearly four decades, which had become for many, especially since the long Mahathir era, a normality. More starkly, excluding the East Malaysian states of Sabah and Sarawak which have different political genealogies, the figures in Peninsular Malaysia show a drastic dilution of its supposed multi-ethnic appeal – only 85 out of 165 parliamentary seats (51.5 per cent) went to Barisan Nasional.[2] Equally groundbreaking, several veteran and senior-ranking leaders of the ethnic-based partner political parties of Barisan Nasional (notably from the Malaysian Indian Congress [MIC] and Chinese-led Gerakan) lost their seats to opposition neophytes and unknown newcomers. Perhaps most significant of all, the majority of voters in five out of thirteen states including the important Federal Territory of Kuala Lumpur gave the mandate to rule to the opposition coalition. In sum, the poll results birthed an uncharted political landscape for Malaysian citizens to countenance and navigate through in the years ahead.

Many political analysts suggest that a conjunction of disparate street protests organized in late 2007 helped to undermine electoral support for Barisan Nasional. In particular, the significant Indian vote swing away from Barisan Nasional, their traditional political choice for several decades, can be traced to the state's heavy handed management and media portrayal of the peaceful Hindraf (Hindu Rights Action Front) rally of November 2007 which galvanized an estimated 30,000 Indians onto the streets of Kuala Lumpur. In this chapter, rather than present a precise account of the myriad factors that converged in the making of the 'political tsunami' event of 2008, I offer a more spectral and diffuse narrative of events, projects and contestations both proximate and distant in keeping with the volume's themes of urban power, dissent and resistance. I argue that the Hindraf rally and the subsequent *Makkal Sakti* ('People Power' in Tamil) movement index a rupture which paradoxically brings together spatial contradictions traceable to the colonial period but which has been inflected in a localized ethnoscape (Appadurai 1996) borne out of a state-driven trajectory of 'developmentalism' (e.g., Kahn and Loh 1992) and an ethnic-based governmentality (e.g., Ong 1999) in more recent times. Said differently, my narrative provides an example of the spatial dialectic argued by scholars like Henri Lefebvre (1991 [1974]) but unfolds in a postcolonial Southeast Asian urban setting. Briefly, Lefebvre paid close analytical attention to the wide-ranging changes brought about by the material and representational re-constitution of space under the imperialistic sign of capitalism. As urban space is both homogenized and fragmented to render it recognizable and exchangeable, cities and the people that inhabit this space undergo various contradictory processes. The emergent contours of new spatial sensibilities and aesthetics segre-gate and disperse differentially people according to rationalized social relations of production and consumption, and in the process bring forth an array of everyday strategies of acceptance, accommodation and resistance among different social classes. In my example of the developmentalist transformation of the spatial entity of Kuala Lumpur, I pay attention to how these processes are played out through a battery of legislative and punitive actions against squatter colonies in general, and in the changing social agency of ethnic Indian-Hindus as embodied in the recent street activities of Hindraf in particular.

Developmentalism and spatial cleansing in Kuala Lumpur

As the capital city of the modern nation-state of Malaysia, the spatial entity of Kuala Lumpur occupies a high symbolic position in social and political imaginar-ies. Contemporary state-driven efforts to cultivate the sentiment of urban patriot-ism towards the city – for example as suggested by the slogan, *Sayangi Kuala Lumpur* (Love Kuala Lumpur) – however, are comparatively recent, and its current status belies a complex and convoluted past. Briefly, the city's genesis and evolu-tion is intimately tied up with the British colonial extractive enterprise. In tandem with British expansive control of the Malay peninsula from the end of the eigh-teenth century to the middle of the twentieth century, a spatial geography of urban centres that manifested the 'colonial-immigrant complex' came into being (Lim 1978). Tin mining and cash crop plantations were the primary economic impetus to embark upon the construction of more efficient and predictable land-based trans-port networks like railways and roads in contrast to rivers prone to the fluctuations of the tropical weather. Revenues from these industries financed the linking up of nodal production and distribution points throughout the country to the coastal ports for relay back to the metropolitan centre. Several new inland settlements were spawned and overtook the older coastal settlements in strategic importance.

Kuala Lumpur was one of many such emergent settlements located about 35 kilometres upstream from the royal coastal capital of Klang. When the British decided to relocate their administrative capital to Kuala Lumpur in 1880, it set into motion the spatial and imaginative transformation of a frontier mining settlement, originally established by a mixture of Sumatran Malay and Chinese traders, into the cosmopolitan political centre first of the Federated Malay States and subsequently of the Federation of Malaya and finally Malaysia.[3] European spatial aesthetics also came into play early as embodied in the planning layout for the town that drew from nascent city planning ideas (e.g., 'Garden City' movement) promoted in the metropolitan centre and implemented to different degrees in the peripheral colonies as experiments in social engineering. In the case of British Malaya, they were also inflected by the contingencies of an essentially racialized and segregationist governmentality to manage the plural demographic spaces because of a liberal policy of immigration that saw the influx of foreign immigrant labour, mainly from India and China, opened up by British capitalist investments. As Joel Kahn puts it,

> Governing Malaya's colonial subjects ... involved various mechanisms aimed at immobilizing them, thus tying them to particular places – peasant villages, forest reserves, plantation belts, factory zones, urban bureaucratic centers – each constructed discursively as the preserve of a particular race. This was done, moreover, not just or even mainly to serve the interests of capital but to facilitate the disciplining of colonial subjects and, therefore, to the benefit of an emergent modern state ...
>
> (Kahn 2006: 140)

In this scheme of things, the bodies of South Indians (mainly Tamils) were particularly valued as a productive source of cheap and pliable labour in the commercially lucrative rural plantation sector, where several generations eventually lived and worked with occasional forays into commercial urban centres. The political and moral economy of the 'total institution' of regimented plantation life has been well researched (e.g., Jain 1970; Ramasamy 1994; Ramachandran 1994). Whilst basic facilities like schools, clinics, temples and residential quarters were provided to the workers and their families, they were also subjected to a disciplinary formation that sought to inculcate and weld a culture of servility and dependency to their patrons. The colonial archives also bear witness to a broad range of everyday subaltern resistance and ruptures against inhumane working conditions (e.g., Ramasamy 1992). Arguably, the most concerted and celebrated period of recorded labour unrest is in the aftermath of the Second World War which saw nascent undercurrents of ethno-nationalist consciousness cross-cutting with multi-ethnic labour movements as inspired by the Malayan Communist Party (MCP) and Malayan General Labour Union (e.g., Harper 1999; Stenson 1980; Tai 2000). Nevertheless, despite various gains in incrementally improving their material conditions and the upward mobility of segments of this ethnic group into the lower middle class, these studies suggest that the lives of plantation workers have been largely relegated to a marginal existence of persistent poverty and material deprivation in the absence of effective institutional intervention in comparison with the rest of Malaysian society.

In the urban centres, large numbers of Indians were similarly targeted as labourers and low-skilled artisans in the infrastructural public works and railway sectors. In Kuala Lumpur, many were provided cramped public housing quarters in working class districts (like Sentul and Brickfields), which became popularly perceived as mono-ethnic 'Little Indias'. Many others, together with other working class ethnic groups, also resorted to erecting their own dwelling houses on vacant land with or without consent from their landowners, and formed an expansive array of 'squatter colonies' that range from mono-ethnic to mixed ethnic groupings. In a milieu when the population of Kuala Lumpur was relatively manageably small and vacant land was plentiful, the colonies' existence was not always considered problematic. Indeed, elsewhere I have argued that whilst the category of 'squatter colonies' draws its salience from legal changes to land tenure which effectively displaced indigenous notions of tenureship during the colonial era, tolerence towards their existence has been checkered and contingent on specific historical circumstances (Yeoh 2001b). For instance, the first major resettlement exercise of 'squatters' in the post-war period was conducted in the mid-stages of 'The Emergency' (1948–1960) in the context of an undeclared civil war between the British Administration and the MCP in an effort to wrest control of the country. In 1953, the Committee on the Kuala Lumpur Squatter Problem was set up to address the widespread phenomenon of squatting. While the committee eventually proposed the policy of clearance and resettlement in order to provide suitable housing for the urban poor, these efforts were also closely related with defusing security problems associated with Chinese squatters who were believed to be 'deeply infested with Communists'. Surveys conducted during that period indicate that, as over 70 per cent of the urban squatter population (estimated at around 70,000 to 140,000) was made up of ethnic Chinese, the clearing of squatter settlements was necessary because their layout 'made police supervision a matter of great difficulty, interfered with public and private development and because they were a real problem from the point of view of the Emergency' (cited in Johnstone 1983: 257). Similarly, the Kuala Lumpur 'race riots' of 1969 sparked off immediately after the poor electoral showing of the Alliance parties (forerunner to Barisan Nasional) also resurfaced concerns about the role that squatter residents may have played in them.[4] The Subcommittee of the National Operations Council on Squatter Re-Housing and Re-Settlement argued that:

> Unchecked squatting challenges the status of government as agencies for maintaining law and order; results in an increase in crime, juvenile delinquency and a wide variety of social problems, a loss of substantial revenues to the government; affects the physical development of Kuala Lumpur, its economic, social, and political stability; inhibits economic growth and investment; and reduces its image both at home and overseas.
>
> (cited in Azizah 1994: 30)

To further strengthen the powers of the municipality for forced eviction, the Emergency (Clearance of Squatters) Regulations 1969 were enacted. Together with the National Land Code (1965), both pieces of legislation were offered as incontrovertible evidence that squatting is a criminal activity. Between 1969 and 1975, about 18,000 people (about 60 per cent of whom was identified as ethnic Chinese) were subsequently evicted in Kuala Lumpur. Only 34 per cent of this number was eventually re-housed in low-cost housing financed by the Federal Government.[5] However, this was only a temporary respite as small-scale academic surveys conducted in the 1970s indicated that the urban squatter population had quickly risen again.

Moreover, from the 1970s, a significant demographic transition became more apparent as ethnic Malays began to constitute an increasing proportion of the urban squatter population.[6] Many were drawn from the rural areas by the possibilities opened up by the government's industrialization policy and by the affirmative action programme of the New Economic Policy (NEP) crafted in the aftermath of the May 13 'race riots'. Rural ethnic Malays were particularly urged to 'modernize' and gravitate to urban centres in order to dissolve the colonial legacy of a spatial duality between the non-Malay urban dwellers and Malay rural *kampung* residents (cf. Kahn 2006). Ong has characterized this milieu as essentially marked by an ethnic-based governmentality buttressed further by an Islamic governmentality. As she puts it, 'an extensive system of graduated sovereignty has come into effect as the government has put more investment into the bio-political improvement of the Malays, awarding them rights and benefits that are largely denied to the Chinese and Indian minorities' (Ong 1999: 214ff). The strategy of the NEP was to help create a sizeable middle and entrepreneurial Malay class to offset the perceived economic imbalance of wealth hitherto held by foreign companies and ethnic Chinese. During his 22-years long tenure as Prime Minister, Mahathir Mohamad initiated or allowed a bundle of policies that helped to accelerate that transformation.[7] With the expiry of the NEP in 1990, the Mahathir Administration announced a New Development Policy (1990) and, subsequently, a New Vision Policy (2001). The key impetus was to propel Malaysia into a developed country status by the year 2020 on the platform of a neo-liberal economic programme requiring the country's economic and social orientation to be re-aligned towards the disciplinary demands and work ethics of a 'privatization' and 'pro-growth' trajectory. Alongside the programmatic and infrastructural morphing of the country was the task of mobilizing a citizenry supposedly fettered by their divisive ethnic origins and divergent desires. For this purpose, the Mahathir Administration recuperated an earlier anti-colonial formulation of *Bangsa Malaysia* (Malaysian Race) to signify the imaginary of a unified trans-racial community and become incorporated together with the vocabulary of 'developmentalism'. With the country's buoyant GNP and developmental projections as a ballast, the Administration further embarked on numerous large-scale and flagship infrastructural (particularly in transportation and communications) and construction projects that required large reserves of cheap and seasonal foreign migrant workers sourced from neighbouring Southeast Asian and South Asian countries. Many companies also capitalized on the liberal migrant labour policy to replace Indian labourers who had worked on their plantations for decades. Subsequently, they were displaced into town centres, particularly in and around Kuala Lumpur, to seek alternative livelihoods in the lower rungs of the urban economy and becoming an underclass of urban Indians.[8]

The fluid labour flows also overlapped with concerted efforts by City Hall to rationalize and plan more comprehensively Kuala Lumpur's spatial morphology through the introduction of a structure plan in 1984. It was from this period that civil society groups have noted that the forced eviction of urban squatters became comparatively more intense and unrelenting as the authorities laboured to contain and manage their spatial expansion within the city administrative limits (e.g., Syed Husin Ali 1998; Mohammad Nasir Hashim 1994; Urban Resource Unit 2002). In these eviction exercises, civil society groups rallied to the support of the squatters leading to numerous face-offs and altercations with the developers or city authorities, and frequent arrests by the police. Basically, they contend that their rights as 'urban pioneers' (rather than squatters), in accordance with international human rights standards, should be recognized and extensive consultations be held before any re-location exercise is conducted. Nevertheless, by the 1990s, the pathological notion of a 'squatter-free city' as a spatial signifier of modernity firmly entered into the official discourse. It worked interchangeably with the teleological and utopic discourse of transforming Malaysia into a 'fully developed' nation by the year 2020 (Vision 2020). Whilst there exists plentiful literature that offers positive appraisals of the developmental progress of the country, more critically nuanced studies also exist (e.g., Gomez and Jomo 2000). They essentially characterize these changes as contributing towards the rise of 'exclusionary populism and clientelist patronage made manifest in a stream of state positions, licenses, contracts, generous lending, and, in the 1990s, a skewed privatization of state assets, followed by re-nationalization amounting to bailouts' (Case 2004: 32). In particular, intense contestations over political largesse and patronage have given rise to endemic 'money politics' within United Malay National Organization (UMNO), the dominant political party of *Barisan Nasional* and replicated to a lesser extent in its other partner parties.

During his tenure as Prime Minister, Mahathir Mohamad was moreover infamously embroiled in two major Constitutional crises that saw the weakening in the powers of the Monarchy (in 1983–1984 and 1992) and the Judiciary (in 1988). Another landmark event which has impacted on the landscape of religious pluralism involved amendments to Article 121 (1A) of the Federal Constitution which removed the jurisdiction of the civil courts over Islamic matters consonant with revising the legal system to make it 'more Islamic'. The amendment effectively created two spheres of jurisdiction between the civil and Syariah criminal courts. Anecdotal evidence suggests that there is a correlation between the kind of developmentalist entrepreneurships noted earlier and the rise of a triumphalist Malay-Muslim public persona which, in accentuating the centrality of a range of Islamic jurisprudence, beliefs and practices, has also impinged on the sensibilities and mundane spaces of non-Muslims in unsettling ways. These range from prohibitions of the use of certain words like *Allah* and *doa* (prayer) in non-Islamic literature, the difficulties of non-Muslims in obtaining land for the construction of places of worship and burial grounds, to the widespread removal and destruction of Hindu roadside shrines and small temples ostensibly for urban re-development. Similarly, recent local council regulations require non-Muslim dog-owners to secure letters of consent from their Muslim neighbours before they can apply for licenses (e.g., Yeoh 2005; Suaram Human Rights Annual Reports). By contrast, the construction of new and conspicuously elaborate mosques or the extensive renovations of older ones to cater for urban Muslims have increasingly dominated the Kuala Lumpur cityscape.[9]

Accusations of an inequitable dispensation of business opportunities to earn a living have sometimes percolated to the realm of commercial street spaces in the capital city. For instance, in a recent study conducted in a thriving and cosmopolitan South Asian business enclave of the old precinct of Kuala Lumpur (Yeoh 2008), I discovered that Indian-Hindu street traders were particularly irate about the manner in which City Hall had disproportionately allocated trading lots to them in comparison to Malay-Muslim traders in a locality where they had conducted their business for several years without any hassle. The experience was particularly poignant as the episode unfolded during a rare temporal conjunction of two religious festivities – between the Hindu festival of *Deepavali* and the Islamic *Hari Raya Puasa* – and when tourist authorities and key political leaders had made great play of the joint celebrations (i.e., 'Deepa-Raya') as an indexical sign of the interreligious harmony and multiculturalism of the country as a whole. Instead of being allowed to have a significant presence in the historically mixed enclave, they were advised to shift their trading to the traditional Indian enclaves of Sentul and Brickfields.

Attempts at the moral and disciplinary re-shaping of the cosmopolitan cityspace of Kuala Lumpur have not spared the personal and intimate spaces of urban Muslims either. Several amendments in Syariah criminal laws since the 1990s have strengthened the enforcement of the moral surveillance and punishment of Muslims who transgress a range of Islamic rulings. These transgressions include straying from obligatory fasting during the holy month of *Ramadhan*, consuming *haram* (forbidden) substances like alcoholic beverages, dressing that exposes one's *aurat* (modesty) in public, and being deemed to be in close physical proximity (*khalwat*) to members of the opposite sex who are not relatives. In the case of *khalwat* involving a non-Muslim, he/she can be detained by the police for further questioning, an action which is problematic from the standpoint of secular civil rights (Yeoh 2005). Islamic departments at state level also monitor closely the activities of myriad grassroots-based Islamic groups that follow or resemble prohibited Shi'ite and other 'deviant' leanings for the purpose of weeding them out and sending them for rehabilitation.

Since the 1980s, the number of civil society groups in Malaysia has risen steadily, many arguably in response to the perceived contradictions of the developmentalist trajectory noted earlier (e.g., Weiss and Saliha 2003). Others were formed with an explicit human rights perspective in a milieu when Mahathir's trademark 'strong authoritarianism' often meant a low priority for civil and political rights in the pursuit of transforming Malaysia into a 'developed country'. Using a battery of laws enacted during the British colonial era to combat communist and anti-British nationalist activism, Mahathir Mohamad infamously invoked the

Internal Security Act (ISA) 1960 for the detention without trial of over a hundred individuals comprising an array of political dissidents, educationists, social activists and evangelists in October 1987 supposedly for national security reasons (code-named 'Operation Lalang') but which commentators read as an exhibition of predatory strength against his political challengers.[10] Nonetheless, members of the opposition political parties together with human rights-based civil society groups have persisted with voicing out their concerns by periodically organizing candle-light vigils, public rallies and street demonstrations at key historical and symbolic public sites in Kuala Lumpur. The reasons for organizing these events have been diverse and range from protests over fuel or toll hikes, building of dams, closing down of Chinese vernacular schools, forced evictions of squatters, commemorating Labour Day to highlighting human rights violations whether occurring in Malaysia or beyond the nation-state borders. Given the strict laws on public assembly and the reluctance of the police to issue permits, these events do not usually last long and require skilful on-the-street negotiations with the presiding police officer for the day. Moreover, turnouts have not usually been large because of public apathy and fear of reprisals. Nor are these events reported favourably in the mainstream media given the state of current press legislations and media ownership entanglement with member parties of the ruling coalition. Though muted in the past, the advent of the Internet has helped to foment stronger 'public' expressions of dissatisfactions with the perceived rise of ethno-religious (Malay-Muslim) supremacy and the undermining of civil liberties as enshrined in the Federal Constitution, albeit anonymously. This, in turn, has attracted thinly veiled threats of recriminations from various politicians and religious leaders should the status quo be challenged.

Nevertheless, in recent years the overlapping effects of the differential legacies of political authoritarianism, legal dualism and a triumphant ethno-nationalist ethos have led to an emboldening of sections of the Malaysian citizenry. For instance, under the rubric of the constitutional guarantee of the freedom of religion, civil society groups comprising both non-Muslims and Muslims have questioned the legality and wisdom of punitive actions taken by Islamic religious authorities prosecuting Malay-Muslims who choose to renounce Islam in order to embrace other faiths or hinder individuals from re-converting to their original faiths after failed mixed marriages with Muslim spouses. In other cases, unilateral decisions by spouses to embrace Islam and subsequently seeking the endorsement of the Syariah court in dissolving their marriages conducted under civil law or obtaining custody of children without the consent of the convert's partner has raised alarm and inter-religious tensions. In these liminal human entanglements, the dominant position of the civil courts has been to accede to the jurisdiction of the Syariah court. A number of these high profile cases had involved Indian-Hindus and contributed to a heightened sense of siege among this particular community.[11] For these groups, marginalization is read not merely as occurring in the public realm of education, work opportunities and earning potential but now also proceeding intrusively and unrelentingly into the private domain of religious beliefs and cultural practices.

Merdeka celebrations and street rallies

By any measure, 2007 was an extraordinary historic and performative moment for Malaysian citizens. Not only did it see an elaborate year-long official celebration of the golden anniversary marking the political independence (*Merdeka*) of the Federation of Malaya from Great Britain, the last quarter of the year also witnessed three anti-establishment public rallies almost in quick succession that caught nationwide, if not worldwide, media attention.[12] Whilst each rally was organized to highlight specific agendas and galvanized different kinds of protestors, they were nevertheless emotively linked by an undercurrent of discontent with the state of affairs in the Malaysian polity and societal fabric.

In late September, the Bar Council defied a police ban to proceed with a 'Walk for Justice'. Some 2,000 individuals – most of whom were lawyers wearing their trademark black suits – congregated in the distant administrative city of Putrajaya and walked 3.5 kilometres in the afternoon sun from the Palace of Justice to the Prime Minister's Department to submit a memorandum calling for the setting up of a Royal Commission of Inquiry to address scandals compromising the independence of the judiciary. This was in response to Anwar Ibrahim releasing a 14-minute amateur video clip recorded, serendipitously, several years earlier of a handphone conversation between lawyer V.K. Lingam and a former Chief Justice in brokering senior judiciary appointments. Although the march was unprecedented in the history of the Bar, coverage in the mainstream media was muted, though it was well covered in the independent online newspaper, *Malaysiakini* and several blogs.[13]

In early November, despite again a police ban on the rally, perimeter roadblocks and the use of water cannons to dissuade marchers from passing through, the Coalition for Clear and Fair Elections (or *Bersih* literally meaning 'clean' in Malay), a group bunching together 67 opposition political parties and civil society groups, was able to mobilize an estimated 40,000 to the streets of Kuala Lumpur historic city centre. Their rendezvous was the Palace to submit a memorandum to the King appealing for his intervention in ensuring a free and fair general election believed then to be imminent. Inspired by the media visuals of the 'Saffron Revolution' of Buddhist monks in Burma a few weeks earlier, participants and supporters were encouraged to wear yellow as a symbolic gesture for freedom. Anecdotal narratives suggest that the sight of a sea of yellow-clad men, women and children of different ethnicities forged a powerful cohesive imagery for many who witnessed the episode either firsthand or on the Internet. Two weeks later, the equally significant rally organized by Hindraf took place, once again in the commercial district of Kuala Lumpur. However, before I go into the specifics of this historic gathering, I will digress to draw attention to an aspect of the avalanche of highly publicized state-organised activities for the *Merdeka* celebrations in order to set the immediate context for the significance of this particular rally.

The golden anniversary of *Merdeka* provided a strategic temporal opportunity for a variety of disparate agendas. One salient strand entailed intertwining the trope of a centripetal nationalist pride with the expansive benefits of consumptive tourism. Thus, the slogan that was coined and promoted globally by the

Figure 7.1 Images of the 50th Anniversary poster.

government authorities, even before 2007 was ushered in, conjoined the patriotic 'Celebrating 50 years of Nationhood' with 'Visit Malaysia Year 2007'. The 'multiculturalism' of the country's diverse Asian ethnic and religious ancestries was represented by a multi-coloured graphic of the national flower of Malaysia – a hibiscus flower – and underscored by another slogan authored a few years earlier, 'Malaysia, Truly Asia'. In more tangible terms, this translated into the target of attracting 20.1 million foreign tourists to spend RM44.5 billion (US$13.9 billion) in the country.[14] Kuala Lumpur assumed a central importance in metonymically showcasing the developmental progress of the country to the world. Months earlier, in addition to the streets of Kuala Lumpur being spruced up with eye-catching and tourist-friendly signages, a campaign was launched to acquaint a broad range of personnel coming into contact with cash-laden tourists with social etiquette befitting the auspicious occasion. Launching off the *Merdeka* celebrations, the Prime Minister rode a 60-metre high Ferris wheel especially erected for the occasion. Oriented towards the iconic Kuala Lumpur City Centre (KLCC) Twin Towers and dubbed the 'Eye on Malaysia', the sponsors promised a ride that offers an 'unforgettable glimpse of Kuala Lumpur'.[15]

The trope of 'multiculturalism' further required that the festivals of the major faiths in the country be listed out for easy identification.[16] The first religious event publicized was the Hindu festival of *Thaipusam* (usually occurring in early February) held in honour of the male deity, Murugan, and as celebrated in the Batu Caves temple complex situated on the outskirts of Kuala Lumpur city (a distance of about 12 kilometres). Over the decades, the Batu Caves temple complex, built around scenic limestone outcrops has increasingly attracted large crowds of pilgrims (and tourists) to become arguably the single largest religious gathering in the country. Crowds in excess of a million have been reported. For the 2007 celebrations, what was a striking departure from the past was the extensive publicity undertaken by state authorities to promote the event as a 'colorful spectacle'. Visual images of pilgrims in a state of trance carrying conspicuous *kavadis* (ritual burden) adorned tourist brochures and billboards. Subsequent mainstream newspaper reports estimated the crowds to be in the region of 1.2 million. More significantly, and in a genre of reporting (accompanied by photographs) that was repeated throughout the year for all other state-identified religious festivals, the generic message conveyed was the exuberance and vitality of a harmonious multi-ethnic and multi-religious Malaysia.

The following year, in 2008, the tone had shifted radically. Two days before the festival, at a highly publicized function, Prime Minister Abdullah Badawi had unexpectedly declared *Thaipusam* to be a public holiday for the Federal Territories of Kuala Lumpur and Putrajaya, an act that was supposedly historically significant if weighed against nearly four decades of unsuccessful appeals by a host of Indian and Hindu-based organizations, including the MIC, for *Thaipusam* to be a national holiday in addition to *Deepavali* (Festival of Lights).[17] However, instead of a collective triumph for Hindus in the country, the gesture by the Prime Minister in that particular moment was assessed by his detractors as hollow. Indeed, for several weeks before the announcement, SMS messages and Internet postings had been in wide circulation appealing to Hindus to boycott the Batu Caves temple complex. The recipients were advised to commemorate *Thaipusam* at other major shrines as a protest against the current MIC leadership. In the evenings, ensconced in the safety of sacred spaces, Hindu temples around the country became

Figure 7.2 Online reporting of the Hindraf Rally (with permission from Premesh Chandran).

venues for lively discussions on the troubled events of recent months. The strategy of the politics of numbers worked for the crowds at the Batu Caves temple complex for *Thaipusam* that year was estimated to be only around the lowly figure of 300,000. Despite claims by the MIC leadership, eye-witness accounts by various Hindu-based civil society groups disputed the alleged large crowds gathered at Batu Caves reported in the mainstream media, contending that they had resorted to recycling tele-visual images of the previous year to bolster their refutations of the relevance and effectiveness of the SMSes.[18]

What had catalyzed this course of action was the proximate sequence of events that culminated on street protests modelled on Gandhi's tactics of mass civil disobedience. On the Sunday morning of 25 November 2007, despite police roadblocks since several days before, an estimated 30,000 Indian protestors congregated in various localities around the iconic KLCC Twin Towers. Hindraf leaders had spent months mobilizing Indians around the country to witness the handing of a petition containing 100,000 signatures over to the British High Commissioner.[19] The petition requested Queen Elizabeth II to appoint a Queen's Counsel for a class action suit filed a few months earlier in August by lawyer P. Waythamoorthy (and chairman of Hindraf) against the British government at the Royal Court of Justice in London. The suit sought compensation to the amount of US$4 trillion – computed at US$2 million for every ethnic Indian currently residing in the country – for transporting Indians from their homeland to British Malaya as indentured labourers and thereafter allowing them to be exploited for over 150 years. The petition further alleged that the postcolonial Malaysian government has in effect practised a systematic programme of 'ethnic cleansing' through their racist discriminatory policies and wilful neglect of Indians since Independence. Many ordinary Hindus – men and women – had prepared for the occasion by going for temple prayers and fasting. Disturbing news of the inappropriateness of the demolition of a Hindu temple in Klang by state authorities just days before another major Hindu festival (*Deepavali*) was held further strengthened their resolve to highlight the urgency of their predicament to the Malaysian public.

In attempts to pre-empt the street protest, authorities had decided to arrest three key Hindraf leaders, including Waythamoorthy, under the Sedition Act (1948) a couple of days before the event. Despite being denied a police permit for legal assembly, the organizers decided to press ahead. The mainstream media carried warnings by police authorities that street protestors would be 'arrested on sight' armed with a little used court order. Even with police roadblocks around the city to stem the in-flow, several thousand Indians residing outside of Kuala Lumpur managed to reach the capital city. Many had gravitated to the Batu Caves temple complex for prayers. Before dawn, the Federal Reserve Unit (FRU) descended onto the place and herded the crowd – many of whom were carrying placards of images of Gandhi – within the temple gates and locked them in. Tear gas and chemical-laced water cannons were directed at the crowd gathered inside the temple to quell their protests.[20] Over 400 demonstrators were arrested of which 99 were subsequently charged for illegal assembly and 31 for alleged attempted murder of a policeman and causing damage to public property.

Later in the day, the same extraordinary scenes of Indians facing off with the FRU lasting several hours were repeated in several localities of the perimeter cordon thrown around the British High Commission. The images of Indian protestors being repeatedly sprayed by water cannons and numerous canisters of tear gas, only to re-group elsewhere to advance again were captured by an array of camera hand phones and video cameras, and disseminated widely in the Internet. Apart from local online newspaper, *Malaysiakini*, and the global news broadcasting entity, *Al-Jazeera*, which carried live coverage of the event, several bloggers uploaded updates onto their portals. Many viewers were unaccustomed to the sight of ordinary Indians carrying placards and demonstrating in large numbers. This contrasted with the more common media visuals propagated during *Thaipusam* – of Hindu pilgrims silently congesting the city streets at dawn whilst accompanying on foot a chariot bearing the deity, Murugan, on their way to the Batu Caves temple complex situated several kilometres away on the outskirts of Kuala Lumpur. Quite significantly, the Hindraf rally troubled the racial stereotype of Indians as 'highly religious', servile, compliant and non-confrontational to the status quo on the one hand, and the sanitized and celebratory versions of multiculturalism as imagined by the state authorities on the other. By foregrounding Indian collective civil disobedience and resistance in the eminently public spaces of the capital city, the organizers of the rally successfully collapsed together in dramatic fashion both the historical contradictions and continuity of the colonial past and postcolonial present, a claim not lost to many as suggested by the immediate backlash it received.

In the days and weeks following the rally, the mainstream media carried stories that essentially sought to discredit and undermine the claims of Hindraf leaders as well as criminalize them. Prime Minister Abdullah Badawi accused Hindraf of wanting 'to destroy the country' by tarnishing peaceful co-existence between various religious and ethnic groups with its 'baseless allegations' and scaring foreign investors away. MIC leaders rebutted as patently untrue that there has been no progress made although they also conceded that much more could be done to uplift the working class Indian community. Hindraf was also said to be linked to the militant Tamil Tigers of Sri Lanka, an allegation denied by its leaders. In response to pleas from Hindraf, a request from the Chief Minister of Tamil Nadu (India) to intervene was publicly rebuked by a Minister of the Prime Minister's Department as meddling in Malaysian affairs.[21] With the moral panic of the breakdown of Malaysian society established by the mainstream media, five key Hindraf leaders were detained under the ISA in mid-December as posing a threat to national security. Several civil society groups, whilst initially ambivalent about the mono-religious and dramatically racialized claims of Hindraf, had not participated in the 25 November rally, but nevertheless rallied together to condemn the use of the ISA as unjust and unwarranted. The spontaneous gathering of largely working class Indians braving formidable odds was read as a legitimate 'cry of the dispossessed' requiring remedial rather than punitive action by the government.[22] Several letters posted to *Malaysiakini* and online discussions on well-known English-language Malaysian blogs echoed fears declared in the mainstream media of the country possibly descending into religious sectarian politics in the manner of other countries in the region if the government authorities did not take firm action. However, in contrast to the monologic discourse evident in the mainstream media, uncensored online debates were more robust and allowed readers to assess the contesting claims posted by anonymous contributors.

The ISA detentions did not dissipate the groundswell of Indian discontent which became eventually well publicized through the media as *Makkal Sakti*. In early January 2008, P. Waythamoorthy, who had gone on self-imposed exile in London, announced that another peaceful assembly would be held outside Parliament on the weekend of Valentine's Day. A parade of mostly children would gift the Prime Minister red and yellow roses as a symbolic petition requesting him to release the Hindraf leaders. For dramatic effect, the 5-year old daughter of Waythamoorthy had made public a letter she had written to the Prime Minister in mid-January requesting him to be present for the ceremony several weeks later.[23] The unreciprocated silence of the Prime Minister to the letter was taken as another proof of the callous attitude of the country's foremost leader.

During this period, the MIC leadership did not remain idle. Realizing that the tide was possibly turning against them, they laboured to re-assert their moral legitimacy to politically represent Indians in the country. Several public relations events at various venues (including Indian commercial enclaves) were organized with the Prime Minister in attendance to assuage perceptions of Indian marginalization and to discredit the claims of Hindraf. It was in one of these events dubbed 'An evening with the Prime Minister' held at a local stadium, that Abdullah Ahmad Badawi announced that *Thaipusam* would be a public holiday in the Federal Territories of Kuala Lumpur and Putrajaya in addition to the states of Perak, Penang, Johore, Selangor and Negri Sembilan where Hindus are populous.

One of the key factors fuelling the decision to boycott *Thaipusam* in early 2008 was the punitive actions taken by the heavily armed FRU against Indian-Hindu men and women gathered at the Batu Caves Temple complex in November 2007. Visual images and anecdotes of the manner in which the FRU had shown wanton disrespect for and desecrated Hindu sacred spaces were circulated widely through cellphones and by word of mouth. That the MIC leadership had not spoken out unequivocally against these actions confirmed that they were aligning themselves firmly on the side of the oppressors. During the General Election campaign period, one of the rallying cries of the amorphous and essentially leaderless *Makkal Sakti* movement and echoed by the Hindraf leaders was for the Indian electorate to vote for any opposition party candidate offered in their constituencies. Despite public optimism by Barisan Nasional leaders that the Indian population has not been won over by the claims of Hindraf, not only was the MIC political leadership decimated at the twelfth General Election but a historic ten Indians in the Opposition party coalition were elected into Parliament.[24] Legal adviser M. Manoharan, one of the Hindraf leaders detained under the ISA, was elected into the Selangor state assembly.

Conclusion

Fears and anxiety that a repeat of the tragic 'race riots' of May 13, 1969 then sparked off by a similar outcome in the Kuala Lumpur electoral results, did not materialize. Optimist commentators hailed that the 'ghosts of May 13' were finally laid to rest. In the immediate weeks and months following the 2008 General Elections, cohorts of political analysts, academics and ordinary Malaysians alike were engrossed in dissecting and plumbing the voting results in order to discern the depth and durability of the ground shifts in voter sentiments.

Indeed, these sentiments were quickly reciprocated in a number of ways. Noteworthy has been the manner in which key leaders of Barisan Nasional has adopted a comparatively more reconciliatory tone than before, some even apologizing for their past strident words and actions. Although facing calls from Mahathir Mohamad and some of his own party members (UMNO) to resign because of the poor election results, Prime Minister Abdullah Badawi has resolved to stay on until 2010 before passing on the reins to his deputy. He promised to make policy changes to address some of the key concerns that have attracted steady criticism over the past few years. Significantly, the first symbolic step he took involved rebuilding the independence and integrity of the judiciary. In April, the Prime Minister's Department further announced that non-Muslims intending to convert to Islam should inform their families beforehand.[25] Several weeks later, an unprecedented Syariah High Court decision allowed a Muslim convert to renounce Islam and revert to her original faith, Buddhism.[26] Members of *Barisan Nasional* have joined the calls of opposition political parties and civil society groups for amendments of the Printing and Publications Act in order to allow for greater press freedom. Even the MIC leadership has begun appealing for the Hindraf Five to be released from ISA detention.

In terms of political representation, more Indians were appointed to prominent leadership positions at the state legislature level, particularly in states won over by the opposition parties, now renamed *Pakatan Rakyat* (People's Coalition). In these states, civil society groups continue to press for the re-instatement of local council elections and for greater transparency and accountability in the appointment of councilors, awarding of contracts, project approvals and so forth. However, these states also face financial and infrastructural challenges as a number of Federal-funded projects have been shelved or put on hold. Other actions took on more circumscribed forms. For instance, in contrast to their earlier position which painted bloggers as threats to national interests, a number of deposed Cabinet Ministers have resorted to setting up personal blogs in the manner of celebrity opposition politicians presumably to assuage their position and to reach younger voters in preparation for the next General Elections.

In the first Parliamentary seating held in early May 2008 the signs of a more robust and keenly contested legislature given the present distribution of power were promisingly indexical of a nascent bi-party political order. In the *Pakatan Raykat*-dominated territory of Kuala Lumpur city, civil society groups have expressed cautious optimism of the dilution of a racialized social order and a movement towards a more trans-ethnic cosmopolitanism that already exists in part in everyday social interactions in juxtaposition to the state's impetus of inculcating a technocratic and developmentalist version of cosmopolitanism. Moreover, they hope to see the mitigation, if not the reversal, of the dominant *habitus* to resort to punitive actions in dissuading divergent expressions of democratic ideals and institutions even whilst celebrating the rich multicultural assets of the country in the same breath.

The initial euphoria over the General Elections results has now abated and the pragmatics of routine governance as embodied in policy debates between the *Barisan Nasional* and *Pakatan Rakyat* political rank-and-file have now taken centre stage in Parliamentary and State Legislative proceedings. For the marginalized in Malaysian society, including working class Tamil-Hindus, whether these fractious ruminations will translate into substantive material changes in the long term is as yet inconclusive. For now (as of July 2008), only time will tell whether the confluence of the massive street demonstrations of 2007 coinciding with the 50th Merdeka anniversary celebrations have ushered in a new political milieu in Malaysia. At least one thing is certain however. Their historic place in Malaysian political folklore, like the iconic May 13 'race riots', is assured. They offer a dramatic counter-narrative of multi-sectoral public dissent and civil disobedience on the streets of Kuala Lumpur.

Notes

1 This was the headline of *Sunday Star*, 9 March 2008, an English daily controlled by the Malaysian Chinese Association, a member of the ruling coalition, *Barisan Nasional*. In contrast, the editor of the independent online newspaper, *Malaysiakini*, called it a 'perfect storm'.

2 The key members of the *Barisan Nasional* are the ethnic-based political parties, United Malay National Organisation (UMNO), Malaysian Chinese Association (MCA) and

Malaysian Indian Congress (MIC). Preliminary analysis indicates ethnic vote swings against the *Barisan Nasional* in Peninsular Malaysia as follows: Indian 35 per cent, Chinese 30 per cent, and Malay 5 per cent. See 'Making sense of the political tsunami', *Malaysiakini*, 11 March 2008.

3 For a useful history of early Kuala Lumpur, see Gullick 2000.

4 For an analysis of the 1969 General Election results, refer to Ratnam and Milne.

5 See table in Johnstone 1983: 260.

6 Elsewhere, I have examined how these demographic changes have impacted upon the Hindu religious practices of a Tamil squatter settlement embedded within a cluster of other settlements on the periphery of Kuala Lumpur (Yeoh 2001a).

7 See Khoo 2003 and Yao 2003 for discussions of Mahathir Mohamad's palpable imprints on the Malaysian polity.

8 See Nadarajah 2004, Loh 2003 and Willford 2006 for recent updates.

9 Arguably, a media event that singularly embodied this ethos was captured on live television during the UMNO Youth Assembly of 2006. Viewers saw the UMNO Youth president (who is also a Cabinet Minister) raising a *keris* (Malay sword) in the opening ceremonies followed by a train of speeches given by delegates that critics argued were racist and seditious in content and tone. Although the leadership attempted later to explain away the act as harmless and an expression of cultural sovereignty, the incident continued to be salient on the Internet and was recalled during the General Election campaign period.

10 Since the 'September 11 incident' in New York, civil society groups have noted that the ISA has been invoked by the Malaysian government to detain Muslim individuals belonging to 'deviationist' and 'religious extremist' groups in the country (see Suaram Human Rights Reports).

11 Space only allows me to recount in brief one major legal case that unfolded in 2007. In May 2007, a majority judgement by the Federal Court ruled against Lina Joy's attempt to remove the word 'Muslim' from her national identity card. Lina Joy was formerly a Muslim with the name of Azlina Jailani but who had converted to Christianity in February 1997. Joy then applied to the National Registration Department (NRD) to change her name on the grounds that she no longer professed Islam and had accepted the Christian faith. The NRD rejected her application in August 1997. She then brought her case to the High Court but was decided against in April 2001. The judge argued that because an ethnic Malay is defined by the constitution as, among other things, 'a person who professes the religion of Islam' and since she is an ethnic Malay she cannot renounce Islam. In September 2005, her request to change the religion designated on her national identity card was again denied by the Court of Appeal. She then appealed the decision further to the Federal Court which ruled that jurisdiction over the matter remained with the Syariah Court.

12 In 1963, when the former British colonies of Sabah, Sarawak and Singapore joined the Federation, the name was changed to the Federation of Malaya.

13 The Royal Commission of Inquiry was subsequently set up and the report of its findings released two months after the General Elections. It confirmed that the video clip was genuine and recommended legal action against those implicated in the phone conversations.

14 See 'Malaysia beckons', *Star Weekender*, 17 March 2007.

15 See advert in *Sunday Star*, 29 April 2007.

16 Namely, Buddhism, Christianity, Hinduism, Islam and the harvest festivals of the indigenous peoples of East and Peninsular Malaysia.

17 *Deepavali* was probably proclaimed a national holiday because the early MIC leadership consisted mainly of people with North Indian ancestry, and it had strong links with the Indian Congress.

18 See 'Celebrations unaffected by SMSes', *The Star*, 24 January 2008.

19 Hindraf is a coalition of 30 Hindu-based organizations committed to 'peaceful struggle

in the pursuit of justice for the poor and underclass ethnic Malaysian Indians'. See their website at http://www.hindraf.org/.

20 For images of the incident posted on a well-known Malaysian blog, see http://www.jeffooi. com/2007/11/hindraf_rally_ethnic_minority_1.php. Refer also to http://www.tamilnation. org/diaspora/malaysia/071125protest.htm.

21 *Interalia*, see 'Don't butt in, says Nazri', *The Star*, 29 November 2007; 'Government doing its best for Indians, says PM', *New Sunday Times*, 2 December 2007; 'Samy: We've always told the truth about Indians', *The Star*, 3 December 2007; 'Hindraf heads with ties to terrorists to be watched', *New Straits Times*, 8 December 2007; 'Hindraf can wreck stability', *The Star*, 10 December 2007; 'Indians have done well, says Samy', *The Star*, 10 December 2007; 'Hindraf hijacked by opposition', *The Star*, 23 December 2007.

22 For example, see 'Hindraf rally: A plea of the dispossessed?', *Aliran Monthly*, Vol. 27, No. 10, 2007.

23 See '160 held after illegal rose rally', *Sunday Star*, 17 February 2008.

24 See 'Trust Barisan, Indians told', *The Star*, 4 February 2008; 'Samy still very much in control of MIC', *The Star*, 22 February 2008; 'Khir: Indians are loyal to BN', *Starmetro*, 5 March 2008.

25 See 'Religious bodies and Bar laud move', *The Star*, 11 April 2008.

26 See 'Allowed to revert', *The Star*, 9 May 2008.

References

www.aliran.com
www.cij.malaysia.org
www.malaysiakini.com
www.suaram.net

Ali, S.H. (1998) 'Squatters and forced evictions in Malaysia'. In K. Fernandes (ed.) *Forced Evictions and Housing Rights Abuses in Asia*, Karachi: CP City Press.

Appadurai, A. (1996) *Modernity at large. Cultural dimensions of globalization*, Minneapolis: University of Minnesota Press.

Azizah, K. (1994) *Coping with slums in Malaysia*, Bangkok: International Labor Organization.

Case, W. (2004) 'Testing Malaysia's pseudo-democracy', in E.T. Gomez (ed.) *The state of Malaysia: Ethnicity, equity and reform*, London: Routledge.

De Certeau, M. (1984) *The practice of everyday life*, Berkeley: University of California Press.

Gomez, E.T. and K.S. Jomo (2000) *Malaysia's political economy: Politics, patronage and profits*, Cambridge: Cambridge University Press.

Gullick, J.M. (2000) *A history of Kuala Lumpur, 1856–1939*, Kuala Lumpur: MBRAS.

Harper, T. (1999) *The end of empire and the making of British Malaya*, Cambridge: Cambridge University Press.

Hashim, M.N. (1994) *Peneroka bandar menuntut keadilan*, Kuala Lumpur: Daya Komunikas.

Jain, R.K. (1970) *South Indians on the plantation frontier in Malaya*, New Haven: Yale University Press.

Johnstone, M. (1983) 'Housing policy and the urban poor in Peninsular Malaysia', *Third World Planning Review*, Vol. 5, No. 3: 249–271.

Kahn, J. (2006) *Other Malays. Nationalism and cosmopolitanism in the modern Malay world*, Singapore: Singapore University Press.

Kahn, J. and Loh K.W. (eds) (1992) *Fragmented visions: Culture and politics in contemporary Malaysia*, Honolulu: University of Hawaii Press.

Khoo, B.T. (2003) *Beyond Mahathir. Malaysian politics and its discontents*, London: Zed.

Kua, K.S. (ed.) (2005) *Policing the Malaysian police*, Petaling Jaya: Suara Komunikasi.

—— (2007) *May 13. Declassified documents in the Malaysian riots of 1969*, Petaling Jaya: Suaram.

Lefebvre, H. (1991 [1974]) *The production of space*, Oxford: Blackwell.

Lim, H.K. (1978) *The evolution of the urban system in Malaya*, Kuala Lumpur: Penerbit University Malaya.

Loh, F.K.W. (2003) 'The marginalization of the Indians in Malaysia. Contesting explanations and the search for alternatives', in J.T. Siegel and A.R. Kahin (eds) *Southeast Asia over three generations. Essays presented to Benedict R O'G Anderson*, Ithaca: Southeast Asian Program, Cornell University.

Mandal, S.K. (2003) 'Creativity in protest: Arts workers and the recasting of politics and society in Indonesia and Malaysia', in A. Heryanto and S.K. Mandal (eds) *Challenging authoritarianism in Southeast Asia*, London: Routledge.

Nadarajah, M. (2004) *Another Malaysia is possible and other essays*, Kuala Lumpur: National Office for Human Development.

Ong, A. (1999) *Flexible citizenship. The cultural logics of transnationality*, Durham; London: Duke University Press.

Ramachandran, S. (1994) *Indian plantation labour in Malaysia*, Kuala Lumpur: S. Abdul Majeed & Co.

Ramasamy, P. (1994) *Plantation labor, unions, capital and the state in Peninsular Malaysia*, Oxford: Oxford University Press.

—— (1992) 'Labour control and labour resistance in the plantations of colonial Malaya', *The Journal of Peasant Studies*, Vol. 19, Nos. 3 & 4: 87–105.

Ratnam, K.S. and R. S. Milne (1970) 'The 1969 Parliamentary Election in West Malaysia', *Pacific Affairs*, Vol. 43, No. 2: 203–226.

Stenson, M. (1970) *Industrial conflict in Malaya: Prelude to the Communist revolt of 1948*, Oxford: Oxford University Press.

Stenson, M. (1980) *Race, class and colonialism in West Malaysia. The Indian case*, St Lucia: University of Queensland Press.

Suaram Human Rights Reports for (2003), (2004), (2005), (2006), Petaling Jaya: Suaram Kommunikasi.

Tai, Y. (2000) *Labour unrest in Malaya, 1934–41*, Kuala Lumpur: Institute of Postgraduate Studies and Research, University of Malaya.

Urban Resource Unit (URU) (2002) *Dossier on squatters and evictions in Malaysia*, Kuala Lumpur: URU.

Weiss, M. and S. Hassan (eds) (2003) *Social movements in Malaysia. From moral communities to NGOs*, London: Routledge Curzon.

Willford, Andrew (2006) *Cage of freedom. Tamil identity and the ethnic fetish in Malaysia*, Michigan: University of Michigan Press.

Wong, T.C. (1991) 'From spontaneous settlement to rational land use planning: The case of Kuala Lumpur, Malaysia', *SOJOURN: Journal of social issues in Southeast Asia*, Vol. 6, No. 2: 240–262.

Yao, S. (2003) 'After the Malay Dilemma: The modern Malay subject and cultural logics of national cosmopolitanism in Malaysia', *SOJOURN*: Journal of social issue in Southeast Asia, Vol. 18, No. 2: 201–229.

Yeoh, S.G. (2008) 'Limiting cosmopolitanism: Streetlife Little India, Kuala Lumpur,' in S. Mayaram (ed.) *The other global city*, Abingdon, Oxon: Routledge.

—— (2005) 'Managing sensitivities: Religious pluralism, civil society and inter-faith relations in Malaysia', *The Round Table: The Commonwealth Journal of International Affairs*, Vol. 94, No. 382: 629–640.

—— (2001a) 'Producing locality: Space, houses and public culture in a Hindu festival in Malaysia', *Contributions to Indian Sociology (n.s.)*, Vol. 35, No. 1: 33–64.

—— (2001b) 'Creolized utopias: Squatter colonies and the post-colonial city in Malaysia', *SOJOURN: Journal of Social Issues in Southeast Asia*, Vol. 16, No. 1: 102–124.

8   Campaigning against its eviction

Local trade in new 'world-class' Delhi

Diya Mehra

Since the opening of the Indian economy to global capital in 1991, documenting the meteoric rise of India to the global stage has become an elaborate daily affair in the English language press in India; the country's new achievements are mapped in loving detail as the economic growth rate rises and rises. The press tends to use the singular 'India' in its documentation, erasing quietly the multifarious lives of the Indians who comprise this entity. Until, that is, such multiplicity reacts to the government-supported transformation of their lived-in landscape as the structures of a once quasi-socialist state are removed and a new hardware for a capitalized and transnational global economy is put in its place.

In what follows I will document one such conflict – over the legal eviction of the indigenous wholesale and retail trade economy in Delhi as part of a larger make-over of the city that has been initiated since economic liberalization. I will examine how the eviction process came to be engendered, the campaign of resistance it generated, and the urban politics that came into play as the conflict spread to cover most of the city's geographical and demographic territory. The framework that I shall use is one of asymmetrical contestation – with the asymmetry based on a number of ideological, aesthetic, economic and postcolonial hierarchies – within which the Delhi traders struggled to make space for their political voice even as such hierarchies are reproduced and reformulated in Delhi's neoliberal terrain. This article is based on 15 months of fieldwork in Delhi following events surrounding the campaign, which started at the end of 2005 and continues today.

The urban and economic setting

Delhi is currently one of the richest regions in India, having the second highest per capita income in the country (Delhi Statistical Handbook 2006) and the largest inflows of foreign direct investment for any state (*The Hindu* 2007). This economic prosperity is not new and has a long-standing history, linked in part to the conti-nuous large investments put into the city by colonial and postcolonial governments to ensure that the city they lived in presented an adequate symbolic centrepiece for the Empire and for the Republic. Such infrastructural and monetary investments have meant that business has flocked to the city, where doing business is feasible and profitable. Delhi is the headquarters for many foreign and large national firms, who produce, export and market from their base in the city for regional, national and international markets.

In this, the city's wealth is also linked to a much older, indigenous, mercantile tradition in manufacturing, wholesaling, redistributing, retailing and exporting a large variety of commodities and finished goods. In the post-Independence period, especially after 1970, this segment of the city expanded as the national government put in policies to encourage the import substitution of goods. Within this economic regime, capital goods were to be produced through large-scale public sector and, less commonly, private units, while consumer goods were (and continue to be) manufactured in vast quantities by the informal/small-scale industrial sector, which grew and flourished in places like Delhi (Dutta 2006).

Physically, such trade and manufacture units historically emanate from the Old City,[1] and have spread to sub-centres across the city's concentric rings of progressive urbanization, many of which have established their own product specialties and trade networks. Wholesale traders receive agricultural produce as well as finished goods supplied by the small-scale and informal manufacturing sectors concentrated in the city, and farmers in the hinterland, and often supply to areas all over the country through the city's well linked and dense transport network. The labour force for these, and many non-manufacturing services such as construction which have also flourished as the city has grown, was and is the city's large numbers of urban migrants, many of who are poor.[2]

Since the opening up of the economy in 1991,[3] while this segment of the economy has also benefited from expanded opportunities, its expansion has been overshadowed by the city's new prominence as a classic entrepot for global capital flows (Sassen 1994). This has led to a number of initiatives to reorganize the city's physical and territorial landscape. The 'shift' in Delhi has been to revisualize the physicality, and lifestyle of the city, from problem-ridden Third World to a globalized 'world class' consumptive Disneyland (Zukin 1991). In this process of 'creative destruction' (Brenner and Theodore 2002), on the 'creative' end, there has been territorial expansion of the metropolitan area by legally and physically linking suburbs within a statutory National Capital Region (NCR) hence opening up new lands for development. Furthermore massive new investments in physical and *especially transport infrastructure* – airports, roads, flyovers, a new metro system, and a high-capacity bus system have been made to manage mobility within the new metropolitan area. The partial privatization of civic utilities to provide 'upgraded' and Western-style civic services, and the restoration of heritage sites, and numerous ongoing projects to create signature public spaces for leisure and recreation centred on 'downtown' Delhi have also been undertaken. All these initiatives are seen been to be a part of the conversion to world-class status.

The makeover has also taken the form of multi-stranded attempts to discipline and evict the extant trade/informal economy which occupies prime land and infrastructural space now deemed necessary for other purposes. Since 1991, an estimated 100,000 slum houses (Mehra and Batra 2005), which once provided cheap housing for migrant labour, have been demolished. Small-scale industrial units (numbering around 200,000 in 2006)[4] have also been asked to relocate outside of the city; cycle rickshaw pullers have been banned from centres of commerce such as Old Delhi – Asia's largest wholesale markets – where they are the main form of transport for people and products, and hawkers are to be zoned and confined to a limited number of designated public spaces. As the new economy expands, the old appears in forced retreat, often finding itself in the way of new plans and policies.

Eviction attempts are embedded in multifaceted discursive forms and practice and are instantiated in different circulatory routes, notably the judiciary, planning and legislative authorities, private investors and middle class citizen groups who have come together conjecturally to collectively demand a rehaul of the city. This process began in the early 1990s.

In the beginning there was a breakdown: A narrative on the coming of new capital

The economic changes ushered in by India's Central government in 1991, favour essentially a generic middle class lifestyle of private consumption generated by a framework of neoliberal state policies (Srivastava 2007, Mazzarella 2003). Global capital arrived in Delhi to amplify the already Westernized 'modern' lifestyle of the city's urban moneyed, who, as several researchers have noted, now saw their future increasingly within newly available globalized imaginaries of what the city and country should look like, and who embraced this vision through a turn from an 'unostentatious' culture of saving to one of spending and display (Rajagopal 2001, Chatterjee 2004, Corbridge and Harriss 2001). In the 1990s, the new visual architecture of the city increasingly began to encompass a global technology-driven design vocabulary, visible in the sleek new buildings which sprung up in downtown Delhi and on the city's outskirts in the form of master planned communities fittingly named for example Malibu Estates and Beverly Park. In shops in up-market areas and on the newly available multi-channel cable TV, newly imported lifestyle goods and styles shimmered. Many authors have commented that this efflorescence of globally linked consumptive culture is coterminous with a social shift that situates the 'consuming class' – the new crop of middle class professionals and entrepreneurs – at the normative centre of the urban and national polity, given that their lifestyle, and refashioning of self-identity are both the engine and the image of anticipated and imagined economic growth (Srivastava 2007, Dutta 2006, Mazzarella 2003). It is also because this consumptive lifestyle symbolizes the arrival of the nation as a meaningful player on the cosmopolitan global stage, knowledgeable of its norms and mores.

But simultaneously, Anees Jung, a columnist writes 'the city I chose to settle in has lost its innocence. The face of boomtown Delhi is garish, distorted, at times frightening' (*Asian Age*, May 20, 2001). And: 'Indian malls and supermarkets are strapped for car parking space. The upshot: mayhem and frayed tempers among visitors in congested car parks' (*Outlook*, October 9, 2000).

Mayhem and modernity followed the first inflows of global capital into the city. A total of 4.3 million people, migrants and residents, were added to the city's population between 1991 and 2001 (Delhi Development Authority 2006). The number of private cars on Delhi roads multiplied[5] and Delhi became the second most polluted city in the world after Mexico City. Urban commentators, cited in newspaper columns, popular journals and the academic press, pointed out repeatedly that the infrastructure of the city was failing and for those living with this embodied failure, a constant battle with municipal authorities ensued. Water and electricity shortages that were once considered routine were now greeted with anger and, if they last long enough, violence.

An editorial on road rage in *The Times of India* states:

> It is time that we admit that something is terribly wrong with [the] capital city of India. Too many cars, unbearable pollution, the worst public transport system in the country, perpetual traffic jams, and aggressive speed maniacs. Add to this the relentless stress and drudgery of urban existence and the recipe for rage becomes almost complete.
>
> (May 4, 2000)

The city, it is generally agreed, needs cleaning up.

The most visible appearance of such discourse was in the English language press, which much before television, had a local presence that expanded quickly as newspapers turned to 'lifestyle' coverage in the city pages which not only multiplied in number but also began to include a series of campaigns on neighbourhood and city issues. These could vary in focus, but commonly themes included the neighbourhood presence of potholes, garbage, dysfunctional taps, overgrown parks, leaking sewers on the one hand and a focus on hip and sleek new products, people, restaurants, cinema, 'culture' on the other. The dynamics and interplay of these dual foci – of breakdown and of phoenix-like revival, of emplacement and displacement, the aesthetic and the reviled, local and modern – are crucial to the story of the transformation of the city. They represent the foci through which eviction takes place. On the one hand there appear new priorities, new infrastructure and a new landscape of leisure and international style that, long desired, now for the first time seem possible and accessible; on the other is the stark visibility of the low-cost informal city, that is, as reported in the press, 'illegal', 'encroaching' on government land (all categories); an 'eyesore', unsafe and unsanitary (slums), having 'nuisance' and 'hazardous' value (small-scale industries), are an impediment to pedestrian and motorized traffic (hawkers and cycle rickshaws), which collectively produce the urban chaos that is Delhi.

Apart from aesthetic and symbolic inadequacy, what made the informal economy particularly vulnerable to critique was the fact that although many segments had received governmental encouragement and recognition in the import-substitution decades, they were 'technically' illegal, and hence informal. Having established a monopoly over the land market in 1957, the state planning authorities have subsequently failed to develop adequate low-cost housing – its central mandate – or build enough commercial real estate or industrial estates – hence slums, 'unauthorized' colonies, industries and shops; just as the municipality has not given municipal licenses to hundreds of thousands of hawkers, and more recently cycle rickshaws. Instead, an informal legality, predicated on political clientage, had existed which allowed this part of the city to grow within and around the interstices of the legal, formal, and until recently, solely bureaucratic national capital. With expanded economic opportunity, the informal economy was expanding ever increasingly in and around the city, attracting millions of migrants, just as the middle class city, and perhaps most importantly the political elite were planning a reshaping of the city that was devoid of hitherto existing urban forms and the social, political and economic landscape that they were attached to.

The response

The response to the amplification of the distressed-yet-desired city can in fact be read at many levels. The earliest response came from the Supreme and High Courts of Delhi, who remain till today one of the three most important players in the redesigning and regulation of Delhi's new urban space and fabric, with the other two being the state government and middle class civil society (comprising the English language media, Resident Welfare Associations [RWAs] and NGOs). The courts intervened in the management of the city largely through a new avenue of legal redressal, the Public Interest Litigation (PIL), which had emerged from the excesses of the Emergency of the mid-1970s, when the Supreme Court was seen as having placidly supported Indira's Gandhi's proclamation of a national Emergency entailing a suspension of democratic rights, the forcible sterilization of hundreds of people, and a sharp crackdown on the political opposition and on dissent in general. As many commentators have noted (Sudarshan 1990), in an attempt to 'refurbish' and 'assert' its role, the Supreme Court: first, positioned itself as the saviour of the disadvantaged, who did not usually have access to legal redress and thus to social justice; second, loosened the rules for petitioners, allowing any form of plea, famously even if on a postcard, to be registered as a PIL, even in cases where the petitioner was not directly affected by the issue petitioned about. PIL would be open to 'any public spirited individual or social action group to bring an action for vindication' on their behalf (*M.C. Mehta v. Union of India and Ors* 1985).

In the 1990s, the Supreme and High Courts turned their attention from the disadvantaged to, especially in the case of Delhi, the environment, tripartitely understood here as: first, *the natural environment* including the air, the city's river, its forests and natural reserves; second, *the built urban environment*, that is, traffic, roads, schools, hospitals, buildings, industry, housing, heritage among others; and finally, *the moral environment*, that is, illegality, corruption, inefficiency, incompetence and significantly the stylistic inadequacy of the 'uneducated', who now stood out as plaguing the city – endless slender brown bodies on the city's miles of roads. In some instances the courts took *suo moto* cognizance of issues, in others they were petitioned. The petitioners – environmentalists, NGOs, public interest lawyers, private citizens and RWAs (neighbourhood associations) – are part of new middle class social movements that emerged in the city in the 1990s and who increasingly used the courts to bring attention to governmental inaction and the decline of Delhi's natural, urban and moral habitats. This phenomenon has commonly been described as the rise of 'bourgeois' environmentalism (Baviskar 2003).

Middle class rising: Creating a civil public sphere

In putting out their judgements, the courts have responded to two kinds of litigation. The first is usually considered 'landmark' as in the case of M.C. Mehta, a lawyer whose petitions have had a far reaching impact on environmental regulation in Delhi, (among other areas), including the eviction of informal economies; the second has come from the pleas of RWAs – neighbourhood associations found across Delhi's lower to upper middle class neighbourhoods who take central charge of neighbourhood civic affairs and who have emerged as central players in the middle class environmentalism that has swept the city. This is largely because they provide a dense network of linked groups across the city's 1,483 square kilometres (Delhi Development Authority 2006), and have given the new civic clean-up depth at the neighbourhood level, which although variable in impact, has meant that a clutch of civic issues – greening, local cleaning-up, removal of hawkers, slums, etc. – have received attention across the city. As it is these associations that filed many of the petitions that have led to the current eviction crisis faced by the traders, I will focus on the RWAs, although it is important to remember that the lead case for the petitions has been filed by M.C. Mehta.

RWAs first emerged in the post-Partition era when Delhi expanded massively as it became home to hundreds of thousands of refugees in the population exchange between India and Pakistan. In this context, RWAs were set up to by new refugee settlers to lobby for land, housing and later, civic amenities. Following these formative years, they would remain involved in neighbourhood affairs, interfacing with government and political parties as representatives of the neighbourhood, and often aligning with one party over the other. Since economic liberalization, however, they have seen a powerful boost in their importance in civic affairs, as they are the cornerstone of a new participatory governance initiative, developed by the current Congress Party regime of Delhi's Chief Minister Sheila Dixit, namely, the *Bhagidari*, or stakeholder partnership scheme inaugurated in 2000.

Officially, *Bhagidari* invites a whole host of civil society organizations in the city – such as corporations, NGOs, Market Traders Associations (MTAs) and women's groups among others – to participate in local city governance. However, in reality, most of the *Bhagidars* (stakeholders) are from lower, middle and upper middle class residential neighbourhoods (that is they are RWAs). The poor and parts of the lower-middle class who live in varieties of semi-legal Delhi housing such as slum clusters and slum resettlement colonies, urbanized village areas and unauthorized colonies, are excluded from the initiative because they are not entirely legal according to city law. It is also because, as Mrs Dixit once remarked in a keynote speech, they cannot be put together with 'educated' citizens in the same programme, as they are not comparably as 'knowledgeable' and thus could not effectively participate in the same process. With the level of their life-knowledge and skills they would require their own initiative, which has yet to be unveiled, she added. Also excluded are associations representing the informal trade and manufacturing sector, which are also often semi-legal and which have tended to support the opposition Hindu nationalist Bhartiya Janata Party (BJP).

In the last seven years, *Bhagidari* has meant a series of NGO-curated workshops in which RWAs participate, meeting face-to-face with local civic agencies and officials to whom they can describe their complaints, and from whom they can learn about new schemes and projects such as sewage disposal systems, power distribution plans, water harvesting, recycling, education and health measures. The ingenuity of the plan is that while it does not require the actual transfer of funds to the RWAs, it still cultivates intense neighbourhood involvement and initiative in identifying and solving localized problems and helps RWAs feel that they are participating in government and getting close attention for their local problems. RWAs are often run by a smaller group of residents in any area who, in effect, become a local consultative and regulatory council. They have been known to run neighbourhood projects that are outside of the *Bhagidari* scheme as the ambitions of active RWAs extend beyond their original remit.

Mrs Dixit has, in effect, managed to build a strong, staunchly middle class constituency through the *Bhagidari* scheme, who are also generally appreciative of her efforts to rebuild the city on a more macro scale in terms of improvements in traffic control, general cleanliness, pollution management, the 'greening' of the city, the maintenance of heritage sites, etc., campaigns which RWAs have actively participated in and supported in the English language press.

In the 1980s and 1990s, as the city began to creak from new capital, RWAs from all the four major sections of the city – East, West, North and South – filed a number of petitions in the Supreme and High Courts of Delhi demanding the removal of slum dwellers, rickshaw pullers and hawkers from their neighbourhoods.[6] They also filed petitions against the commercialization of their neighbourhoods, as retail areas once confined to marketplaces began to spread through residential colonies to meet the rising demand for merchandise and commercial space. In the case of slum dwellers, rickshaw pullers and hawkers, the call was to remove those that were illegal and the cause of filth and crime from middle class areas. In the case of shops, the RWAs' sense was that their neighbourhoods had been much quieter, lacking crowds and traffic, when the quantity and quality of consumer goods were limited. RWAs now expressed a nostalgia for the solely residential character of their neighbourhoods in earlier years. However, as stated earlier, 'official' space for any of these segments of the economy was scarcely developed by the Delhi Development Authority and so, increasingly, areas marked as residential in the city's Master Plan were being converted into commercial space, space for hawkers, rickshaw pullers as well as for slum housing.

The courts sided with the RWAs on many of these petitions – leading to a series of court orders evicting the old local economy from the city. Such evictions have come in waves starting with slums in the late 1990s (which continues to the present) and small-scale industries in 2001. In February 2006, the Supreme Court of India ruled that between 50,000 to 500,000 small, medium and large retail businesses in

Delhi would have to be 'sealed' or shut down because they were illegally operating from their premises. They were in violation of 'permitted land-use'; a technical term denoting that Delhi is legally zoned into separate and distinct commercial, industrial and residential zones.

The conspiracy

In the 13 months since this first Supreme Court ruling in February 2006, there has been a massive campaign against the order that involved tens of thousands of people organized under the banner of Delhi's 'trading' community. The primary organizing group has been the Confederation of All-India Traders (CAIT), based in a traditional stronghold of New Delhi's traders, the colonial suburb of Karol Bagh. While the CAIT, like many of the other 'associations', was established in the post-liberalization 1990s, in actuality it is one of a long stream of associations that have represented Delhi's trading communities since at least the turn of the century. Narayani Gupta (1998) writes extensively on the role of such Traders' Associations in the civic politics of Delhi in the colonial era, representing as they do the massive economic presence of the city's retail and wholesale networks. Indeed, the fact that the state authorities are challenging the traders is testament to the strength of the new template of urban planning and design that is being put into place.

In the conspiracy world of the traders, their imminent eviction is financed by private real estate developers who had bought out the elected and judicial arms of government. Private developers were allowed for the first time in 2000 to build new 'mega-projects' including shopping malls. Subsequently, in Delhi and especially in the surrounding NCR, private developers have built hundreds of malls promising a new kind of shopping experience with 'world-class brands', English speaking staff, restaurants, cinemas and parking lots all enclosed within a cool air-conditioned bubble. However, until recently, newspaper reports noted that although the average, and highly price sensitive, Indian shopper enjoyed visiting the malls, in actuality he/she still spends most of his/her money at the local traders (*International Herald Tribune* 2005).

The traders believed that their eviction would direct their customers to the suffering shopping malls, while also allowing for the 'decongestion' of central Delhi of its original residents many of whom are rooted in the city's matrix of informality, so that this prime location and land could begin to be redeveloped, as the government line goes, to begin to look like Paris – symbolic here of a 'traditional' global megacity. This Delhi/Paris would be home in its central areas to a far richer and more powerful urbane elite as is usually the case, with the lower and middle classes[7] that now populated most of the city dispersed to the larger and emergent NCR, where increased private development had led to the large-scale construction of residential apartments, shopping malls, private schools and private hospitals. The decongestion of the city would thus, achieve the dual ends of opening up land in the elite centre and providing customers for the newly developing outlying areas of the NCR.

The traders' campaign

Despite orders from the highest court in the land, it seemed the traders were not going down without a fight. They have traditionally formed the core constituency of the Hindu nationalist BJP, which has alternated power with Mrs Dixit's Congress party in Delhi since Independence. However, in this case the traders chose to carve out their own platform, seeking support from all political parties, working with the BJP but not under the BJP's name. This decision partly reflects the different party affiliations of the people who ran the campaign and also a general recognition that sealing and demolition had first started under the BJP's regime in 1998. The BJP thus, was a part of the consensus among Delhi's political elite that the city should be extensively 'upgraded' and redeveloped. Finally, it also meant the possibility of easier negotiation with the Congress party, currently in power at the state and national levels (the latter controls urban development in Delhi as part of the British legacy of protecting the central Delhi area they built in elaborate style).

In building a campaign, the CAIT drew on the collective strength of existing MTAs and trade groups composed of retailers, who, not unlike their RWA counterparts, had proliferated in number across middle class and lower middle class neighbourhoods in the 1990s, as markets and the number of shopping areas and shops grew. Part of the campaign thus involved bringing these groups together to act collectively, not an easy feat given that the city's markets were spread over 1,483 square kilometres and 12 million people (Delhi Development Authority 2006), and that CAIT had not been in touch with many of these market associations before the campaign started. After the first initial set of informal meetings between a few concerned traders at the end of 2005, a core working group was formed with a loose structure wherein different traders were given responsibility for bringing together their geographic and commodity-based constituencies. In some areas this was easier than in others. The leadership of the CAIT itself comprised individuals with political affiliations with the Congress and the BJP, which they drew on. In some instances they also came from geographic areas of the city where traders' networks and associations were established and strong. In other areas, CAIT had to build a campaign, sometimes facing a denial of the problem among local shopkeepers, suspicion of CAIT's own motives, a general wait-and-see attitude to the Supreme Court's order, as well as a general lack of resources and knowledge of how to contact many associations.

As a strategy, CAIT worked through the public face of one extremely articulate spokesperson who became the figurative head of the campaign, presenting in his words the consolidated city-wide voice of the traders. He would be the chief strategizer of the campaign, the main intermediary and negotiator with the bureaucracy, government and the Courts, as well as a compiler of alternative proposals to solve the city's civic woes.

The campaign intensifies

The CAIT's campaign, hesitant and low-key at first, grew as the legal case proceeded. By August 2006, the Supreme Court had ruled that shops on 180 of the widest

streets in Delhi would be sealed. As was the case in the sealing matter, the PIL structure usually involves the setting up of a system of parallel government – namely a
'monitoring committee' staffed by a certain number of court-appointed commissioners who are legally charged with implementing the court's orders and who are
provided staff, offices, transport, and monies to do so. Typically, the monitoring
committee first investigates the situation on the ground and submits reports through
an *amicus curiae* to the judges. The *amicus curiae* is responsible for indexing the
large number of petitions and reports that come in on any subject and providing a
procedural framework as well as a summary of facts during hearings. The court on
its part, with these inputs, then serves notice to the different government agencies,
frames new regulations to ameliorate the issue at hand, and orders the government
and bureaucratic agencies to implement court orders under the supervision and
regulation of the monitoring committee, often with deputations of police force. The
monitoring committee then submits regular reports to the court on how work is
progressing. The court in turn, takes actions on its recommendations.

The sealing monitoring committee was soon given institutional space and staff,
and chalked out a sealing schedule in consultation with the civic agencies. On any
given day, the committee would set out, accompanied by officials from the
Municipal Corporation of Delhi (MCD), water and power engineers, police force
and a videographer. As the group walked down a street, they would enter and examine every floor in every 'residence' on the street for signs of commercial activity.
The videographer would shoot the scene, and if commercial activity was found, the
water and power engineers would cut off both supplies. Finally, a padlock covered
in white gauze would be affixed to the closed shop or office's shutters and affixed
with a red wax seal. If the seal was broken, the shop/office owner was in contempt
of court, and could be imprisoned.

Once passive shopkeepers were now caught in a dilemma: in its judgement the
Court had provided the option of individual shopkeepers submitting an affidavit on
the monitoring committee stating that they themselves would shut shop by a date
three months in the future, but this entailed giving up without a fight, as well as
being caught in the legal tentacles of the monitoring committee and the court – an
entanglement which could prove lengthy and costly. It would mean, as some traders tell me, that one brought attention to oneself – 'come and get me'. This was
especially worrying given that the monitoring committee appeared unsympathetic,
unresponsive and unimpressed by the traders' different pleas, while highly responsive to RWAs' reports about continuing commercialization in their areas. The other
option, taken by some, was to fight through the local initiatives of the CAIT.

Eventually, many shopkeepers adopted a flexible mix of all these strategies to
resist the clutches of the sealing squad and the monitoring committee. For local
shopkeepers, one of the primary difficulties was understanding how they were to be
affected for there was a considerable distance between local realities and the broad
categories that the Supreme Court was carving out in its orders on what would be
sealed. Local shopkeepers networked heavily between themselves and other trade
networks to get information about what the status of their area or neighbourhood
was, what was happening in the city, what was expected and what was the best

strategy to avoid sealing in their own colonies. In some instances, this meant meeting with their own local officials – District Commissioners, Police Commissioners, Municipal Corporation and Delhi Development Authority officials, the monitoring committee, members of the State Legislative Assembly and of Parliament to whom they made representations. In others, it meant collectively bribing different officials to understand what the monitoring committee had planned so they could sufficiently disguise their shops just before the sealing squad hit their areas. Often on the day of sealing, entire commercial blocks worked overnight to erase shop facades, building a brick wall to block incriminating shop windows, removing all signage and emptying their shops of all merchandise and display fixtures. When the sealing squad arrived then, they would find boarded up shops and the empty shells of gutted-out shops. Shopkeepers also started attending CAIT's meetings and responding to their calls to action in large numbers spreading its campaign to ever-larger geographic areas, as well as trade groups.

For CAIT, at the city-wide level, the biggest problem was addressing the conceptual question of their illegality, as this was the main accusation against the traders. It was commonly held and well known in the city, for example, that traders had bribed municipal officials for their permissions to build beyond what was legally permissible and in areas that were marked in the city's Master Plan as residential; all this in defiance of 'law-abiding' RWAs who had tried to stop them, in vain, until they were forced to put in PILs. Not only were the traders not 'law-abiding', they were also subject to a number of other stereotypes that did not play in their favour. For in the lived encounters of the city, in its physical and sentient reality, it is populated much more by creole (impure, hybrid) 'Hinglish' and a proliferation of stereotypes mark the various multiplicities amongst its large citizenry. In this language, the traders were seriously disadvantaged on many axes. As money makers (*lalas*) in trade (*dhandha*), they were considered conservative, stagnant, physically obese, secretive and stingy – willing to make money at all costs, paying scant attention to legal regulations (especially those that required them to spend money) or to the humanitarian concerns of the city and other people around them. As troublemakers (*goondas*), the traders, lacking the requisite style and demeanour of the professional middle classes overwhelmingly present in the RWAs, were also seen as uneducated, rough, aggressive, lacking finesse and nuance, vernacular rather than Western and willing to take on any fight or use force to solve their problems. Finally, prospering in boomtown Delhi they were also considered the 'out-of-control' 'Big Fish', awash with 'black money' hidden from the taxman, whose showy, opulent and over-the-top showrooms now crowded the city. Their rich sons aggressively drove their zippy sportscars proclaiming their entitlement to the city even though they remained fundamentally uncouth. The traders knew that these were the prevailing images in the city of their communities, admitting themselves that of two trader sons, the brighter one got educated and slower one was asked to sit in the shop.

As a way to counter this, the CAIT leadership tried to build an alternative discourse. Primarily, they were interested in building 'trader' as an identity, since they realized that there would be other economic policy decisions in the future that would adversely affect indigenous mercantile trade such as the opening up of retail to foreign companies and the Food Safety Bill, which contained provisions that aimed to dramatically alter the way the retail and food business was carried out, moving from a series of traders, or middlemen, to a much larger-scale economic venture. Locally, there had already been a long-standing local struggle concerning the Old City with the area's many commodity markets being expected to move out so that the area's heritage value could be restored for the Commonwealth Games which are to be held in 2010 and for boosting general tourism.

As a result, adopting the slogan 'Say it with Pride, I am a Trader', the CAIT leadership spent a great deal of time explaining the historical depth of trading in Delhi, how strong the trader community was when united, and how much strength was required to fight the various assaults which the government was planning; sealing being only one of many. This was done publicly at non-trader events, but also in internal meetings, where it was used as strategy to cohere a united front of traders' associations, which in fact was being formed even as it was being projected.

On the sealing drive itself, the CAIT leadership positioned the plight of the traders within the languages of India's poor. These are languages that have traditionally been used in political struggle and campaigns but rarely by the middle class of whom the traders are firmly a part. Such language usually involves references to needing *roti*, *kapda* and *makan* (food, clothes and shelter), that is, basic survival needs. It involves asking how one's cooking fires will be lit after shops are closed or alternatively how one's children will be fed. At the most elaborate it suggests the question of how any of Hinduism's fundamental rituals – birth, marriage and death – be carried out once one's livelihood has been lost. This rhetoric was generally treated with scepticism as no one in the city could imagine that the traders were actually poor. However, it should also be read as a way of marking one's place in a hierarchy. In local imaginaries, traders were smaller in status and stature, less powerful and more needy, subject to the hegemony of the more-Westernized middle class, which in this case would be RWAs and their members who were positioned as the 'bigger' people, not perhaps in terms of money, but certainly in terms of style, education, aesthetics and the desirability of their morality. For in the public debate over the necessity of sealing, it was really these qualities of the traders and of their shops that were being questioned.

The traders also pushed the issue of the livelihoods of their employees, documenting in the press releases and conferences, how many jobs would be lost by the urban poor and highlighting how their businesses were the only ones that actually hired such people. Far from being parasitic, another long-standing image of the trading community, they pointed out that hiring the 'uneducated' working class was one more contribution of the 'patriotic' traders to the nation and its development.

The campaign continues

As more and more markets and buildings on major roads and streets began to get sealed, and more significantly the Supreme Court rejected emergency legislation brought in by the political machinery – in this case the Ministry of Urban

Development – to forestall sealing, the CAIT campaign heightened in terms of both pitch and numbers. At the traders' meetings, the number of MTAs as well as associations representing trades, commodities and services increased manifold as the government stumbled in its efforts to end the sealing drive. In their public discourse at these meetings, the traders started increasingly to use the language of economic nationalism, positioning their struggle in terms of the loss of livelihood as similar to the coming of the *Angrez*, the English, and the current hegemony of the postcolonial Englishmen or *kale sahib*, as no different from colonial economic Imperialism. In some ways this rhetoric matched a discourse emergent in popular culture, specifically through the popularity of two 'blockbuster' Bollywood films: *Lage Raho Munna Bhai* and *Rang De Basanti*. Both were centred on a surprising cinematic revival of nationalist heroes (Gandhi, Bhagat Singh) at a time when nationalism seemed almost in jeopardy from processes of globalization.[8] In part, the success of these films can be interpreted as a call to rebuild the nation through popular struggle and social introspection at a time of flux. The traders attempted to co-opt these metaphors, clarifying that although they usually did not come down onto the street to protest (an activity associated with the lumpen), they were compelled by the actions of the courts, the government, and the imperative to save themselves and their employees, both of whom they supported with little help from the state and who were now to be displaced in favour of foreign capital as had happened in the time of British colonialism. In this way, the trading community was re-enacting the patriotic acts of nationalist pasts, as was their right and obligation.

The traders' use of nationalist rhetoric was not limited to discourse, indeed it was most visible in its street form. As 2006 progressed, traders tried every form of popular and public protest common in nationalist Indian politics. These included local and mass meetings, sit-ins, roadblocks, hunger strikes, the burning of effigies, processions, protests by women and children, motorcycle rallies, rallies in costumes; once even parading the CAIT leadership dressed as Gandhi, in white loincloths with tall walking sticks.

The importance of such street-based protest cannot be underestimated, for various reasons. For one it was a visual and numeric assertion of *the sovereignty of the popular* in the city, obligating by its size and strength the elected government who represented 'the people' to respond. Indeed, until quite late in the process the traders refused to directly engage with the court, saying that they would only engage with their democratically elected representatives.

Protests also had an important effect on galvanizing dispersed traders' associations into a coherent campaign, especially in conjunction with the local Delhi press. As protests increased, they received steadily increasing media coverage especially on Hindi language local news channels that, at the height of the conflict, broadcast little else. Indeed, while the politics of performance and the performance of politics have a long history in India (see Freitag 1989), in this case the media (along with meetings) emerged as a vital form of communication between the central leadership and local associations to create a geographically wide and visible campaign. In effect, what was created was a feedback loop: as traders and trader-led events captured more TV time, more and more trade associations participated in the

Figure 8.1 Traders at a street-side meeting (photograph by the author).

campaign, using the 24/7 news cycle to keep in touch with the plans and pro-grammes of the CAIT, producing them in copycat form in their neighbourhoods when required.

One important reason for the growing ire of the traders were the machinations of the Government of India, which engendered months of uncertainty and instability on the fate of shops.

The Central government[9] was caught in a strange place. Although both the Chief Minister of Delhi State and the central Minister for Urban Development were from the Congress Party, they were political rivals in Delhi, both vying for the post of Chief Minister and control over the reshaping of the city. The Chief Minister, archi-tect of the *Bhagidari* movement, was not sympathetic to the traders' cause. All meetings with her were reported as being marked by disdain for both the markets and their physical shape, as well as for the traders. Although she did come out and eventually support the traders' cause it was only at the point where it was politically unsafe not to do so.

The Minister and Ministry of Urban Development played a more significant role in politically managing the crisis. In the courts, the Ministry put forward various amnesty and deferment notifications for the courts' consideration but they were all struck down barring one set of notifications regularizing shops on 2000 Delhi roads; a temporary provision barring sealing on the streets until the legality of the notification is determined. Faced with this belligerence on the part of the courts, as well as a countervailing tendency within the central cabinet as a whole that 'the rule of law must be preserved' (Zee News, October 25, 2006) to reassure foreign investors that the city *did* require upgrading, the ministry never philosophically countered the court either during oral arguments or in the proposals they drew up.

Eventually, this led to a strong duality in their dealings with the traders' campaign. On the one hand, the traders' anger and desperation grew – protests engulfed the city as the ramifications of what was to happen began to sink in and more and more businesses and individuals found themselves facing possible sealing. This included private schools, banks, hospitals, clinics, guest houses, cramming centres, chemists, IT services, NGOs, lawyers, doctors and other self-employed professionals, all of whom were operating in residential areas. As the panic grew, the Ministry strengthened its public professions that it would ensure that everyone would survive and their shops and offices be regularized, but made milder and milder arguments in the courts, where the bench remained intransigent in demanding that its orders be complied with, taking every political assurance that the Ministry made outside of the courtroom as disdain for its rulings.

To the traders then, the government's assurances did not appear to remove the 'sword' of sealing that was hanging over their heads. The Supreme Court did not seem to relent, encounters with the monitoring committee revealed that it was determined to seal as many shops as possible, and sealing squads visited more and more neighbourhoods in the city. As this scenario became clearer, the rhetoric and actions of the traders grew stronger and more disruptive. There were more and more disturbances in the city as buses and tyres were burnt, strikes and work stoppages were called, roads were jammed, civic officials beaten-up and the police attacked by stone pelting wherever and whenever they went to try and seal shops. The traders thundered on TV channels that there was more violence and disruption to come as they rejected the entire new vision of the city that the government was putting forward, warning of increased strikes, city-paralyzing disturbances and eventually wholesale violence; for this, the traders said, was the only language that the government understood.

Violence

By mid-September, Delhi was in chaos and on September 20, 2006, four people were killed in a culminating copycat protest event. It was what the mainstream, middle class traders had been privately hoping for – serious violence that shook the government from its passivity and proved that the traders were a force to be taken seriously. Ironically, it came in an area that had been entirely left out of the campaign so far. Seelampur is an unauthorized colony, largely populated by small shops and more importantly small manufacturing industries making incense, iron and wood, among other products, that supplied not only the city but the country and an international export market.

Seelampur had not been included in the campaign because its Hindu market associations were divided and weak and had little linkage with CAIT. Its

Figure 8.2 A trader after his arrest at a demonstration (photograph by the author).

considerable Muslim population was disconnected from the traders' campaign which had been couched entirely in the language of Hindu nationalism, making room only for the large Sikh community that was also found among the city's major trading communities. This communal division was not surprising given the ethnic background of many merchants. Most come from communities traditionally aligned to the BJP and its mother organization the Rashtriya Swayamsevak Sangh (Vidal 2000, Dorin 2003, Jaffrelot 2000). Not only did their business practice form a part of the much older tradition of enmeshing economic, religious (Hindu) and cultural (caste, ethnicity) identity (Haynes 1991), but many were also post-Partition refugees with little empathy for the city's Muslim community.

When the sealing squads came to Seelampur, the small manufacturers who had already seen various assaults on their businesses largely through the process of industrial relocation, and who themselves inhabited 'unauthorized' land, started throwing stones at the police, who overreacted and opened fire on the collected crowds killing four people. As the news spread, the Central government moved quickly to stop all sealing, and for a moment it seemed like the traders' victory was assured.

It was at this juncture that the court began to respond with its own brand of flexibility, carving out in its orders conditions for regularizing a substantial number of small shops and retail areas that it would accept (in some cases pending an examination of the legality of the conditions of their regulation), while coming down harshly on all others. In light of this, the Ministry of Urban Development made its weakest argument yet against the Court's intransigence on permanent regularization, then came out and informed the public that despite their best efforts they were unable to entirely stop the sealing. Instead, all the main trader leaders were arrested, along with many from local MTAs, and company after company of the Border Security Force were provided to cover the monitoring committee and the sealing teams when they started their actions again. This was the Ministry's way of conveying to the Court that its orders would actually be carried out. With the Court having relented on regularizing some shops, the two arms of government appeared to be at compromise designed to calm the spiralling panic and chaos in the city.

After these events in the fall of 2007, the case went into legal limbo for a few months. Then quietly, and in small numbers, the sealing started again in peripheral areas. Cycle rickshaws were banned from the Old City, as were food hawkers from the city at large, along with many of the city's private bus operators, all of whom came from the small-scale non-formal sector. The process of cleaning up had started in earnest again. It is possible in the next few months that the Court will strike down the earlier notification that provided protection to the 2000 roads previously noted, which had been a major gain of the traders' campaign. The conclusion to this story, in that case, will be that one more segment of the old Delhi economy will find itself evicted.

How did the protests, so visible and vocal, produce such a limited outcome for the traders? Over the course of 2006 and 2007, CAIT and local MTAs put in hundreds of hours, negotiating, protesting, appealing, strategizing and keeping themselves informed of the court's verdicts and of the government's plans. They are now – as they describe themselves – tired, wanting a decision to be made once and for all, instead of making the continual move and effort and counter move and effort that has marked the campaign.

This is how, they tell me, the Government of India keeps control: it kills you with its bureaucratic mass and morass, its sluggish temporality; with its omnipresent yet dispersed might and intricate legal processes constructed in opaque corridors, with calculations which are both unfathomable and unquantifiable, and which appear to shift seamlessly. As one trader told me, in a country like India after 50 years of quasi-socialist rule and the huge investment into the image and structuring of the modern nation, the state is in every part of all our lives, impossible to remove or to challenge. If it is not direct force, it is the endless waiting for a concrete decision, the wait for a piece of credible and stable information, for clarity on rules and procedures, the fathoming of Janus-like talk, and finally what we are seeing now, and so well described by Rob Jenkins (2000), its politics of stealth which in this case involves bringing back the sealing of shops after the campaign had died down, seemingly, after some sort of victory, but in many ways exhausted by its own steam.

Conclusion

Throughout 2006, the traders attempted to build a decentralized but highly media savvy campaign with localized protests spread across the city eventually culminating in days of shut-downs and violent protest. In building the campaign, traders sought to mobilize 'trader' as an identity and community, one with a long history in Delhi as a centre for retail and distribution. They attempted to reopen a dialogue on what it means to be a citizen, distilled through the experience of anti-colonial nationalist struggle and its language of protest. And they tried repeatedly to evoke a 'space of disruption', utilizing, they argued, the only language that the government of India is responsive to, overt resistance in the form of street protest and violence against property and those regarded as agents of the state.

The traders are not the only ones who have dissented against economic liberalization in India and its concomitant ordering of urban and rural space. With the introduction of free trade special economic zones (SEZs) as well as various other large infrastructural and real estate projects (such as townships, highways, airports, metros), eviction to make available land for development and resistance to these moves through different social movements have become a staple narrative in the documentation of 'India Rising'. There is of course, a great deal of cultural difference in how these movements develop and coalesce, however, the underlying critique of the state shows a great deal of constancy which perhaps emerges from the common experience of being entangled in the machinations of the Indian state and its repertoire of tools to induce and defuse crises in the ongoing process of modernization. The uneven success of movements can be attributed perhaps to their incapacity to neutralize this.

Notes

1 The Old City is the name given to Old Delhi, Mughal capital, which is the counterpart of New Delhi built first in colonial times.
2 According to the 2001 economic survey of Delhi, 8 per cent of Delhi's population lives below the poverty line. This estimate is based on a monthly per capita poverty line of Rs 454.11. There has been a great deal of discussion and arguments in policy and academic circles on whether this benchmark figure is unreasonably low and thus gravely underestimates the levels of poverty in Delhi as in other parts of the country where it is used as a statistical indicator. For a more detailed argument on how it is calculated and the problems with the calculation see Utsa Patnaik's *The Republic of Hunger and Other Essays*, 2007.
3 In 1991, the Congress government under P.V. Narasimha Rao initiated a series of reforms to open up the Indian economy to global competition and capital as part of a structural adjustment deal made with the IMF, to avert a balance of payments crisis.
4 Planning Department, *Economic Survey of Delhi, 2005–2006*.
5 From 573,000 in 1985 (NCRPB 1999) to 4,551,000 in 2005–2006 (Delhi Development Authority 2006).
6 The actual statistics for how many RWAs have filed cases are not collated and available. However, during fieldwork it was observed that there was an existing PIL against every major market, industrial cluster and slum settlement in South Delhi, where a great deal of the fieldwork for this article was done. Similar PILs had also been filed in other parts of the city. This is not to suggest a complete uniformity in the positions of RWAs; this topic is subject of further research and publication.
7 The definition of class, and especially, the middle class has been subject to considerable debate in India primarily because of the difficulty of using income as an indicator (Deshpande 2003). Following Sanjay Joshi (2001) and Deshpande (2003), I use a

definition here which is not necessarily statistical or based on economic criteria, but refers instead to processes of aspirational self-fashioning and acquiring cultural capital, within which there are considerable gradations. One example of such gradations can be found in the categories used by professionals marketers who divide urban communities into different 'socio-economic' groups (SECs) – A, B, C, D, E – based primarily on education and occupation. In this hierarchy, professionals, entrepreneurs and the self-employed with advanced degrees are at the top of the class pyramid (SEC AI), and are always of a higher class than similarly educated shopkeepers, traders, and workers (SEC A2, B and D, respectively) who in turn are of a higher class than their less-educated 'classmates'. This in effect is a short-hand for the different degrees of cultural capital.

8 Much research indicates that globalization actually increased a sense of nationalism or at least nationalist rhetoric in India (e.g., Butcher 2003).

9 Constitutionally, India is a federal republic. The Central government is the term used to denote the government at the national level, as differentiated from state governments.

References

Asian Age, (2001). 'Delhi O Delhi!', *Asian Age*, May 20.

Baviskar, A. (2003). 'Between violence and desire: space, power and identity in the making of metropolitan Delhi', *International social science journal*, vol. 55, pp. 89–98.

Brenner, N. and Theodore, N. (2002). 'Cities and the geographies of "actually existing neoliberalism"', *Antipode*, vol. 34, no. 3, pp. 356–386.

Butcher, M. (2003). *Transnational television, cultural identity and change: when STAR came to India*. Delhi: Sage.

Chatterjee, P. (2004). *The politics of the governed: reflections on popular politics in most of the world*. New York: Columbia University Press.

Corbridge, S. and Harriss, J. (2001). *Reinventing India: liberalization, Hindu nationalism and popular democracy*. Delhi: Oxford University Press.

Delhi Development Authority (2006). *Draft Master Plan for Delhi – 2021*. Delhi: Delhi Development Authority.

Deshpande, S. (2003). *Contemporary India: a sociological view*. Delhi: Viking.

Directorate of Economics and Statistics, Government of the National Capital Territory of Delhi (2006). *Delhi Statistical Handbook 2006*. Delhi: Directorate of Economics and Statistics

Dorin, B. ed. (2003). *The Indian entrepreneur*. Delhi: Manohar.

Dutta, Pradip Kumar (2006). 'Hindutva and the re-formation of the Indian middle class subject', in John, M.E., Jha, P.K. and Jodhka, S.S. (eds) *Contested transformation: changing economies and identities in contemporary India*. Delhi: Tulika Books.

Freitag, S.B. (1989). *Collective action and community: public arenas and the emergence of communalism in North India*. Berkeley: University of California Press.

Gupta, N. (1998). *Delhi between two empires, 1803–1931: society, government and urban growth*. Delhi: Oxford University Press.

Haynes, D.E. (1991). *Rhetoric and ritual in colonial India: the shaping of a public culture in Surat City, 1852–1928*. Berkeley: University of California Press.

International Herald Tribune (2005). 'India's malls pull in people who aren't buying', *International Herald Tribune*, May 11.

Jaffrelot, C. (2000). 'The Hindu nationalist movement in Delhi: From "locals" to refugees – and towards peripheral groups', in Dupont, V., Tarlo, E. and Vidal, D. (eds) *Delhi: urban space and human destinies*. Delhi: Manohar.

Jenkins, R. (2000). *Democratic politics and economic reform in India*. Cambridge: Cambridge University Press.

Joshi, S. (2001). *Fractured modernity: making of a middle class in colonial North India*. Oxford: Oxford University Press.

Mazzarella, W. (2003). *Shovelling smoke: advertising and globalization in contemporary India*. Durham: Duke University Press.

M. C. Mehta v. Union of India and Ors, CWP 12739/1985

Mehra, Diya and Batra, L. (2005). 'Neoliberal Delhi: through the Lens of the Yamuna Pushta Demolitions', in Ahuja, R. and Brosius, C. (eds) *Megastädte. Zugänge (Annäherungen?) zu den Metropolen Indiens* (Megacities: Approaches to Metropolitan Cities in India). Heidelberg: Draupadi Verlag.

National Capital Region Planning Board (NCRPB) (1999). *Delhi: a fact sheet*. Delhi: NCRPB.

Outlook, (2000). 'Talking shop', *Outlook* October 9.

Patnaik, U. (2007). *The Republic of Hunger and other essays*. Delhi: Three Essays Collective.

Planning Department, Government of the National Capital Region of Delhi. *Economic Survey of Delhi 2005–2006*. Delhi: Planning Department.

Rajagopal, A. (2001). *Politics after television: religious nationalism and the reshaping of the Indian public*. Cambridge, UK; New York: Cambridge University Press.

Sassen, Saskia (1994). *Cities in a world economy*. Thousand Oaks, California : Pine Forge Press.

Srivastava, Sanjay (2007). *Passionate modernity: sexuality, class and consumption in India*. Routledge: New Delhi.

Sudarshan, R. (1990). 'In quest of the state: politics and judiciary in India', *Journal of commonwealth and comparative politics*, vol. 28, no. 1, pp. 44–69

The Hindu (2007). 'Delhi region tops in FDI', *The Hindu*, January 1.

The Times of India (2000). 'Drive them mad', *The Times of India*, May 4.

Vidal, D. (2000). 'Markets and intermediaries: an enquiry about the principles of market economy in the grain market of Delhi', in Dupont, V., Tarlo, E. and Vidal, D. (eds) *Delhi: Urban space and human destinies*. Delhi: Manohar.

Zukin, S. (1991). *Landscapes of power: from Detroit to Disneyworld*. Berkeley: University of California Press.

9   Re-writing Delhi

Cultural resistance and cosmopolitan texts

Melissa Butcher

'What is Delhi?' I ask myself. I reply, 'The world is a body, and Delhi, the soul'.

Mirza Ghalib

For over ten years, I've been travelling in and out of Delhi where I've situated much of my work on the spatial and cultural transformations that result when local every-day practices meet global mobility. And I've watched the city grow and fracture during that time.

It's the Eid after-party in the old part of Delhi. I feel like I'm having a heart attack. Collectively I think we ate an entire goat and drank a litre of boiled milk, dipping our ghee and rose syrup soaked jalebis in it just to add to the coronary carnage. I am penned in on all sides by pairs of eyes and hands and feet and qamiz, by smells of kebabs, raw meat, sweets in clay pots, the smoke from brasseries, stepping over mother and child, begging for alms, and around tables of Q'urans, calendars, and monuments to Mecca. The sweet seller remembers me from my last visit 18 months ago. He has been there almost every night for as long as he can remember. This is Chandni Chowk – Old Delhi – with the mighty ochre, flood-lit Jama Masjid at its heart. Chaotic cables and electricity wires are as entangled overhead as its laneways and knotted communities.

Crossing the round-about at Delhi Gate is New Delhi, with its 'Barista' café chains, hip clubs, neon signs, new Metro railway, mega-malls with premium high-street brands at European prices, and construction sites. Next to the broken walls and parapets, reminders of thousands of years of history, Delhi Development Authority apartments are gutted and renovated by a new middle class. In the wealthier suburbs another storey is added, an old building razed and a new one built. High Capacity Bus Service corridors mark the main arteries into the city cen-tre. With almost 300 000 new cars on the roads in 2006, traffic is now a constant crawl, giving commuters time to read the billboards that line the flyovers, promis-ing 'world class lifestyles' in satellite cities that are green oases on the outskirts of this megalopolis of almost 14 million. Newspaper advertising highlights the 'global experience' of living in these new enclaves.

As a consequence of converging global capital, technology and migration Delhi is a prime example of the transformations and spatial inequalities that are marking cities in Asia and, I would argue, Europe. There have been ongoing campaigns against this remodelling into a 'Global City' that has involved the displacement of tens of thousands from 'unauthorised' settlements that suddenly found themselves on prime real estate. Bureaucracy and state power have worn many of these protests out (seen Mehra's chapter in this volume). But in the face of the state's ability to contain overt protest, there have emerged alternative forms of resistance taking place in interstitial spaces, in the gaps of the city, staying below the radar of state authorities.

An example of this is the work of the Delhi-based non-government organisation (NGO), Cybermohalla (Cyber-Neighbourhood); a multi-media project working with young people living in two Delhi resettlement colonies marked by 'unauthorised' settlement, transience and socio-economic deprivation. While the objectives of the project were something debated between myself and participants, this article will first argue that the work of Cybermohalla not only represents the 'politics of lived space' (Pile 1997), or the 'politics of location' as Mohanty (1987) refers to it, but a particular form of cultural resistance in the shape of an alternative narrative to the marginalisation of these colonies and their residents within Delhi's dominant discourse. Second, to extend Kothari's (2008) work with illegal street traders in Spain, the article will argue that Cybermohalla's work is an example of 'cosmopolitanism from below', although in this case developing creative competencies, including translation skills and imagination to manage processes of urban transformation and segmentation.

Theoretically, the analysis of these arguments contributes to our understanding of power relations in urban space, the types of power associated with distinct spatial formations, and broadens our understanding of what resistance can entail including the use of creative cultural production and imagination to redefine the meaning of a place. From interviews with facilitators and participants (March and December 2007)[1] and an analysis of content produced by Cybermohalla's practitioners,[2] the article will examine their re-interpretation of the neighbourhood, whether this has the potential to instigate change at levels wider than the personal and the local, and whether this is, or should be, the point. First, however, the following section will provide an outline of what Cybermohalla is providing an alternative narrative to.

'India shining'

'India Shining' has become a tag line to describe the country's post-liberalisation (1991) economic development. There is new found confidence from its booming global industries, such as information technology, and economic growth rates of around 9 per cent (2006–7). It was in fact the slogan of the cultural nationalist political party, the Bharatiya Janata Party (BJP) (Indian People's Party) during the 2004 election. Yet it is widely argued that the BJP lost that contest because, while poverty rates in India have declined, many, particularly in rural areas, had yet to benefit from economic liberalisation. As social and economic segregation remains, India is anything but 'shining' for some sectors of the population, as development following a neo-liberal model has concentrated investment in urban areas.

While Delhi as the capital of India mediates global economic activity, chan-nelling the movement of transnational goods, capital, technology and people into the country (Knox 2002), it does so under conditions of intense inequality concen-trating global capital and disadvantaged populations within its boundaries (Sassen 2007). This urban segmentation is, according to Wilson (2007: 36), affecting cities globally as they attempt to fit within an imaginative model of 'global city' in order to attract further economic investment along the following lines:

- concentrating investment in gentrification enclaves;
- intensifying state intervention (such as the sealings and demolitions in Delhi); and
- introducing policies that explicitly fragment cities into 'deserving' and 'undeserving' terrains, with those areas in Delhi marked as undeserving also being marked for demolition.

On this last point, the operation of top-down hierarchies remains significant in the hegemony of a particular model of urban planning, of the aesthetics of a 'global city' and forms of social control that deem particular spaces of less worth than other urban areas marked out as sophisticated and cosmopolitan. Here cosmopolitan is used in Hannerz's elitist definition of a transnational class consuming other cultures, including their 'ethnic' own, as an 'artform' (1996: 236). Sibley (1995) identifies the defining and maintaining of clear boundaries to ensure internal homo-geneity and order as forces that purify space 'in order to keep out objects or people who do not fit the dominant classifications' (Malone 2002: 5). Boundaries of inclu-sion and exclusion are drawn (Drudy and Punch 2000), and we see the physical removal of those that don't fit within Delhi's Master Plan (Ministry of Urban Development 2007) or the city's desired global image.

This process of 'clearing out' space is predicated on a shared idea of values that constitute that space and what should go on within it, and that these values and asso-ciated practices should be maintained. The acceptance of this dominant set of val-ues determines what is normal and what is deviant, who is included and who is excluded (Butcher 2003). For example, the city's local authorities have begun a process of remodelling Delhi to mould it within an imagined aesthetics of a 'global city', to attract global flows of capital, human resources and an international sports spectacular (the Commonwealth Games in 2010). Edge cities such as Noida and Gurgaon have been created to cater for the flow of transnational corporations and transnational professionals into India as well as the burgeoning middle class. These edge cities are marked by new condominiums, villas, proximity to malls and multi-plexes, and facilities such as health, education and leisure centres, crèches, lawns and landscaped gardens, yoga centres and spas, with clearly delineated boundaries and internal homogeneity maintained by gated surrounds.

But there are other types of edge cities being created as well. 'Cleaning up' the city required the removal of shanty towns, *jhuggis*, the closure of small traders, and whole neighbourhoods of what were predominantly resettlement colonies of rural migrants and socio-economically marginalised populations being demolished and their inhabitants forced to move to outlying areas of the city. Those that have been displaced from settlements such as Nangla Maanchi (an area demolished in 2006, displacing some 30 000 people) have been resettled in outlying areas such as Ghevra, some 50 kilometres from the city centre. For 7 000 rupees (€140), if you can prove you lived in Nangla Maanchi prior to 1998 you can be given a plot of land of approximately 12.5 square metres in Ghevra; perhaps a larger plot up to 18 square metres if you lived in Nangla Maanchi before 1990 (Dupont 2008). During a site visit in March 2007, there was little infrastructure in place: water was trucked in, there was yet to be a school built, and latrines were portable, made of metal, shimmering in 40 degrees of early summer heat. Most of the inhabitants were unemployed, removed from informal employment networks when they were moved out of the city and away from trading centres such as Old Delhi. Sassen's geographies of margins and centres are clearly played out in Delhi in this spatial marginalisation of those already at the economic periphery of the city.

Power is explicit in this process; first, a cultural hegemony in the acceptance of a particular aesthetic in urban planning, and second, as we are seeing in other cities throughout Asia and Europe (see Drudy and Punch, 2000, and Brudell *et al*. 2004, for their work on urban regeneration in Dublin), the removal of poor and working class inhabitants who are made increasingly invisible. In this sense globalisation is also, as Wilson argues, 'a powerful rhetorical device whose invoking can be a potent political tool for capital in its drive to transform cities' (Wilson 2007: 29).

However, as a result of this displacement, the city is also generating a new kind of politics, a politics of locality and presence (Sassen 2007) that creates a distinction between being powerless, and an actor even though lacking in power who seeks to create action outside of existing, prescribed power relations. This analysis aligns with Pile's (1997) and Hasson's (1997) arguments for a need to redefine the relationship between power and powerlessness. There is a recognition that capital and class are not the only centres of power but that the built environment itself, the city, is part of interacting fields of power with inhabitants positioned differently between capital, local, state and regional politics, public and private sectors, religion and communal identity (Pile 1997: 3). Oppressive practices of authority attempt to confine people to a circumscribed space but resistance, including resistance centred on cultural production, can be the act of transforming the meaning of that space.

Diverse struggles have adopted this approach to resistance by developing an 'alternative politics that seeks to create autonomous spaces of action outside of the state arena' (Routledge 2002: 318), often challenging the state-centred character of development. They have formed around issues of gender, class, the environment, identity, kinship, neighbourhood and 'the social networks of everyday life'. These are 'frequently cultural struggles' not only over material conditions and needs, but also over 'the practices and meanings of everyday life' (Routledge 2002: 318), including the use of urban space. For this reason I describe these activities as a form of cultural resistance: counter-hegemonic, place based, often articulating alternative development practice, using cultural resources embedded in particular localities and that can therefore only be understood in the context of the locality that produced them (see Skuse and Cousins 2007 for their work on similar themes in South African townships). Culture in this way represents a boundary defining mechanism that circumscribes particular spaces of belonging and contested terrains as different stakeholders give that locality different meaning and use value.

For example, urban protest movements from disadvantaged neighbourhoods have been associated 'with the creation of new social spaces in which ethnic groups and underprivileged social classes challenge the dominant political, economic and cultural system, assert their identity and seek to advance their civil and social rights' (Hasson 1997: 236). Hasson argues that everyday life experience, biographies, local characteristics, interactions between groups and the environment, and learning processes shape actors' interpretations of their environment, and, consequently, the means and manifestation of protest. In the case of Cybermohalla it would appear that local experience and learning processes, in particular a pedagogy of critical thinking, coalesce in the form of texts. In various media formats, these texts have come to reify the everyday life of these communities for an audience in other fragments of the city that previously ignored their presence.

Cybermohalla

... to write the pages of history is also to make a new map of the world
(Pile 1997: 22).

The 'urban regeneration' or reconstruction of Delhi, its segmentation and the creation of the possibility for new forms of political agency, form the backdrop to the activity within Cybermohalla. It is engaged in its own process of trying to, as Shveta, Cybermohalla's content editor and translator put it,

Figure it out; what is it we are in the midst of [the changing city]. How will we flow in the city? Because Cybermohalla is not a space of judgement. It's a positive possibility to find ways to flow through [the city].

Cybermohalla began in 2001 as a joint project between an education NGO[3] and the research centre Sarai,[4] with the support of external donor funding, as a means of intervening in the process of urban development in Delhi. They established multimedia labs in two resettlement colonies to begin working with young people in the locality using both technology and creative pedagogy but with an open idea of how the project would develop and what it would produce.

The labs began by developing text-based practices that aimed to create a new language (including a visual vocabulary) to redefine the city and the place of these resettlement colonies within it. The result has been a startling collection of media work including essays, photography, animation, sound-scapes, blogs, street murals and multimedia art. Utilising cultural resources from 'traditional' and contemporary popular culture, this work has become an alternative narrative to the economic, political and social conditions that marginalise its creators. It reflects the contested environment of the city and its converging global flows by focusing on everyday practices, material objects and the environment in their locality.

The first lab began in LNJP colony in 2001 and is still operating. A new lab was established in Dakshinpuri (DP) Resettlement Colony in 2002, while a third lab was demolished along with its neighbourhood, Nangla Maanchi, in 2006. These are very much locality based multi-media labs, with a different 'feel' and content being generated in each reflecting the fact that the colonies are physically and demographically different. Reinforcing the idea of the importance of locality, Love Anand, a lab coordinator in DP, refers to *sandarbh* (context) as an element that influences their work. 'The idea of *sandarbh* is like, is very close, is much related to the space, the locality, the local, where people are. It's not exactly context but it's the local, where people are.' LNJP has 'illegally' and organically established itself since 1969 at the crossroads between old and new Delhi but is now marked for demolition. I have driven past this locality dozens of times in the past and not realised that thousands of people live behind the crowded, jumbled shop-fronts (sealed in 2006 but which local traders later illegally reopened). LNJP is predominantly a Muslim community. DP was legally established as a resettlement colony of predominantly Dalit communities relocated during Indira Gandhi's authoritarian government of the mid-1970s when a previous round of slum clearances took place that have become part of the constant ebb and flow marking Delhi over thousands of years. The labs are situated in rented space in a community centre (LNJP) and residence (DP). Without romanticising these spaces, they are dense, cluttered and dirty with high levels of unemployment, crime and at times violence. But the argument is that if content can be circulated that redefines this space as home, as community, as having an intellectual life, then it can be engaged with differently. And if it is engaged with differently then these localities can no longer be regarded as somehow of less worth than other parts of the city, and cannot therefore be so easily made invisible.

There were at the time of interviews (2007) some 80 practitioners, young men and women,[5] but this is a rolling population with some staying on for years, others coming for a short time, and others coming and going. Many participants came to the labs through other projects being run by the education NGO in the localities, for example, *Bal* (Youth) Clubs. The labs are 'self regulated spaces' (run by participants themselves) with lab coordinators from the locality who have worked in the centres over a period of time. Every participant contributes a small amount, for example, 20 rupees (€0.50) a month towards the upkeep of the centres.

There is a general routine of work six days a week centred on *Sunna-Sunana* (listening and being heard) sessions. Practitioners will write a text each week, generally starting with what they hear in their home or their neighbourhood, designed to start a process of critical literacy that facilitates thinking differently about the space they live in. Texts are then brought into the lab where they are read out to others (the *Sunna-Sunana* session). There are giant ears painted on the ceilings on both labs to remind us of the importance of listening in this process. The ceilings and walls of both centres are covered in photographs, posters, snippets of conversations and ideas. These are highly generative spaces as texts are critically reviewed by other participants, or 'imploded' as a Sarai facilitator put it, worked on further by the practitioner or taken by smaller groups and animated, turned into an audio-visual or sound-scape, for example. The material can be added to the website or published in magazines and broadsheets created by practitioners, translated into English and published in high quality book format for a wider audience in Delhi. There is an emphasis on interaction with the local community through public murals, wall magazines, and a mobile trailer on market days that distributes audio programmes or text material.

Interaction between practitioners focuses on dialogue, discussion and questioning, none of which have to be resolved; an aspect of the project, I argue, that challenges the hegemony of outcomes-based models of development. The texts are designed to have an intermediary quality, an incompleteness, to encourage continuous thinking and the mutability of ideas, with the aim that it will eventually be impossible to write about the city without accessing this vocabulary being created in Cybermohalla labs. As one of the facilitators put it in almost Freirian terms, 'I will change the terms in which you render me legible, I will not be legible the way you want me to be legible' (Jeebesh, Sarai facilitator).

The focus is on 'minor practices', that is, small-scale, everyday practices that already existed in these localities, such as storytelling, keeping diaries or journals, photography and videomaking which are well-established media in India. These in turn are used to capture the everyday life of the community, the banal (market days, leisure activities, work). More importantly they move away from the image of these working class, economically disadvantaged, formerly known as 'slum', areas as being intellectually sparse. I would add the observation that the project also recreates a virtual community as the built environment is radically altered around the participants; alterations over which they have no control. In the case of Nangla Maanchi, where Cybermohalla maintained a lab until its demolition in 2006, the archive kept of this settlement is the only record of that community left.

The focus on descriptions of everyday life within the localities include stories of intimacy, pleasure, sadness, mischief and violence. They talk about interstitial spaces: windows, doors, stairs, cupboards; Yashoda's bed room, for example.

My Room

At night, having spent yet another day of my life, when I lie down on this bed, I feel there is no one closer to me than it is. Because during the day there are many things I can do, many people with whom, so as to maintain a relationship, I have to spend, if not much, then a little time. Because according to me if one does not invest time in relationships, the feelings of intimacy weaken. But when I lie on my bed, there is nothing else for me to do. Just me, my bed, remembrances of things past, thoughts related to these memories, questions related to these thoughts. Questions to which I sometimes find answers, but in which, at other times, I get completely entangled.

(Yashoda Singh, Book Box 2003)[6]

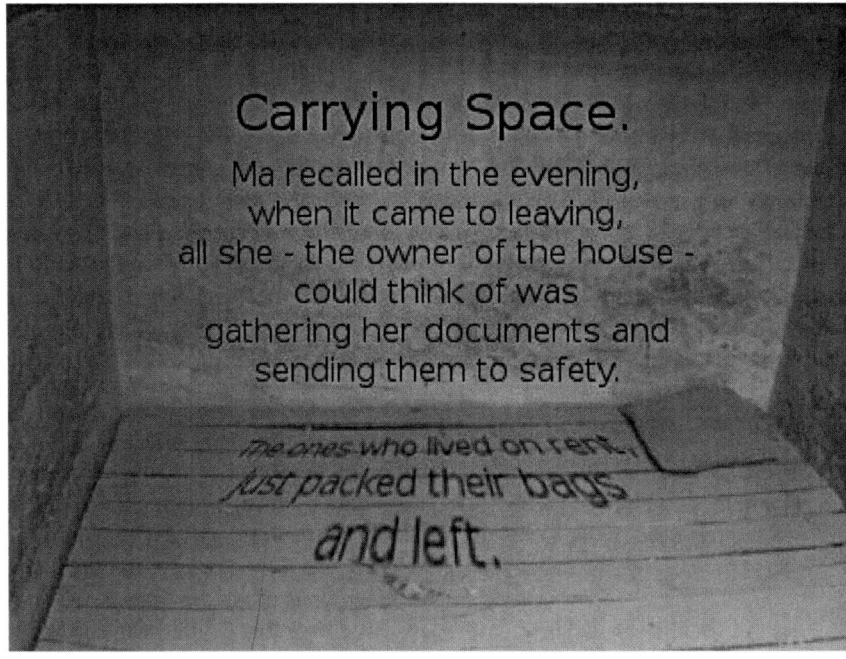

Figure 9.1 Carrying Space (with permission from Cybermohalla Ensemble, 2006, http://nangla.freeflux.net/gallery/bed_pillow2.JPG).

The content expresses an imagination of the world from the ground up, focusing on the minutiae of daily life. This emphasis on material practice continues in the photograph of a bare room from a home emptied in preparation for demolition (Figure 9.1). In this scenario of vulnerability and transience the most precious artefacts a resident of a settlement can have are the documents that prove they lived there pre-1998 (for example, a ration card or a bill receipt). This guarantees at least a plot of land at some point in a new resettlement area, like Ghevra. This image is the only record of how important these bits of paper are.

As part of a blog that documented the demolition of Nangla Maanchi, a looped animation of photographs captures a woman and two small children trying to cross the Ring Road, a main artery encircling Delhi. They dash between the traffic, which is exponentially increasing on Delhi's roads in number and make of vehicle. A text accompanies the video:

> A cooling river and a pair of hissing serpents flank Nangla Maanchi. The river is the Yamuna, and the serpents are the two wide lanes of the Ring Road with their speeding traffic. Even strangers clasp each others' hands to navigate across the Ring Road.
>
> (Jaanu Nagar, 2006)[7]

While the video captures the difficulty of navigating through the city, even within the midst of this hardness there's an intimacy described in the idea of strangers holding hands. This seemingly simple visualisation of an everyday occurrence subsequently evokes wider debates around access, equality, the environment and the space of the city as generating both fear and intimacy.

Texts not only describe events but demonstrate a developing process of questioning the changes in the city, and a collective empathy with those who are being displaced. In keeping with the emphasis on 'radical incompleteness' there is a diversity of opinion in the writing. Suraj's following text, for example, expresses less concern with wider power structures in the city that have enforced the demolition of Nangla Maanchi and that threaten LNJP, but instead celebrates opportunities the city can bring and valorises the resilience of those being forced to move ('daring and without fear') who find their place in the city.

A Corner in the City

There is fear in the city, but there is also something that allays fears. Something that makes one free of worry. A woman who has always been in a veil in her village can head towards the city with her two-year-old child. The search for progress, earning, money, name, fame bring people to the city. But the interesting thing is, whether he gets any of these things or not, he finds a corner in the city that he can call his own. Where this corner that is your own can begin is not pre-decided. Giving time to a space for long creates a value in that person. The value of the person brings a value to the space. This is the reason that Ghevra has become the rightful corner of people in Nangla. They have given thirty years of their lives to Nangla. Ghevra is the corner of the city where people who came to the city with daring and without fear have found a location. People who entered the life of uncertainty in the city have found their corner in the city.

(Suraj Rai 2006)[8]

Lakhmi's piece, which follows, is perhaps an example of more critical work, expressing the hardship of marginalisation and dislocation. However, both texts represent the fragmentation of the city, the anguish of those who have been moved yet again and the relief of those who have managed to stay, or at least find a corner of stability, creating an 'infinite' space between communities. This remoteness is not only physical, Ghevra being some 75 kilometres from DP, but a metaphorical distance between the different imaginations of the city.

Ghevra is at a Distance of 75 km from Dakshinpuri

Ghevra is discussed often in Dakshinpuri. How can it be otherwise? When a settlement in the city is faced with demolition and there is talk of relocation, a resettlement colony like Dakshinpuri begins to reminisce. Images and memories from its own past emerge. The thought of every moment passing in the settlement that is being demolished begins to evoke moments that constitute its own past. Narrations begin about what the city had felt like when one was being evicted from one's own home. The tension in the city becomes near to the self. In moments like this, the only difference between Dakshinpuri and Ghevra seems to be that with the passage of time, Dakshinpuri has reclaimed its place in the city, whereas Ghevra has just begun on this journey. "Where have they brought and left us, so far!" When I hear someone in Ghevra saying this, I feel the distance between Dakshinpuri and Ghevra has stretched and become infinite. It seems then that Ghevra is not only distant from the present moment of Dakshinpuri, but also from the imagination of the emerging city.

(Lakhmi Kohli 2006)[9]

While the previous texts contested the physical displacement of people within the city, Arish's text highlights economic displacement and marginalisation through his evocative descriptions of the everyday act of work.

Arish's Shop

Today is my sixteenth day. It's 4:00 am, at home everyone is asleep. Every day at this hour I wear my dirty work clothes, put a fresh set of clothes in a bag and set out for the shop by quarter past four. I read the *kalma* under my breath each day as I go. First, I take a three wheeler to the market. The driver takes five passengers in one vehicle and takes five rupees from each passenger. I always sit between two people so that I am protected from the cold. [...] I'm going to the hen market. [...] There were fourteen of us in all that morning. Four were from Nepal, seven from Bihar and three, including me, were locals. [...] By 7:00 am we have between 300 to 400 hens ready in the net for cutting. Two drums are kept next to these nets. As the hens are cut, they are thrown inside these drums. One person holds the hen, the other cuts it. [...] The man from Bihar who was holding down the hens for me said, 'Arish, empty the drums'. [...] I went and stood near the drum. Immediately, the smell – no not the smell but the vapours from the drum – they hit my brain. I felt dizzy. [...] Hens had fallen one on top of the other, all of them wet with the red blood; mouths were open, eyes shut and the veins from the necks protruded out. [...] [Afterwards] [s]itting there [having tea] I suddenly thought for a moment, "If only I was here by myself and not here on work. I would have had no worry nor anxiety about work, and would have sat here comfortably drinking my cup of tea, watching others doing their work. There, someone is out in the sun, pulling hens out of crates and cutting them, someone is packing them, someone is taking the packed parcels and loading them onto rickshas, someone is passing on his way to somewhere else, someone is rushing past. [...] The way to peel a hen is very specific. First hold the hen in one hand and pull one of its legs. Its skin will tear. Insert four fingers under the skin and pull with abrupt force. The skin will come off from one side. Then do the same thing with the other leg. Now turn the hen over and break its head from the neck. Push your fingers into its stomach and pull out its intestines and discard them to one side. [...]

Because in the beginning I had found it very difficult as well and I threw up. I didn't like being in this environment at all. But work is work, after all, and I had to endure. I didn't have any options. [...] I take a bus home. At home, I eat and lie down to sleep, thinking, 'Why do the hens have to be thrown around so much?'

(Arish Qureshi, to be published)

Embedded in this content generation is an imaginative exposition of the city, an idea of its cruelties and possibilities, in the built environment and in the writer's ability to access a sense of belonging to it. Prabhat, a coordinator with the education NGO, describes the labs as enabling participants 'to be in love with the space that you're in and to allow for it to emerge in your imagination from time to time' (recounted by Shveta). According to Gow (2005: 403), 'imaginaries are a necessary navigational means – not fantasies unrestricted by reality'. The content produced in Cybermohalla, or perhaps more importantly the process of its generation, then becomes a map to navigate contested place and reconstructed meaning in a rapidly transforming Delhi.

Cultural resistance to definition

While it is perhaps too soon to assess the impact of Cybermohalla on the imagination of those responsible for restructuring the city, practitioners and coordinators were at pains to emphasize that they did not regard Cybermohalla as a form of 'resistance' as I initially used the term in discussion with them.

It's not that we are here to take flags in our hands and march on the road. We are here just to say that we are here to understand the things in a different way, not in terms of good and bad, not in terms of fights. [...] It gives you a different perspective. [...] You will get to know the place and start thinking about things in a different way.

(Raju, 22 years, three years with DP Lab, Coordinator)

Love Anand made a clear distinction between deliberately trying to change someone, the didactic approach, and change that occurs organically through sharing and listening.

Think about the different people who enter into this lab. [...] So the one who speaks a lot will have to develop this skill to listen to the other, and the person who is not speaking in the beginning will have to start speaking, in the interaction, in the sharing mode. They will have to start thinking at some point about locality, about their project, about the research. And this involvement will be there at some point and then things will change and things will not remain the same. That would be through the process of sharing. That would not be as if we want to change someone.

(Love Anand, 20 years, three years with DP Lab, Coordinator).

Yet I would argue that developing the competencies of listening and speaking are a form of intervention. For example, Cybermohalla did not counter the demolition of Nangla Maanchi; there was an understanding that they could not contest state power at that level and overt demonstrations didn't stop the demolitions either. Instead they attempted to change the terms of the demolition.

> The blogs were discomfort producing because there was sadness in them, the communication of someone else's indignation, but never a plea for help. For a reader, the way to respond to this may have needed working out, outside of the known forms of participation of rally, protest etcetera.
>
> (Shveta, content editor/translator)[10]

The same could be argued for how the project addresses the marginality of existence at the city's periphery. While Arish in his text eloquently described this reality he makes no request for 'help', complicating the standard notion of intervention on behalf of the poor often made by NGOs and development policy. The text asks merely to be read and what the reader does with that story is up to them.

However, while Love Anand noted earlier that they were not interested in 'changing anyone' he did recognise that a 'ripple effect' was possible, and several participants remarked that the project had impacted on them in various ways. There is a recognition that even in the catalytic moment of asking a question change may occur in others.

> We are not social reformers, we are not working for social change, but yeah, it does change at an individual level. [...] So when I started talking to a lady she might not have thought of it earlier, but now that I have asked her these questions and I have asked her to respond to these questions she would of course go and think about 'what is different today?'
>
> (Rabia, 21 years old, four years with LNJP Lab, Coordinator)

It's impossible to assess where the impact of Cybermohalla begins and ends as change occurs not only because of the lab: access to media, education and friend-ship networks (that can also come about because of their involvement in the lab) engage participants in different conversations. Nevertheless, interviewees directly attributed participation in Cybermohalla with increasing confidence and self-esteem, greater involvement in family and community debate, and the development of imagination, writing and technology skills.

> I was never involved in my family issues but now I not only intervene during a discussion in my family but I also try to bring out my opinion and put my opin-ion forward. [...] I used to think very little but now I think a lot. I think I have this capacity to reflect and think.
>
> (Pinky, 16 years, one year with DP lab)

Earlier I used to write about things that are there but now I can think, imagine and write.

(Raja, 16 years, one year with DP lab)

Bushra revealed that her family and others in the locality perceived her differently. Talk of her marriage had declined, people called her by her own name,[11] and she felt she was allowed more freedom to move around the locality without being questioned as to where she was going. She could move outside the neighbourhood, more so than her sisters, even as far as India Gate (a popular site for tourists and Delhiites).

So that's how I see myself, as someone who has become important and who has got some identity now.

(Bushra, 19 years, two years with LNJP lab)

The texts appear to have produced a legitimacy for the practitioners in the locality, where power relations were also being challenged just as Bushra's movement challenged the city's segregation. At a third level, she embodies Sassen's (2007) argument that mobilities are blurring the line between Global North and South, evident in the fragmented Global City. Bushra's reflection on space opening outwards was a recurring motif for several participants. For Raju space shifted in tandem with the movement of content from the lab to the locality to the city.

And in the whole process you feel, […] there is something which is changing, in sharing, in discussion. […] it has gone to the locality and then to the city, so this gradual shift with the lab and you could relate this shift happening somewhere inside you, on the personal level also, there is this shift going on as the lab shifts from the lab to the locality and then to the city, you also feel that something is changing within you, and that's how I see the change happening in me and that's how I feel with the sharing and with the learning. There is something which is changed in me.

(Raju, 22 years, three years with DP Lab, Coordinator)

For Love Anand, there's also a sense that the horizon has shifted.

When I came I realised as your thinking grows, as it goes more deeper, you are no more just an operator. […] But here you have the freedom to think much more freely, and work according to the way you want after interacting with others in the lab, after discussing it, and that's how you do your *riyaz*, your practice. […] Very early, after coming to the lab, I realised that it's not just computers and that it's other things as well here, and I started writing, listening to sounds and photographs, and I started making sense out of all these and now I think the horizon has become much wider for me, it has opened up a bit.

(20 years, three years with DP, Lab Coordinator)

On reflection, some participants began to see themselves connected to places even further away, to other cities and other countries, again a process marked by imagination.

> Think about a situation where you go to a shop and the shopkeeper tells you that this commodity is from China and this one is from Mumbai. So suddenly you are associated with China and with Mumbai from a different city, through imagination.
>
> (Saifuddin, 20 years, three years with LNJP Lab, Coordinator)

The city has become 'small', especially for the young men interviewed. This gendered experience of change created an intense debate in LNJP when raised in the discussion.

> The city is something very small for the guys. I have visited so many places ... it seems that there's no place to visit any more. Like when I was earlier with my friends we would discuss which is the new place to visit. But now there's no such place to visit. So the city has become somehow very small for me.
>
> (Saifuddin, 20 years, 3 years with LNJP Lab, Coordinator)

> Now that we find it very small, the city, we want to go away from the city, outside the city. We want to visit different places like Nepal.
>
> (Arish, 21 years, 2.5 years with LNJP lab)

> I think it's big enough, it's not small, it's very big. Especially when you are going to a new place. How do you imagine, at times if you don't know the place, it might be scary to go to a new place. [...] The city is scary at times.
>
> (Nasreen, 20 years, four years with LNJP Lab, Coordinator)

While change was articulated this appeared at times as an accidental part of the process from the practitioners' perspective, although I would argue not wholly unexpected on the part of the NGO coordinators. For some, the motivation for working at the labs was simply 'fun' and to learn computer skills. This technology, the idea of the computer, now represents possibility and economic opportunity for young people in India in areas of chronic unemployment. Computers in the labs are also used to write CVs and to look for work, not only by the practitioners but by many others in the localities as well.

Conclusion

Cybermohalla is, by its own definition, not a broad-based protest movement. Given the opposition to using that word by practitioners perhaps then the emphasis is more on intervention, redefining 'resistance' as a process of managing change; managing the impact of globalisation and neo-liberal economic development, rather than overtly resisting it. In this sense, the analytical framework of cosmopolitanism is useful as it highlights the development of particular competencies to manage positions of difference and, as Kothari (2008) has demonstrated in her elaboration of 'cosmopolitanism from below', positions of inequality. In particular, I would argue that participants in this study have expressed increased confidence and self-esteem (for example, Bushra's sense that she has 'become someone important'), and imaginative possibility that redefines the space not only for an outsider but for themselves.

The content generated in Cybermohalla demonstrates a possibility for dialogue outside former circumscribed spaces of knowledge in the city; there's the possibility to carve out a space using a language developed from the bottom up. This is a vernacular representation of the city, technologically re-versioned. The production is in the language of the city's elite and I argue that this is the means by which Cybermohalla bridges socio-economic divides: by finding a common creative, aesthetic, cosmopolitan language. The material they produce is of a high quality, they at times collaborate with professional artists, and everything that is written is translated into English to reach as wide an audience as possible as part of the deliberate strategy to establish the existence of these formerly invisible settlements. The focus on common material objects and emotional resonances also creates the possibility for a form of translation of these imagined spaces between Delhi's segmented localities.

The focus on developing new language in their emphasis on 'incompleteness' overcomes a discursive impasse; to not use the language of dominant discourse or the hegemonic criteria of 'India Shining' cities that classifies these settlements as dirty and dispensable, they are literally re-writing it. It is not a slum, it is a locality. They are not slum dwellers, they are practitioners. Stigmatised identities (poor, working class, low caste, and even to be labelled 'traditional' as opposed to 'modern', 'global', 'shining' India) are re-written through revitalised cultural practices in line with transforming the meaning of that space. This reinforces the earlier point of increased confidence, enabling them to move into spaces they were previously excluded from by power relations within the colonies (patriarchal family institutions, for example) and the invisible barriers of the city. According to Shveta,

> stepping out [of the locality] always also meant not saying you are from DP in the CV. Now they figure out how they want to write, what they want to write, questions, descriptions, it has a value and will find a circulation. They don't counter the meta-discourse of criminality [that surrounds this area] but it gives them confidence about being able to flow through the city.

Facilitating a process whereby the participants have the confidence to flow through the city, to move into spaces in the city where formerly they would not have gone, to be seen by others in different localities, is, I would argue, to contest isolation and immobility, and certainly challenge terrains of ownership within Delhi's hierarchies of power manifest in urban planning. The process of translation becomes part of the discovery of a way to 'flow' through this space, to absorb the friction that their presence can create in spaces formerly designated as unavailable to them. Cybermohalla then appears to take on the role proposed by Fanon, that '[r]esistance cannot simply address itself to changing external physical space, but must also engage the colonised spaces of people's inner worlds' (Pile 1997: 17). The process of redefining the meaning of these colonies, shifting inner worlds in the process, is intimately connected to imagination, as noted in several of their narratives (imaginary connections to new countries, to new opportunities, to new social roles).

Returning to Sassen's (2007) idea of a new politics of place through emphasising 'presence', while these may be regarded as informal, unregulated, lawless settlements, there is an 'idea' of them created in the work of Cybermohalla. And as long as there is an idea that these places exist, or existed (in the case of the demolished settlements), they can't be ignored. Using what Cole (1990) has described as the 'hooks and linkages' of cultural resources attached to everyday practices (for example, local histories captured in storytelling), 'the outline of a community' is created that has a right to exist and claim a legitimate part of the city (Skuse and Cousins 2007: 992).

Cybermohalla is then a story of converging global flows, of imagination and cultural transformation seen in everyday practices of living in these localities, that contest established power relations as well as shift the spaces of belonging within which these young people can move defined as much by affective and imaginative dimensions as physical ones.

Acknowledgements

The author would like to express her gratitude to the practitioners in Cybermohalla, to Kamal Kumar Mishra for translation, and Priya and Shveta for all their patience and assistance in this project.

Notes

1 Interviews with participants were conducted in Hindi with the assistance of a translator, Kamal Kumar Mishra.
2 'Practitioners' is the preferred nomenclature used by those working in the labs.
3 Ankur (Society for Alternatives in Education) had worked in these localities for many years before the establishment of Cybermohalla, providing a familiar connection with the community. Their activities include establishing learning centres, children's clubs and libraries.
4 Sarai is a coalition of researchers and practitioners based at the Centre for the Study of Developing Societies, Delhi. Their work focuses on the transformation of urban space and contemporary life, particularly the interaction between cities, technology and culture.
5 From early teens to early 30s although most participants would be 15 to 23 according to Sarai.
6 The story in full can be found at: http://www.sarai.net/practices/cybermohalla/public-dialogue/ books/book-box/before_coming_eng.pdf.
7 Nangla Maanchi Blog, 27/05/2006; http://nangla.freeflux.net/blog/archive/2006/05/27/the-road-opposite-nangla.html
8 Nangla Maanchi Blog, 04/09/2006; http://nangla.freeflux.net/blog/archive/2006/09/04/a-corner-in-the-city-suraj-rai.html.
9 Nangla Maanchi Blog, 08/09/2006; http://nangla.freeflux.net/blog/archive/2006/09/08/75-kilometers.html

10 For example, http://nangla.freeflux.net/blog/eviction/
11 In LNJP it is common for younger family members to be known by their father or older brother's name.

References

The Cybermohalla network (2003) *Book Box*, Delhi: Sarai.

Brudell, P., Hammond, C. and Henry, J. (2004) 'Urban Planning and Regeneration: A Community Perspective', *Journal of Irish Urban Studies,* 3 (1): 65–87.

Butcher, M. (2003) 'Breaking Away: Youth Culture and Public Space', in M. Butcher and M. Thomas (eds), *Ingenious: Emerging Youth Cultures in Urban Australia*, Sydney: Pluto Press. pp. 124–141.

Cole, J. (1990) 'Crossroads: The Politics of Reform and Repression 1976–1986' *Review of African Political Economy*, 17 (48): 121–126.

Drudy, P.J. and Punch, M. (2000) 'Economic Restructuring, Urban Change and Regeneration: The Case of Dublin', *Journal of the Statistical and Social Inquiry Society of Ireland*, Vol. XXIX: 215–287.

Dupont, V. (2008) 'Slum Demolitions in Delhi since the 1990s: An Appraisal', *Economic and Political Weekly*, 43 (28): 79–87.

Gow, G. (2005) 'Rubbing Shoulders in the Global City: Refugees, Citizenship and Multicultural Alliance in Fairfield, Sydney', *Ethnicities*, 5 (3): 386–405.

Hannerz, U. (1996) *Transnational Connections: Culture, People, Places*, London: Routledge.

Hasson, S. (1997) 'Local Cultures and Urban Protests', in S. Pile and M. Keith (eds), *Geographies of Resistance*, London: Routledge.

Knox, P. (2002) 'World Cities and the Organisation of Global space', in R. J. Johnston, P. J. Taylor and M.J. Watts (eds), *Geographies of Global Change Remapping the World*, 2nd edn, Oxford: Blackwell Publishing.

Kothari, U. (2008) 'Global Peddlers and Local Networks: Migrant Cosmopolitanisms', *Society and Space*, 26 (3): 500–516.

Malone, K. (2002) 'Exposing Intolerance and Exclusion, and Building Communities of Difference', Keynote address, *Youth and Public Space*, Youth Coalition Symposium, Canberra, Australia, April 8, 2002.

Ministry of Urban Development (2007) *Master Plan for Delhi 2021*, Delhi: JBA Publishers.

Mohanty, C.T. (1987) 'Feminist Encounters: Locating the Politics of Experience', *Copyright* 1 (1): 30–44.

Pile, S. (1997) 'Introduction', in S. Pile and M. Keith (eds) *Geographies of Resistance*, London: Routledge.

Routledge, P. (2002) 'Resisting and Reshaping Destructive Development: Social Movements and Globalising Networks', in R. Johnston, P. Taylor and M. Watts (eds), *Geographies of Global Change: Remapping the World*, USA: Blackwell.

Sassen, S. (2007) Keynote Address, *BodyTalkCity Conference*, organised by Dublin Docklands Development Authority, 17 November 2007, Dublin, Ireland.

Sibley, D. (1995) *Geographies of Exclusion*, London: Routledge.

Skuse, A. and Cousins, T. (2007) 'Spaces of Resistance: Informal Settlement, Communication and Community Organisation in a Cape Town Township', *Urban Studies*, 44 (5/6): 979–995.

Wilson, D. (2007) 'City Transformation and the Global Trope: Indianapolis and Cleveland', *Globalisations*, 4 (1): 29–44.

10 Why loiter? Radical possibilities for gendered dissent

Shilpa Phadke, Shilpa Ranade and Sameera Khan

I wish to ... just be myself ... not think about who's watching me ... if I want to just sing to my heart's content ... swing about and walk the streets ... laugh ... express myself ... without anybody misconstruing anything I do or say!!!!!

I wish I could go to a tea/paan/cigarette stall at any time of day or night and not have only men flock around it and make me feel like I am intruding on their space.

– The Blank Noise project[1]

Why loiter?

As educated, employed, middle-class, urban Indian women in our thirties, when we express a desire to seek pleasure in the city by loitering it might seem problematic to some. It might seem as though (a) as beneficiaries of the women's movement who have access to education, healthcare and employment, *we are asking for too much,* (b) given that most women in India don't have access to even basic facilities, *we are being frivolous* and (c) our desire to loiter is peculiar, for in any case *loitering itself is an offensive activity.* For loitering, the lack of demonstration of a visible purpose, is usually perceived as a marginal, sometimes downright anti-social, even extra-legal, act of being in public city space.

Yet, we would like to stick our necks out to suggest that not only *do* we desire to loiter, we in fact believe that this act of pleasure-seeking holds the possibility of not just expanding women's access to public space but also of transforming women's relationship with the city and re-envisioning citizenship in more inclusive terms.

Even within the women's movement, the desire for pleasure has never been as legitimate as the struggle against violence. In India, for instance, the contemporary women's movement (1970s onwards) has focused on issues of overt violence against women: rape, dowry deaths, sexual harassment, domestic violence and sati; raising awareness and reforming the law (Agnes 1992, Dave 2006, Kannabiran 2006, Kumar 1993). From our perspective however, the quest for pleasure and the struggle against violence are deeply inter-connected. The quest for pleasure actually strengthens our struggle against violence, framing it in the language of rights rather than protection. The struggle against violence as an end in itself is fundamentally premised on exclusion and can only be maintained through violence, in that, it tends to divide people into 'us' and 'them', and actually sanctions violence against 'them' in order to protect 'us'. The quest for pleasure on the other hand, when framed in inclusive terms, does not divide people into aggressors and victims and is therefore non-divisive. Furthermore, the right to pleasure by default must encompass the right against violence. This right includes the provision of infra-structure like transport, street lighting, public toilets, and policies that enable more sensitive law enforcement by recognizing people's fundamental right to access public space.

This article draws substantially on insights and findings of the Gender & Space Project (2003–2006) at PUKAR (Partners in Urban Knowledge, Action & Research) on which all three of us collaborated. This research project sought to exa-mine women's access to public space in Mumbai. In the course of our research we spoke to women, individually and in groups, across class, community, profession and geographical divisions; ethnographically studied women's use of public spaces including but not limited to parks, railway stations, and even new spaces of consumption such as malls and coffee shops; graphically mapped the use of public spaces by women; and engaged intensively with students through our pedagogic initiatives.[2] This research demonstrates unequivocally that, despite the fact that in 21st-century global Mumbai certain women are both visible and desirable in the public, particularly in their roles as professionals and consumers, women have only conditional access and not claim to public city spaces. This is true even though Mumbai is unanimously considered the friendliest city for women in the country.

Our research shows that though political and economic visibility has brought increased access to public space, it has not automatically translated into greater *rights* to public space for women. We suggest that concerns regarding safety for women are articulated in a language of exclusion and premised on the elimination of other marginal citizens.

So long as women's presence in public space continues to be framed within the binary of public/private and within the complexly layered hierarchies of class, community and gender, an unconditional right to public space will remain a fan-tasy. In this article, we make a case for loitering as a fundamental act of claiming public space and ultimately a more inclusive citizenship. For the right to loiter for all, we believe, has the potential to undermine public space hierarchies. Pushing this proposition further, we suggest that loitering is a politics of publicly visible dis-sent that offers possibilities to envision a radically altered city.

Loitering, we argue, immediately disrupts the post-feminist assumption of equal access to the public. Even as an imagined intervention it upsets the complacency that is often engendered by the visibility of middle-class women in the public sphere especially in education and employment. By doing so it also brings into focus otherwise taken-for-granted limitations to women's access to public space.

Our call for loitering as a strategy of dissent reflects our politics and is founded on our research which enabled us to understand the modalities of gendered spatiality in Mumbai. The position we take on loitering in this article is then primarily a conceptual rather than an empirical one. While our work focuses on Mumbai, our understanding of gendered public space and the transformative potential of loitering might resonate in the everyday realities and experiences of other globalizing cities in Asia.

Ordering the global city: The respectable woman and the *tapori*

"Whoever is found between sunset and sunrise ... laying or loitering in any street, yard or any other place ... and without being able to give a satisfactory account of himself ... shall on conviction, be punished ..."
– Bombay Police Act, 1951

Contemporary Mumbai is a metropolis of almost 5.5 million women and 6.5 million men.[3] Since the early 1990s, the liberalization of the Indian economy has led to the infusion of capital into the country and Mumbai, India's commercial capital, is at the centre of this development. This has included a shift from a manufacturing to a service economy, tellingly symbolized in the conversion of its historic textile mills to glitzy shopping malls, a process that has systematically marginalized the city's working classes.[4] Simultaneously, the rise of Hindu right-wing politics has substantially altered what was once a relatively liberal religious environment, a change underscored by the communal riots the city witnessed in 1992–1993.[5] The global 'war on terror' has only exacerbated this process, manifest as it is in a politics of morality and a deep suspicion of those seen not to belong.[6]

Further, globalization and the resultant socio-economic changes have ossified hierarchical divisions in the city to make it not just anti-all-marginal citizens but, more importantly, to make their marginalization more acceptable. Slum demolition drives, the removal of street hawkers and the closure of dance bars are just some examples of this marginalization.[7] This impulse to exclude the poor is also reflected in the spatial geography of the city: in the increasing security, the symbolic high walls of gated communities, and the glass barriers of malls and coffee shops.

As suggested earlier, as Mumbai strives to take its place among the global cities of the world, the presence of women in public space, as professionals and consumers, increasingly signals a desirable modernity. As a result, even if women in general don't have unconditional claim to public space, in the narrative of the global city, women of a particular class and demonstrable respectability have greater legitimacy in public than many men of a lower class.

It is then the most desirable among these women, the urban, young, middle-class, able-bodied, Hindu, upper-caste, heterosexual, married or marriageable woman around whom the narratives of respectability are structured in contemporary India. This woman is the bearer of all moral and cultural values that define the family/community/nation (Bacchetta 2003, Chakravarti 2006, Sarkar 2000). Her virtue, sexual choices and matrimonial alliances are fraught with questions of appropriateness based on the insistence on caste, community and class endogamy. In contrast, lower-class men are looked upon as an undesirable presence in public space. Their lack of legitimacy is underscored by locating them as a potential source of the threat faced by women, as putative perpetrators of sexual harassment and assault. Interestingly, women themselves internalize these narratives as is apparent from interviews across the city wherein women identified poor men (and Muslim men) as the threat. Women's restricted mobility in public space is often rationalized in relation to the presence of this 'dangerous' 'other'. Lower-class men and middle-class women are then the oppositional figures around whom the discourse of safety, legitimacy and illegitimacy in public space is structured (Phadke 2007). This narrative defines the intersection of class and gender hierarchies in Mumbai.

To foreground this opposition it is interesting to consider the figure of the Mumbai *tapori*, a lower-class vagrant male, the closest counterpart to the Parisian flâneur in the Mumbai context.[8] A *tapori* is usually a youngish lower-class male who spends much of his time hanging out at street corners with others like him. He is often peripherally connected to a neighbourhood politician or don which shores up his bravado as a figure of fear and awe. While occupationally he may be either unemployed or engaged in small-time businesses, his primary identity in action comes from solving the neighbourhood problems, from resolving fights over water to recovering bad loans, using fear or coercion. The *tapori* postures as masculine but often has no real power and can claim little more than his particular street. The presence of the *tapori,* as represented in Bollywood films such as *Rangeela* and *Ghulam,* is about the performance of an attitude.[9] This performance causes many women using public space some anxiety since the presence of the *tapori* leader and his cronies often brings with it cat-calls, comments and loudly sung film songs. A group of young men regularly loitering at a particular street corner or tea stall immediately marks that space as being unsafe for women.

While the explicit fear is the possibility that lower-class men will attack women in public space, implicit is the anxiety that they may form consensual sexual relationships with middle-class women thus violating class, caste and community norms of sexual endogamy.[10] The burden that is carried by both middle-class women and lower-class men in public is that of maintaining an appropriate distance from each other. In this process they enact and reinscribe the status quo of class and gender hierarchies.

The people who have the most access to public space in Mumbai are middle-and upper-class men though they often don't need to, choose not to, are too busy to, or too fastidious to actually *be* in public space.[11] Interestingly, it seems that in a context where access to public space is contested, the more legitimacy you have in public spaces the less likely it is that you actually access it. Lower-class men may be able to access public space but are often objects of surveillance. On the other hand, middle-class women despite their ostensible desirability actually have very circumscribed access to public space.

Situating safety for women in opposition to the presence of others has the effect of rendering both, women and other marginal citizens, outsiders to public space (Phadke 2007). So long as lower-class men are cast as the threat, women will never have open access to public space as citizens. A claim to public space (rather than conditional access) can only come when all women and all men can walk the streets, for women's access to public space cannot come at the cost of the exclusion of others.

The tyranny of purpose: The window-shopper and the street-walker

'Whoever, in any public place or within sight of, and in such manner as to be seen or heard from, any public place ... by words, gestures, willful exposure of her person ... tempts or endeavours to tempt, or attracts or endeavours to attract the attention of, any person for the purpose of prostitution; or solicits or molests any person, or loiters or acts in such manner as to cause obstruction or annoyance to persons residing nearby or passing by such public place or to offend against public decency, for the purpose of prostitution, shall be punishable on first conviction with imprisonment.'
– Immoral Traffic (Prevention) Act, (1988) under the Indian Penal Code

The visible Mumbai woman accesses public space purposefully, she carries large bags, parcels and babies to illustrate her purpose, uses her cell phone as a barrier between herself and the world, and heads unerringly for the ladies compartment of the local train. Women's demeanour in public is almost always full of a sense of purpose; one rarely sees them sitting in a park, standing at a street corner smoking or simply watching the world go by as men might. Our research demonstrates that women's access to public space involves a complex series of strategies involving appropriate clothing, symbolic markers, bulky accessories, and contained body language designed to demonstrate that despite their apparent transgression into public space, they remain respectable women, essentially located in the private.

Manufacturing respectability primarily involves illustrating linkages to familial structures and masculine protection. Women often wear traditional markers and signifiers of matrimony, particularly Hindu matrimony, on their bodies to underscore their connection to private spaces.[12] In fact sometimes unmarried women also wear them in order to appear more respectable. Women are also required to reflect respectability in the contained way in which they hold their bodies such as occupying the least possible space in public transport.[13]

Since education and employment are legitimate reasons to be in public space, women in Mumbai often use their identity as students or workers in order to enhance access to public space. Women also legitimize their presence in public space by exploiting acceptable notions of femininity that connect them to motherhood and religion. In our mapping of a large public playground in the mill-district of Mumbai, for example, we found that the only time women were found 'hanging out' was around the time the school, flanking the playground, ends for the day. These are mothers many of whom come much before school closes to spend some 'official' time in public space with friends.

Similarly, older Hindu women often form *bhajan mandalis* (groups that chant devotional songs) and gather in public parks. The celebration of festivals like Ganeshotsav, Navratri and the month of Ramzan/Ramadan, as also visits to temples sometimes late in the night (such as to Mumbai's famous Siddhi Vinayak Temple), offer women opportunities to access the celebratory public outside of their everyday lives. Some of these women acknowledge meeting friends for dinner before heading out to join the temple queue. These occasions offer spaces for

Figure 10.1 Waiting at a Mumbai bus stop (photo credit: Poulomi Basu).

momentary subversion and pleasure in the public that might otherwise be denied to them. At the same time, these spaces continue to be circumscribed by the performance of normative femininity.

Woman's fundamental out-of-placeness in public space is maintained through the hegemonic discourse which sets up an opposition between the 'good' private woman and the 'bad' public woman.[14] This binary dominates the perception of all women in public space; being in public without a purpose – that is, loitering – would automatically mark a woman as belonging to the latter category.[15]

There are however two kinds of women in Mumbai who do appear in public space without an apparent purpose; the window-shopper and the street-walker. The former, as consumer, embodies the raison d'être of the global city. The latter is there for work, but is not just undesirable but also illegitimate. In reality, neither is there without purpose, for both shopping and sex-work are productive activities.[16] Despite this apparent similarity the two are perceived very differently.

In a consumption-driven economy, shopping is an act that is both respectable and respected. The buyer therefore occupies a very privileged position. In our research on Mumbai we found that the spaces where women, especially middle-class women, are visible are inevitably spaces of consumption: shopping malls, coffee shops, lounge bars, nightclubs and discos. While many women articulate pleasure in these spaces, nonetheless, access to spaces of consumption demands a demonstration of the capacity to buy, and obvious, if unspoken, codes of dress and conduct underwrite women's presence there. Moreover, while most of these spaces masquerade as public spaces, they are actually private spaces. Women's presence in these spaces thus remains circumscribed and fails to adequately challenge the hegemonic narrative of the public/private binary.

The tyranny of manufacturing purpose then regulates women's access to the public. In our research mapping the paths of women and men in Nariman Point (a business district) in Mumbai, we observed that during lunchtime, most women who come down from their offices to get lunch (relatively few compared to men) go straight to the vendor, pick up their food and head back inside. Men on the other hand will dawdle outside, not only eating at the stalls but often hanging around on the street, before and after eating (Ranade 2007).

Failing in an adequate demonstration of purpose might leave the woman open to conjecture and the assumption that she is soliciting. Ironically, under the provisions of Indian law, sex-work is not illegal, but soliciting in public is, clearly demonstrating the desire for neat public/ private boundaries and a conservative morality that would like to keep all sexual activities indoors.[17]

Sex-workers are seen to be engaging in work that is inherently risky and non-respectable and are therefore seen to be outside the purview of protection available to other women. Consider the Abhishek Kasliwal case in March 2006, in Mumbai, when a woman accused Kasliwal, a wealthy businessman, of repeatedly raping her inside his car. The media showed great interest in the case until police investigations suggested that the woman was probably a sex-worker who had been sexually assaulted in the process of selling sex. The tone of the reportage and investigation then changed. Once the victim was cast as a sex-worker she was seen unworthy of protection from a violent sexual assault and merited little media and police attention.

The public woman is not so much directly a threat to 'good' women as much as a warning to them of the consequences of violating the rules, namely, if they break the rules, they are no longer deemed worthy of 'protection' from society. In fact, society is perceived to be in need of protection from the risk of the contamination that sex-workers present (Phadke 2005).

The main cause for the anxiety posed by the presence of sex-workers in public space is the potential for confusion in distinguishing the respectable women from the unrespectable. To offer an example of how this plays out, in May 2006, the local police in an up-market suburb of north-western Mumbai alleged that they had received complaints that women sex-workers were conducting 'business' by fixing up clients in the open seating spaces outside some popular neighbourhood coffee shops. As a result, the police prohibited the coffee shops from serving customers in the open yards outside their restaurants. Women patrons, in particular, were discouraged from sitting out. The connotation was clear: we are not sure which women are soliciting in such spaces and defiling them, so we shall ban all women from using these spaces.

All women are compelled to carry the burden of this anxiety when accessing public space. In using the demonstration of respectability as a strategy to access public space, women are not only circumscribed by the discourse of the public/private binary but go on to reinscribe it. For all women to be able to access public space unconditionally, we first need to dismantle the discourse of respectability.

The right to public space (rather than conditional access) can only come when all women can walk the streets without being compelled to demonstrate purpose or respectability, without being categorized into public or private women.[18] What would change if women preferred to exercise a right to public space rather than demand provisional access, or demanded pleasure without rationale or access without boundaries, or chose *to loiter*?

Loitering: Pleasure without purpose?

> *As we collectively produce our cities, so we collectively produce ourselves. ... [If] we accept that 'society is made and imagined', then we can also believe that it can be 'remade and reimagined'.*
>
> – Harvey (2000, p 159)

When one thinks of people loitering in Mumbai, the image it conjures up is of messy, difficult to navigate street corners, the smell of low-cost tobacco, the sight of *paan* (betel nut) stains, the sound of boiling tea and unmodulated male voices. Etched into our imaginations is the vision of the unwashed male masses huddled together, unmistakably lower-class in attire and demeanour. Underlying this image is deep class prejudice.

Like the *tapori, lukkha, lafanga, vella, bekaar* are other Indian terms used to describe a kind of purposelessness akin to loitering. They are all uncomplimentary terms suggesting not just the lack of employment but also the unease that the loiterer is potentially up to no good. Loitering then, as suggested in our discussion of the Mumbai *tapori,* is read as a suspicious performance of non-productivity. Women are not even in the reckoning since the assumption is that 'even good men don't loiter'.

Our intention in this chapter is to rethink the meanings implicit in loitering and to recast it not as an act of loss of choice but in fact as the very opposite, as an act of agency and desire. When we say loitering we mean not doing anything that has an apparent purpose, or as the dictionary definition suggests, 'to linger aimlessly'. Loitering unlike flânerie or *tapori-giri* is not attached to an identity. Its engagement with the city is not voyeuristic but rather organic and visceral for unlike voyeurism loitering implicates the loiterer as actor rather than surveyor. Loitering is an act one can indulge in without professing allegiance to any particular group, morality or ideology. It is a process that is temporally present. You are a loiterer only while you are loitering.

Loitering is fundamentally a voluntary act undertaken for pure self-gratification; it's not forced and has no visible productivity. Loitering can have no purpose other than pleasure. Pleasure which is not linked to consumption has the power to challenge the unspoken notion that only those who can afford it are entitled to pleasure, thus ensuring that marginal citizens are kept in their place. The possibility of a pleasure that does not cost anything and at the same time brings the 'undesirables' out into the streets making them visible, threatens to undermine established notions of urban social order.

Figure 10.2 Hanging out at Marine Drive, Mumbai (photo credit: Poulomi Basu).

This idea of apparent urban anarchy might be threatening to the maintenance of the status quo but for women it represents the possibility of redefining the terms of their access to public space, not as clients seeking protection but as citizens claiming their rights.

Imagine varied street corners full of women sitting around talking, strolling, feeding children, exchanging recipes and books or planning the neighbourhood festival. Imagine street corners full of young women watching the world go by as they sip tea and discuss politics, soap operas and the latest financial budget. Imagine street corners full of older women contemplating the state of the world and reminiscing about their lives. Imagine street corners full of female domestic workers planning their next strike for a raise in minimum wage. *If one can imagine all of this, one can imagine a radically altered city.*

We articulate four propositions to suggest exactly how loitering might succeed where other strategies fail, in creating a more inclusive city.

1. Loitering holds the possibilities of disrupting the everyday performances of normative respectable femininity in public space through which an oppressive gender-space formation is maintained.

To fully recognize the extent of these possibilities, it is essential to view gendered space as a constant *process* of *becoming*; gender as something we *do* rather than something we *are* (Ainley 1998). In doing so, we draw on the conception of gender as being a 'regulatory fiction' in society (Butler 1990) and space as being a social practice (Lefebvre 1991); both, in effect, being discursive formations or 'practices that systematically form the objects of which they speak' (Foucault 1972). When we see hegemonic gender-space as something that is not just contested but also constantly being *brought into being* through the everyday actions of men and women in space, rather than something women are *subjected to* by external totalitarian forces, it allows us to imagine possibilities of interrupting and opening up gaps in the relentless replication of unequal gender formations; gaps within which we can re-imagine a rightful place for women in the city.

One might therefore propose loitering as an act that has the possibility to allow the subject to renegotiate sedimented roles, to contest societal and personal expectations, and to enable interventions that fulfil and subvert definitional 'practices' of being. In this context, then, the errant, arbitrary, circuitous routes of the loiterer mark out a kinetic map of pleasure.

In the dialectical relationship between social structure and space, it is the body that becomes the medium through which socio-spatial formations are not just experienced, but produced, reproduced, represented and transformed. Bodies that challenge hegemonic notions of masculinity and femininity, or transgress the boundaries of appropriateness, pose a threat to the 'normalized' social order. Many lesbian women in our discussions articulated that when they chose to dress in less feminine, more 'butch' attire, they encountered hostility – ranging from staring to loud comments and occasionally attempts to physically evict them – mostly in all women spaces like the ladies compartments of trains and women's toilets.

In a relative sense the female body, located 'properly' in the private space of the home, has the greatest potential to disrupt the structures of power in public space. The bubble of private respectability that women are expected to cloak themselves in cannot withstand the act of loitering because the two are based on contradictory imperatives – the former, one of maintaining privacy even in the public and the latter, that of taking pleasure in the public for its own sake. The presence of the loitering female body can then challenge the hegemonic discourse of gendered public space by reconstructing the connotative chains of association that connect loitering, respectability and normative femininity. This has the capacity to create a new set of relationships within and with public space through the ensemble of practices associated with women; relationships, which have the power to not just disrupt the dominant order in public space but to have a more long-term impact on how space itself is visualized.

The subversive potential of a visceral and 'subjective' engagement with the city has been explored by social thinkers starting from the second half of the twentieth century, ostensibly in reaction to the totalitarian master narratives that characterized the early part of the century. The potential in loitering might be visualized as an extension of the power of walking itself so eloquently imagined by de Certeau (1984) whose vision of walking as being simultaneously an organic act of belonging and a subversive engagement with the city informs our idea of loitering. For de Certeau, as people walk they reinscribe the city again and again, often in defiance of established patterns of urban order, each time differently making new meanings. Walking, according to him, is fundamentally an act of 'enunciation' through which the city, and in effect, social order is personalized, and in the process, altered.[19] Similarly, Scalway (2001) suggests that walking, which is an act of negotiation when it incorporates regard for the 'other', creates the possibility of meaningful citizenship right there on the streets.

In a variety of languages the terms used for transgressive women in public space are related to the act of being on the streets without purpose – strolling, roaming, wandering, straying, rambling – all terms that Solnit (2000) points out suggest that women's travel is invariably sexual or that their sexuality is inevitably transgressive when it travels.[20] Since it is street-walking – and the need to draw boundaries, to banish the ambiguities between street-walkers and women walking the street – that is the greatest source of anxiety in relation to public space, loitering in public space, not as respectable virtuous women but as citizens, transforms the very nature of engagement making the case that both the woman in the street and the street-walker are making exactly the same claim to space.

It is precisely because loitering is an embodied practice that seeks to transform the everyday acts of walking and looking in the city from acts that are means to an end to acts that are meaningful in themselves, that loitering becomes a compelling tool for change, allowing us to re-imagine the gendered experience of city spaces.

2. Loitering encompasses a politics of visibility that is different from the subterfuges that women engage in to access the city anonymously.

Women have often sought to access the pleasures of public city spaces by slipping into the city, merging with the crowd and not drawing attention to themselves. Scholars such as Wilson (1991) and Young (1995) suggest that large cities offer women some access to public space through anonymity.[21] At the same time, this brings with it only temporary and invisibilized access. Wilson also points out that, within the heterosexual discourse, the male gaze is focused largely on young and therefore sexually desirable women. It is women who are old or eschew the 'masquerade of womanliness' who could potentially become invisible, an act that brings a 'kind of negative freedom; but also a kind of social extinction' (2001: 93). Garber (2000) also underscores the limitations of the liberating potential of anonymity, arguing that even for women, whose sexed identity is often obviously visible, the capacity to claim space rests on political organization and the ability to make the transition from invisibility to identity. For although in the short term, anonymity may be the obvious choice for women to enhance access to public space, the potential longer term risk of seeking anonymity could well mean the loss of substantive freedom and eventually a kind of political death wherein women forever remain outsiders to public space (Phadke 2005).

Expanding access through anonymity is not the same as staking a claim as citizens and will not in any way change women's location in or relationship to public space. Loitering, on the other hand, might often be unobtrusive but it is far from invisible. This means that the loiterer might sometimes merge into a crowd and at other times stand out. The loiterer is often unidentified but not anonymous. In fact, by the very act of doing nothing in public space, the loiterer demands identification. Loitering then has the potential to challenge gendered restrictions of access to public space by its very visibility.

3. Loitering has the capacity to challenge the new global order of the city by compelling an engagement with the idea that the right to public spaces is a core component of citizenship.

Urban scholars studying cities across the industrial and developing world have argued that people's access to public space and its resources reflects various hierarchies and patterns of discrimination. Access to public space is often sacrificed at the altar of safeguarding 'law and order'. Safety and order are prized in the new global city, and both are presented as the antithesis of what is embodied, literally and metaphorically, by the poor: their slums are unsanitary, their homes makeshift, their bodies unhygienic, and their very existence a source of threat not just to the middle classes but to the city itself. However, as historical evidence shows, attempts to cleanse and sanitize cities have often had the opposite effect of making cities even more fraught, violent and unsafe (Appadurai 2000, Davis 1990, 1992, Mitchell 2003).

The global claims of Mumbai are still new and fragile and therefore to be guarded zealously. One of the ways these claims can be buttressed is by clear definition of spaces as being inside–outside; public–private; recreational–commercial.[22] Loitering disrupts this imagined order of the global city. The act of loitering, in its very lack of structure, renders a space simultaneously inside and outside; public and private; recreational and commercial, rendering it in a constant state of liminality or transition. We submit that it is precisely this ambiguity that makes loitering potentially liberating. The very power of the liminal state lies in its lack of definition, in its defiance of being named. Loitering mocks the authority of any one group of people to determine the future of the city by speaking with visceral bodies and through the indeterminate nature of the identity of the loiterer.

The presence of the loiterer acts to rupture the controlled socio-cultural order of the global city by refusing to conform to desired forms of movement and location, instead creating alternate maps of movement, and thus new kinds of everyday interaction. It thwarts the desire for clean lines and structured spaces by inserting the ostensibly private into the obviously public. The liminality of loitering is seen as an act of contamination, defiling space. Loitering is a reminder of what is perceived as the lowest common denominator of the local and thus is a threat to the desired image of a global city: sanitized, glamorous and homogenous. Loitering then as a subversive activity has the potential to raise questions not just of 'desirable image' but also of citizenship: Who owns the city? Who can access city public spaces as a right?

In a time when the performance of a consumerist hyper-productivity is becoming deeply significant in global-aspirational Mumbai, the *choice* to demonstrate non-productivity can be profoundly unsettling. Loitering is a threat to the global order of production in that people are visibly doing nothing. It disrupts the image of the desirable productive body – taut, vigorous, purposeful – moving precisely towards the 'greater global good'.

Loitering is also a threat to the desired visibility of capitalist consumption in that there is no recognizable product; if a beverage is being consumed it is likely to be unbranded roadside *cutting chai* (three-quarter-cup tea). Loitering, in its defiant demonstration of lack of purpose, immediately refutes the possibility of being co-opted within global practices of consumerist inclusion.

4. Finally, loitering makes possible the dream of an inclusive citizenship by disrupting existent hierarchies and refusing to view the claims of one group against the claims of another.

   Young (1995) suggests that the ideal of city life is not communities, for communities by their very nature are exclusive, but a vision of social relations as affirming group difference which would allow for different groups to dwell together in the city without forming a community. She argues that reactions to city life that call for local, decentralized, autonomous communities reproduce the problems of exclusion. Instead, Young imagines a city life premised on difference that allows groups and individuals to overlap without becoming homogenous.

The kind of exclusion that Young suggests is seen clearly in the local citizens' groups in Mumbai which are often founded on a corporate vision for the city built around zoning, segregation and finally exclusion.[23]

   Building on Young's ideas, we would like to propose that the act of loitering has the potential to make such a vision of diverse city life possible. Our understanding of loitering in public space is based on the right of each individual, irrespective of their group affiliations, to take pleasure in the city as an act of claim and belonging. This is, however, not a notion that is located in a crude understanding of capitalism where each individual maximizes her pleasure in the city leading to the greater pleasure of society. Loitering is an act that could be solitary or in groups. At no point do we perceive the individual as divorced from her multiple locations and identities.

When we ask to loiter then, the intent is to rehabilitate this act of hanging out without purpose not just for women, but for all marginal groups. The celebration of loitering envisages an inclusive city where people have a right to city public spaces, creating the possibility for all to stake a claim not just to the property they own, nor to use the ownership of property as grounds for being more equal citizens, but to claim undifferentiated rights to public space.

This is the potential we see when we seek to reclaim the act of loitering as an act of the most basic citizenship. Here, we not only see citizenship as being linked to cities rather than nations (Holston and Appadurai 1996) but also understand it, not as an *a priori* position sanctioned by the state or collective agreement, but as a space to be claimed through performance (Donald 1999).[24] So when we ask to loiter then, we see loitering as a performance with the capacity to enable a subjectivity that can claim the position of a 'legitimate citizen'. This enactment of citizenship through loitering is further premised on the quest for pleasure, which, as suggested earlier, has the potential of being both non-divisive and inclusive.

It is only when the city belongs to everyone that it can ever belong to all women. The unconditional claim to public space will only be possible when all women and all men can walk the streets without being compelled to demonstrate purpose or respectability, for women's access to public space is fundamentally linked to the access of all citizens. Equally crucially, we feel the litmus test of this right to public space is the right to loiter, especially for women across classes. Loiter without purpose and meaning. Loiter without being asked what time of the day it was, why we were there, what we were wearing and whom we were with.

Acknowledgements

The PUKAR Gender & Space Project (2003–2006) was funded by the Indo-Dutch Programme on Alternatives in Development (IDPAD). For more information on the project, please see www.genderandspace.org. We would like to thank Lakshmi Lingam, Mary John, Tejaswini Niranjana, Kalpana Sharma, Mustansir Dalvi and George Jose, whose comments pushed us to clarify and complicate our understanding of loitering. Very special thanks to Rahul Srivastava for his sustained and multi-layered engagement with our work. We would also like to thank Abhay Sardesai and Amit Rai for their thoughtful comments on a draft of this article.

Notes

1 Responses to the online blog campaign 'I Wish, I Want, I Believe' (February 2007) run by the Blank Noise project, which campaigns against sexual harassment on Indian streets. See http://blanknoiseproject.blogspot.com/2007/02/wish-list.html
2 For detailed arguments and information see Phadke, Khan and Ranade (2006), Khan 2007, Phadke 2007, Ranade 2007.
3 The population of the city, which is under the jurisdiction of the Municipal Corporation of Greater Mumbai, is 11.9 million (Census of India, 2001, www.censusindia.net). For a discussion on Mumbai's history see Dossal 1991, Dwivedi and Mehrotra 1995.
4 For more on the debate surrounding the closure of the textile mills in Mumbai, see Chandavarkar 2004, D'Monte 2002, Menon and Adarkar 2004.
5 For a discussion on the impact of these riots on Mumbai, see Appadurai 2000, Chandavarkar 2004, Hansen 2001, Masselos 1994, Robinson 2005 and others. For an account of how the vilification of Muslims impacts Muslim women's access to public space, see Khan 2007.
6 The latest group seen to not belong to Mumbai are the North Indians. In February 2008, Raj Thackeray, leader of the Maharashtra Navnirman Sena (MNS), launched a particularly virulent attack on the city's North Indian population with physical attacks on North Indian taxi drivers and their cabs. These attacks continued for several days in Mumbai and also spread to other towns in Maharashtra. In April 2008, Raj Thackeray asked industrialists in Maharashtra to reserve 80 per cent of jobs in their factories and offices for *bhoomiputras* or sons of the soil. Earlier in January 2008, Shiv Sena leader Bal

Thackeray in a long interview to his party's newspaper, *Saamna,* had also raised the issue of a 'permit system' for all outsiders to live and work in Mumbai.

7 For slum demolitions, see Burra 2005, Srivastava *et al.* 2004; for the hawkers question in Mumbai see Anjaria 2006, Bhowmik 2003; for dance bars see Agnes 2006.

8 For more on flânerie see for instance Benjamin 1999, Wilson 2001, Donald 1999, Massey 1994, Wolff 1985.

9 See for instance Ranjani Mazumdar's (2006) engagement with the figure of the *tapori* in Bollywood cinema.

10 The fear of inter-caste and inter-religious relationships and marriages is so acute that violence is often an end result. Couples daring to cross these boundaries are hounded, harassed and even killed. In April 2007, a young Hindu-Muslim couple (Priyanka Wadhwani and Mohammed Umer) created a furore when they fled from Bhopal to Mumbai seeking police protection after marriage. Not only their families but the larger community were up in arms. A new group called the Hindu Kanya Bachao Samiti (Save Hindu Girls Front) organized protests and threatened to lynch the couple if they returned home. The local Sindhi Panchayat came out with a code of conduct for Sindhi girls (Priyanka was Sindhi) including a list of instructions for parents to 'keep their daughters in check' such as curbing their use of mobile phones and two-wheelers. There is also the more recent case of Hindu-Muslim couple Priyanka Todi and Rizwanur Rahman. Rahman's dead body was found beside the Patipukur railway tracks in Kolkata on September 21, 2007. Todi's wealthy father has been booked as the prime accused in the case for allegedly organizing the killing of his lower-middle class Muslim son-in-law.

11 The leisure to 'hang-out', among the middle and upper classes, once considered a sign of prosperity, is increasingly seen as unproductive, even anti-social. See Chakrabarty (1999) for a discussion of one such disappearing practice, the *adda* in Calcutta.

12 These symbols of matrimony include the *mangalsutra, sindhoor* and *chooda,* all meant to be worn by Indian Hindu women with some regional variations across the country. *Sindhoor* is the red vermillion powder smeared in the parting of one's hair, *mangalsutra* is the necklace of black and gold beads, and *chooda* refers to the red and white bangles worn on the arms.

13 For a discussion on the containment of women's bodies, see Bartky 1990, Butler 1990, Young 1990.

14 For more on the public/private women debate see Mitchell 2000, Rose 1993, Walkowitz 1992, Wilson 1991, 2001.

15 The control of the presence of 'respectable' women in public space is written into the law through a time regulation in the Factories Act of 1948 in India, which made it illegal for women to be employed/work between 7 p.m. and 6 a.m. As recently as 2003, the government proposed an amendment to this Act which would provide flexibility in the employment of women during night-shifts. This was done largely in response to the needs of new globally linked businesses like the software industry and call-centres.

16 For a discussion of women and consumption, see Friedberg 1993, Domosh and Seager 2001, McRobbie 1997, Morris 2000, Wilson 2001, Wolff 1985. For a discussion of sex-work and its implications for public space, see Nord 1995, Walkowitz 1992, Wilson 1991.

17 This is visible even when couples in public space are booked for obscene behaviour and fined. There has been a visible increase in the policing of couples in parks and on promenades in Mumbai. Couples are often censured for holding hands, and ostensibly threatening the moral fibre of Indian society. Some years ago in the Five Gardens area of Dadar, all park benches were made into single-seaters by the local corporation to discourage couples from engaging in what he termed as 'indecent behaviour'.

18 We are well aware of the limitations of using the discourse of rights when we make a case for loitering. The feminist critique of rights as being individualistic, reifying liberalism and often reflecting existing hierarchies of all kinds and thus limiting the terms of the debate, is both valid and valuable. At the same time, the language of rights is also a

powerful tool to promote greater inclusion in quest of a more egalitarian citizenship. In this article, we use the terminology of rights largely because of the absence of another way of expressing the entitlement of people to loiter. The language of rights, because of its widespread acceptance, offers a space, however inadequate, to make this claim.

19 Besides de Certeau, ideas of the Situationist Internationale (SI) continue to influence attempts to re-personalize the practice of urbanism.

20 While conducting a pedagogic exercise on where women would 'wait' for a friend on the street we find that most women sought the legitimacy of bus-stops where they might pretend to be commuters, for *waiting,* particularly at street corners, was an act synonymous with soliciting.

21 When we say anonymity here we refer to spatial and social elements of large and populous cities that allow for people to remain strangers to each other. For instance, some women in Baiganwadi, a slum in North-east Mumbai, pointed out that their own street was both a familiar and safe space but they still had to behave themselves. The road outside the slum was an intermediate space where they might be recognized, a space many of them described as threatening. Further beyond in the city was the space where they were anonymous, where they often felt the greatest degree of freedom. While anonymity does allow them to be in public space it does little to address the fact that each time they or women elsewhere in the city go out, particularly at night, the masquerade has to begin anew. Furthermore, for women, being intimately part of a homogenous community group often results in greater surveillance and restriction of their movements (Khan 2007, Phadke 2007). Our research suggests that women living in neighbourhoods peopled by their own communities often felt the most restricted while those women who were individual migrants from other towns and cities felt the greatest degree of freedom. This is interesting considering that women living on their own in the city have the least access to support structures that would enable them to produce safety for themselves.

22 The lack of modernist planning in Mumbai, where residential and commercial spaces are mixed, has been an important factor in making public spaces in the city more accessible to women. Our mapping of spaces demonstrated clearly that the number of women in one of the city's few business districts, Nariman Point, drops substantially before and after work hours as compared to other mixed-use areas like Chembur and Kalachowki.

23 In an attempt to cleanse and beautify city neighbourhoods and control local open spaces, middle-class residents groups have sprung up all over Mumbai. In many cases these are known as Advanced Locality Management or ALMs, which is a concept of citizen's involvement with local governance. These often tend to focus on 'beautifying' their neighbourhoods by getting rid of hawkers or slum encroachments.

24 Donald (1999) argues that the question of personhood is central to the definition of citizenship, and this personhood being historically contingent, citizenship is in perennial deferral. Being a citizen, then is not the occupation of a universal or institutionalized position but is a performance.

References

Agnes, Flavia (1992) 'Protecting Women against Violence: Review of a Decade of Legislation, 1980–89', *Economic and Political Weekly,* 25 April, WS19–33.

—— 'Dance Bars: The Right to Dance' in *Manushi,* Issue 154, reprinted 25 July 2006 in *India Together,* http://www.indiatogether.org/2006/jul/soc-dancebar.htm (accessed in June 2007).

Ainley, Rosa (1998) 'Introduction' in Rosa Ainley (ed.) *New Frontiers of Space Bodies and Gender,* Routledge, London, pp. xiii–xvii.

Anjaria, Jonathan S. (2006) 'Street Hawkers and Public Space in Mumbai', *Economic and Political Weekly,* Vol. 41, No. 21, 40–46.

Appadurai, Arjun (2000) 'Spectral Housing and Urban Cleansing: Notes on Millennial Mumbai', *Public Culture*, Vol. 12, No. 3, 627–651.

Bacchetta, Paola (2003) *Gender in the Hindu Nation: RSS Women as Ideologues*, Women Unlimited, New Delhi.

Bartky, Sandra (1990) *Femininity and Domination: Studies in the Phenomenology of Oppression*, Routledge, New York.

Benjamin, Walter (1999) *The Arcades Project*, translated by Howard Eiland and Kevin McLaughlin, Belknap Press, Cambridge, Massachusetts.

Bhowmik, Sharit K. (2003) 'National Policy for Street Vendors', *Economic and Political Weekly*, Vol. 38, No. 16, 1543–1546.

Burra, Sundar (2005) 'Towards a Pro-poor Framework for Slum Upgrading in Mumbai, India', *Environment and Urbanization*, Vol. 17, No. 1, 67–88.

Butler, Judith (1990) *Gender Trouble: Feminism and the Subversion of Identity*, Routledge, London.

Chakrabarty, Dipesh (1999) 'Adda, Calcutta: Dwelling in Modernity', *Public Culture*, Vol. 11, No. 1, 109–145.

Chakravarti, Uma. (2006) 'From Fathers to Husbands: Of Love, Death and Marriage in North India' in Lynn Welchman and Sara Hossain (eds), *'Honour': Crimes, Paradigms, and Violence Against Women*, Zubaan, New Delhi, pp. 308–331.

Chandavarkar, Rajnarayan (2004) 'Introduction' in Meena Menon and Neera Adarkar (eds) (2004).

Dave, Anjali (2006) 'Feminist Social Work Intervention: Special Cells for Women and Children' in Kalpana Kannabiran (ed.), *The Violence of Normal Times: Essays on Women's Lived Realities*, Women Unlimited, New Delhi, pp. 172–196.

Davis, Mike (1990) *City of Quartz: Excavating the Future in Los Angeles*, Verso, New York.

—— (1992) 'Fortress Los Angeles: The Militarization of Urban Space', in Michael Sorokin (ed.), *Variations on a Theme Park: The New American City and the End of Public Space*, Hill and Wang, New York, pp. 154–180.

De Certeau, Michel (1984) *The Practice of Everyday Life*, University of California Press, Berkeley.

D'Monte, Darryl (2002) *Ripping the Fabric: The Decline of Mumbai and its Mills*, Oxford University Press, New Delhi.

Domosh, Mona and Joni Seager (2001) *Putting Women in Place: Feminist Geographers make Sense of the World*, The Guildford Press, New York.

Donald, James (1999) *Imagining the Modern City*, University of Minnesota Press, Minneapolis.

Dossal, Mariam (1991) *Imperial Designs and Indian Realities: The Planning of Bombay City*, Oxford University Press, New Delhi.

Dwivedi, Sharada and Rahul Mehrotra (1995) *Bombay: The Cities Within*, India Book House, Bombay,

Foucault, Michel (1972) *The Archeology of Knowledge*, translated by A. M. Sheridan Smith, Tavistock, London.

Friedberg, Anne (1993) *Window Shopping: Cinema and the Postmodern*, University of California Press, Berkeley.

Garber, Judith A. (2000) '"Not Named or Identified": Politics and the Search for Anonymity in the City' in Kristine B. Miranna and Alma H. Young (eds), *Gendering the City: Women, Boundaries and Visions of Urban Life*, Rowman and Littlefield, Lanham, pp. 19–40.

Hansen, Thomas Blom (2001) *Wages of Violence: Naming and Identity in Postcolonial Bombay*, Princeton University Press, Princeton.

Harvey, David (2000) *Spaces of Hope*, University of Edinburgh Press, Edinburgh.

Holston, James and Arjun Appadurai (1996) 'Cities and Citizenship', *Public Culture*, Vol. 8, No. 2, 187–204.

Kannabiran, Kalpana (2006) 'Introduction' in Kalpana Kannabiran (ed.), *The Violence of Normal Times: Essays on Women's Lived Realities*, Women Unlimited, New Delhi, pp. 1–45.

Khan, Sameera (2007) 'Negotiating the Mohalla: Exclusion, Identity and Muslim Women in Mumbai', Review of Women's Studies, *Economic and Political Weekly*, Vol. 42, No. 17, 1527–1533.

Kumar, Radha (1993) *The History of Doing: An Illustrated Account of Movements for Women's Rights and Feminism in India 1800–1990*, Kali for Women, New Delhi.

Lefebvre, Henri (1991) *The Production of Space*, Blackwell, Oxford.

Low, Setha M. (2003) 'Embodied Space(s): Anthropological Theories of Body, Space and Culture', *Space and Culture*, Vol. 6 No. 1, 9–18.

McRobbie, Angela (1997) 'Bridging the Gap: Feminism, Fashion and Consumption', *Feminist Review*, Vol. 55, Spring, 73–89.

Masselos, Jim (1994) 'Postmodern Bombay: Fractured Discourses' in Sophie Watson and Kathie Gibson (eds), *Postmodern Cities and Spaces*, Blackwell, Oxford, pp.199–215.

Massey, Doreen (1994) *Space, Place and Gender*, University of Minnesota Press, Minneapolis, pp. 199–215.

Mazumdar, Ranjani (2006) 'The Figure of the Bombay *Tapori*: Language, Gesture and the Cinematic City' in Sujata Patel and Kushal Deb (eds) *Urban Studies*, Oxford University Press, New Delhi, pp. 440–464.

Menon, Meena and Neera Adarkar (2004) *One Hundred Years, One Hundred Voices: The Millworkers of Girangaon: An Oral History*, Seagull Books Calcutta.

Mitchell, Don. (2000) *Cultural Geography: A Critical Introduction*, Blackwell, Oxford, pp. 201–223.

—— (2003) *The Right to the City: Social Justice and the Fight for Public Space*, Guilford, New York.

Morris, Meaghan (2000): 'Things to Do with Shopping Centres' in Jane Rendell, Barbara Penner and Iain Borden (eds), *Gender, Space, Architecture*, Routledge, London, pp. 168–181.

Nord, Deborah Epstein (1995) *Walking the Victorian Streets: Women, Representation and the City*, Cornell University Press, Ithaca.

Phadke, Shilpa (2005) 'You can be Lonely in a Crowd: The Production of Safety in Mumbai', *Indian Journal of Gender Studies*, Vol. 12, No. 1, 41–62.

—— (2007) 'Dangerous Liaisons: Women and Men; Risk and Reputation in Mumbai', Review of Women's Studies, *Economic and Political Weekly*, Vol. 42, No. 17, 1510–1518.

Phadke, Shilpa, Sameera Khan and Shilpa Ranade (2006) *Women in Public: Safety in Mumbai*. Unpublished Report submitted to the Indo-Dutch Programme on Alternatives in Development (IDPAD).

Ranade, Shilpa (2007) 'The Way She Moves: Mapping the Everyday Production of Gender-Space', Review of Women's Studies, *Economic and Political Weekly*, Vol. 42, No. 17, 1519–1526.

Robinson, Rowena (2005) *Tremors of Violence: Muslim Survivors of Ethnic Strife in Western India*, Sage, New Delhi.

Rose, Gillian (1993) *Feminism and Geography: The Limits of Geographical Knowledge*, Polity Press, Cambridge.

Sarkar, Tanika (2000) *Hindu Wife, Hindu Nation: Community, Religion and Cultural Nationalism,* Permanent Black, New Delhi.

Scalway, Helen (2001) 'The Contemporary Flâneuse – Exploring Strategies for the Drifter in a Feminine Mode', *The Journal of Psychogeography and Urban Research,* Vol. 1, No. 1. http://www.psychogeography.co.uk/contemporary_flâneuse.html. (accessed in June 2003).

Solnit, Rebecca (2000) *Wanderlust: A History of Walking,* Penguin, New York.

Srivastava, Rahul, Pankaj Joshi, and Vyjayanthi Rao (2004) 'Habitat Heritage & Diversity', unpublished report produced by PUKAR for UNESCO.

Walkowitz, Judith (1992) *City of Dreadful Delight: Narratives of Sexual Danger in Late-Victorian London,* University of Chicago Press, Chicago.

Wilson, Elizabeth (1991) *The Sphinx in the City: Urban Life, the Control of Disorder and Women,* University of California Press, Berkeley.

—— (2001) 'The Invisible Flâneur' and 'The Invisible Flâneur: Afterword' *The Contradictions of Culture: Cities, Culture, Women,* Sage, London, pp. 72–94.

Wolff, Janet (1985) 'The Invisible Flâneuse. Women and the Literature of Modernity', *Theory, Culture and Society,* Vol. 2, No. 3, 37–46.

Young, Iris Marion (1990) 'Throwing Like a Girl: A Phenomenology of Feminine Body Comportment, Motility and Spatiality' in *Throwing Like a Girl and Other Essays in Feminist Philosophy and Social Theory,* Indiana Univ. Press, Bloomington, pp. 141–159.

—— (1995) 'City Life and Difference' in Philip Kasinitz (ed.), *Metropolis: Center and Symbol of Our Times,* New York University Press, New York, pp. 250–270.

Index